ROUTLEDGE LIBRARY EDITIONS: ADULT EDUCATION

Volume 26

ADULT EDUCATION FOR A CHANGE

ADULT EDUCATION
FOR A CHANGE

Edited by
JANE L. THOMPSON

LONDON AND NEW YORK

First published in 1980 by Hutchinson & Co. (Publishers) Ltd

This edition first published in 2019
by Routledge
2 Park Square, Milton Park, Abingdon, Oxon OX14 4RN

and by Routledge
52 Vanderbilt Avenue, New York, NY 10017

Routledge is an imprint of the Taylor & Francis Group, an informa business

British Library Cataloguing in Publication Data
A catalogue record for this book is available from the British Library

ISBN: 978-1-138-32224-0 (Set)
ISBN: 978-0-429-43000-8 (Set) (ebk)
ISBN: 978-1-138-36589-6 (Volume 26) (hbk)
ISBN: 978-0-429-43053-4 (Volume 26) (ebk)

Publisher's Note
The publisher has gone to great lengths to ensure the quality of this reprint but points out that some imperfections in the original copies may be apparent.

Disclaimer
The publisher has made every effort to trace copyright holders and would welcome correspondence from those they have been unable to trace.

Adult Education for a Change

Edited by Jane L. Thompson

Hutchinson

London Melbourne Sydney Auckland Johannesburg

Hutchinson & Co. (Publishers) Ltd
An imprint of the Hutchinson Publishing Group
17–21 Conway Street, London W1P 5HL

Hutchinson Group (Australia) Pty Ltd
30–32 Cremorne Street, Richmond South, Victoria 3121
PO Box 151, Broadway, New South Wales 2007

Hutchinson Group (NZ) Ltd
32–34 View Road, PO Box 40-086, Glenfield, Auckland 10

Hutchinson Group (SA) (Pty) Ltd
PO Box 337, Bergvlei 2012, South Africa

First published 1980
Reprinted 1981
Editorial matter, selection and arrangement © Jane L. Thompson 1980
Individual chapters © their authors 1980
Photoset in 10 on 12 pt. Times

Printed in Great Britain by The Anchor Press Ltd
and bound by Wm Brendon & Son Ltd,
both of Tiptree, Essex

British Library Cataloguing in Publication Data
Adult education for a change.
  1. Adult education – Great Britain – Addresses,
essays, lectures
  I. Thompson, Jane Lindsay
  374.9'41   LC5256.G7

ISBN 0 09 141620 5   cased
      0 09 141621 3   paper

Adult Education Publications

Jane L. Thompson

The editor has written or edited the following books about Adult Education

Adult Education for a Change (ed), Hutchinson,1980.

Learning Liberation: women's response to men's education, Croom Helm, 1983.

Learning the Hard Way: women's oppression in men's education (ed with the Taking Liberties Collective), MacMillan,1989.

Adult Education, Critical Intelligence and Social Change (ed with Marjorie Mayo), The National Institute of Adult Education (NIACE), 1995.

Words in Edgeways: radical learning for social change, NIACE, 1997.

Ruskin College: contesting knowledge, dissenting politics (ed with Geoff Andrews and Hilda Kean) , Lawrence and Wishart ,1999.

Women, Class and Education, Routledge, 2000.

Stretching the Academy: the politics and practice of widening participation in higher education (ed) NIACE, 2000.

Bread and Roses: arts, culture and lifelong learning, NIACE, 2002.

Lifelong Learning in Museums: a european handbook (ed with Kirsten Gibbs and Margherita Sani), EDISAI srl, 2007.

More Words in Edgeways: rediscovering adult education, NIACE 2007

Learning Liberation (reissue) Routledge, 2017.

Adult Education for a Change, (reissue), 2018

Contents

Preface

The idea for this collection of papers belongs to Lionel Paris and came as the consequence of a conference on Non-Formal Education, in which it became abundantly clear that any radical variation on the prevailing orthodoxy in adult education philosophy and practice was all too readily dismissed as 'unreasonably subversive' and 'misguided' by those representing the official and authoritative position. It might have been any one of countless similar occasions.

In *Adult Education for a Change*, we have taken the opportunity to present not an alternative orthodoxy but to initiate a serious debate, which we trust will be taken seriously by those who have grown accustomed to believing that the way things are is, more or less, the way they ought to stay.

Foreword

Keith Jackson, Senior Tutor, Northern College, South Yorkshire

This book is part of a welcome new development among those who work in adult education and think carefully about what they do. There is now a widespread questioning of the concepts and practices which have dominated adult education for a quarter of a century.

A liberal progressive movement for educational change thrived from 1945 to the early 1970s. It was a major project of social engineering whose main platform was that education could be a primary factor in reshaping the world for the better. Education would both promote equality and enable every person to develop to their full potential. What happened in schools would stand as an example to society at large, and form the attitudes of all future citizens who, in the liberal view, democratically control the nation's destiny.

For many in the generation to which I belong, the liberal education movement was a natural cause to support. As eleven plus and grammar school 'successes', we were some of the most fortunate beneficiaries of the 1944 Education Act and other post-war reforms. We grew up during the long boom to see our own lives apparently justifying the claims of the educationalists.

Those who worked in schools had a harder time in fighting the progressive battle than we in adult education, but they had the satisfaction of greater victories. Grammar schools fell to comprehensives, and the best examples of English primary education soon suggested that the state could, after all, support Robert Owen's classroom utopias.

Victories on this scale were inconceivable in the smaller territory of adult education, with its infinitesimal budget. Indeed in the 'liberal adult education' sponsored by the Workers' Educational Association and university extra-mural departments it was argued that the terrain must be held rather than conquered. This was part of the original homeland of the progressive movement. I remember scores of self-congratulatory conferences in which the virtues of liberal adult education were extolled: its freedom and open debate; its rigour combined with relaxed presentation; the friendly relationship between teachers and students who joined together in a disinterested search after truth. Progressives strove to maintain their hold over the central fortress of adult education (that is the responsible bodies) as they saw it, and also to expand their influence over new and growing areas of importance such as local education authority adult education services.

The liberal progressive movement held us firmly because its ideology — 'the language of the purposes of the social group'[1] — was coherent and was reinforced by our experience. We were able to make sense of society in progressive educational terms and to translate our 'understanding' into policies which promoted our own interests. It seemed that reformed, Keynesian, mixed-economy capitalism would work if only people were able to break through their ignorance and prejudice. Expand education, give us the resources, and we would give people the opportunity they required.

This point of view is no longer tenable. Education cannot produce the results intended by the progressive movement. More importantly, reformed Keynesian mixed-economy capitalism does not provide a sufficient basis for a more just and equal society after all. Migrant workers, immigrants, workers in the declining regions and inner cities had always known this. Whole sections of the working class also remained sceptical and now have their worst fears confirmed as unemployment rises and their collective standard of living declines through public expenditure cuts. Peter Wilby has ably summarized the conclusion reached by research and by experience:

We must accept that education is an ineffective form of social engineering. We can then escape from the liberal blind-alley by accepting two simple propositions. First, that if we want to redistribute wealth and power in our society, we should redistribute it by direct political means. Second, we should see education, not as a means of redistributing the national cake, but as part of the cake itself.[2]

Such statements are, indeed, becoming commonplace; a satisfied liberal consensus has steadily disintegrated since the late 1960s. Why then make the point again here?

First, because the different kinds of intellectual and practical experience which have followed a questioning of the liberal tradition also grew out of it, and must be examined and compared in that light. They have taken many shapes: community development projects; community education; education for the disadvantaged; arts workshops; specially developed trade union education.

Second, because the strengths of the liberal tradition must be recognized along with its limitations. In particular, liberal progressives in education have failed not because they set themselves a social purpose. They have failed because they reduced that purpose to a largely educational affair, thus losing much of its meaning in material terms for ordinary men and women.

Third, because the progressive liberal tradition in disarray has not answered conservative reaction in a manner which convinces working-class men, women and children. These are the people who have most to lose from both progressive and reactionary excesses. A radical critique of the Black Papers must include a critique of the progressivism which they attack. The right target has sometimes been hit by reactionaries for the wrong reasons.

Those who seek to overcome the contradictions of liberal education (reflecting the contradictions of the economic and political order which contains them) can best do so by a constant interpretation of their educational practice in the light of theory. I do not mean an inward looking, purely educational theory but a careful exposition of the implications for education of social and political analysis.

This process of praxis [3] (courses of action continually developed and interpreted through interaction with theory) can be seen in broad historical terms, for groups or whole societies. Every worker in academia and in education should also recognize the significance of a more personal praxis. Interpretations of adult education should be judged by the effectiveness of their contribution to that process.

Such a personal process of interpreting practice in the light of theory has been described brilliantly by the geographer David Harvey in his book, *Social Justice and the City*:

The essays assembled in this volume [he writes] were written at various points along an evolutionary path and therefore represent the history of an evolving path. I do not regard this history as idiosyncratic to myself (although there are probably some features in it that may be so interpreted). It is the sort of history that seems inevitable if anyone seeks an adequate and appropriate way to bring together a view point established in social and moral philosophy on the one hand and material questions that the condition of the urban centres in the western world point to on the other.[4]

It was the material conditions of the city which concerned Harvey as he moved to Baltimore while becoming interested in the relevance of the principles of social justice in applying spatial analysis and geographical principles to urban and regional planning. It is in relation to his concern with these material problems that he notes, 'The evolution which occurs in these essays is from a liberal to a socialist (Marxist) conception'[5], since liberal formulations pose irreconcilable dilemmas which 'degenerate into a helpless formless relativism to which no solution, apart from opinionated moral exhortation, seems possible'.[6] Only through socialist formulations could he find the liberation which began 'the process of reformulating problems as solutions and solutions as problems'.[7]

There are many people in adult education who, like Harvey as a geographer and planner, have been convinced as much by practical experience as by intellectual argument that the liberal formulations in education have degenerated into 'opinionated moral exhortation'. This book contributes to the debate in adult education which has resulted over the last few years and I hope it will help to prevent the debate becoming a sterile academic one. Since two of the chapters refer to experience I shared with a group of colleagues and with many others struggling to achieve social justice in Liverpool's not-so-fair city, it will serve both to make my point and to explain one or two references in those chapters, if I acknowledge here the debt I owe to the people of Liverpool's Scotland Road. Their political praxis clarified my own early hesitant questioning of the liberal adult education tradition, which began to seem increasingly inadequate after I had worked in Liverpool for five or six years.

When our family first moved to Liverpool and looked for somewhere to live in the central areas we were stirred by a mixture of horror, pity and bitter anger. We had lived in other working-class industrial areas with high unemployment and/or low wages but there is something savage about the historical level of exploitation in Liverpool which we had not experienced before. Of course we were not the first to notice this. For us, like others, time and familiarity dulled first impressions: compensations were found. But I have never been able to avoid asking whether my work in adult education should cool the anger or reflect it, indeed fortify it as part of my responsibility to oppose the forces which created and create Liverpool.

The liberal adult education tradition had long proved virtually meaningless for the working class in the city. Courses must have seemed more like academic parlour games than a search for understanding within the reality of life in the city. Recognizing this, the WEA and the university adult education department both used specially obtained resources to try out new forms of work. These were only valuable to others besides the educationists when they cast aside the bland and neutral liberal approach for something which was more committed, more objective and more open and truthful.

Working in Scotland Road, when the area was alive with a fight to stop a further massive withdrawal of resources from the area by the 1972 Housing Finance Act, we found that if workers in adult education were prepared to be associated with that fight, then the meaning of adult education changed for a number of significant people: solutions became problems and problems solutions. We concluded:

There can be no doubt that when a working class organisation such as the Tenants' Campaign really began to make progress some of its leading members clearly appreciated and understood the contribution education could make to its members and supporters, both directly and indirectly. Under these circumstances adult education was defined by them imaginatively, flexibly and comprehensively, and not sloppily or loosely without a necessary discipline. There was a clear challenge to those divisions in society: Literature classes for the better off, literacy classes for others. And the challenge was made more confidently and less stridently than it often is by progressive professionals because it reflected the normal reality of working class experience and organisation. People who could not read very well were considered as important as those who like to read history because they were not 'clients' or 'problems', but neighbours and equals who shared the same basic conditions and without whose support and solidarity no progress could be made (by the people of the area) . . . .
The second 'discovery' which could not be separated from the first concerned the nature of a particular kind of repression. This proved to be the real problem in developing adult education for the working class in Scotland Road, not the problem of communication or 'social disadvantage'.[8]

In short, while liberal adult education was supported for helping to develop and reinforce the ideas of social workers in Liverpool, by explicitly confirming them in their professional prejudices, liberal adult education was attacked both by members of a government sponsored Community Development Project, and by members of the university for helping council house tenants in Scotland Road to place their views and actions in a wider political and economic context and thereby giving them greater significance and force. These events and the reaction to them had both practical and theoretical results, of which the chapters by David Evans and Martin Yarnit are part.

Much of what I have read about adult education bears no relationship to political and intellectual experiences like this. It is inward looking and tries to understand adult education only in its own terms. Education is reified as if it has its own significance and meaning. I welcome this book because it contributes to a different kind of debate about the nature of adult education which could be theoretically productive.

That theoretical debate must be historical. Not producing histories of adult education but locating adult education in history. Geoff Brown's chapter is an important example of what the historian can do for theoretical debate which has practical consequences. The people of Scotland Road caused us to search widely in history for our understanding. Like Brown we found that the liberal tradition has more to offer than the last thirty years would suggest. The leaders of liberal adult education canonized Tawney but they chose not to listen to some of his words, particularly those about the relationship of adult education to social and political movements:

If I were asked [he wrote] what is the creative force which has carried forward educational movements, I should reply: the rise of new classes, of new forms of social structure, of new cultural and economic relationships. All these movements have regarded education not simply as an interest or an ornament. They have regarded it as a dynamic, and there is nothing at all surprising or regrettable in that. Knowledge has been sought in fact to meet a need. That need has been sometimes intellectual, it has been sometimes religious, it has been social, it has been technical, but the process by which it is satisfied is as much educational in the latter case as it is the first.[9]

The problem with most liberal adult education since the Second World War is that it has concentrated on satisfying intellectual need alone. With a few notable exceptions, including some adult education for trade unions and industrial workers, it has been too far removed from the processes by which ordinary men and women can meet their collective economic and social needs. Tawney again predicted the consequences of this error.

If you want flowers you must have flowers, *roots and all* — unless you are satisfied, as many people are satisfied, with flowers made of paper and tinsel. And if you want education you must not cut it off from the social interests in which it has its living and perennial sources. [10]

If Scotland Road taught us to look carefully again at Tawney and the kind of liberal adult education he represented, it also led us to seek further for an explanation of the way in which political parties and a government Community Development Project behaved in Scotland Road. They were so noticeably frightened of *ideas* being put abroad for open discussion in the area.

A hundred years ago James Hole, Secretary of the Yorkshire Union of Mechanics' Institutes wrote:

No teacher in this country will gain the ear of the working-man, unless he is willing to have his opinions and statements canvassed, to invite the utterance of conflicting opinions, and to give truth 'a fair field and no favour'. This course has not been and cannot be, adopted in mechanics' institutes, and, therefore, any attempt to convey economical doctrine 'sound or unsound', through their media must prove a failure. [11]

Then it was the mechanics' institutes, controlled directly by the ruling elite of the day; now it is state employees who refused to give truth a 'fair field and no favour'. Then it was the Chartists who fought for an education committed to working-class interests; what now, when the labour movement had turned to the state to collect resources and distribute them for educational proposes?

Like others following the same path we found the period following Chartist sponsorship of independent working-class adult education, when state education began its first major development, a fruitful source of insight. Among modern theorists Gramsci's exploration of the educative role of the state has been for me particularly useful and I hope some of the points made in this book will lead others to gather more concrete information to which his analysis points.

In short Tawney's remarks provide the right framework for thinking about adult education's relationship to society but they do not make it clear why some 'social movements' are given state resources freely while others are not. The movements which workers in adult education decide or are allowed to support, and the terms on which this takes place, are determined not by educational criteria but by political values. Within the state the development of community work and contrived public participation structures, with a substantial body of voluntary and paid activists may itself be regarded as a movement. [12] Education may then, as we have indicated already, support the material interests of those who sponsor and benefit from that movement, in direct opposition to the interests of most people living in the 'areas of special need' where the community movement flourishes. The story which began with nineteenth-century state provision of working-class schooling continues in ever more intricate forms. Gramsci's educative state becomes increasingly assertive.

This book is dominated by people who work in the liberal sector of adult education. Some of the chapters seek, however, to examine adult education as a whole. It is important that this should be done, not in order to unify something called adult education but so that the whole 'arena for struggle' within contemporary state supported education might be brought into view. There are important gaps in the record of this struggle which the book should stimulate others to fill. There is not enough on trade union education, particularly the massive expansion of TUC education to which a Conservative government has recently given half a million pounds. More is needed on the theory and practice of literacy programmes, and on developments in the most progressive local education authorities where the contradictions and the struggle within the state are often apparent.

I repeat, we should all beware the pitfalls when analysing adult education as a whole in this way. It is easy to slip into justifying ideas which have less value to society than to those with a vested interest in promoting adult education as an entity in its own right, or as a special part of continuing or recurrent education in the present vogue. Considering the complex nature of concepts such as maturity and intellectual development a theory of education based on age (unless it does denote entirely contingent administrative arrangements) needs very careful scrutiny. The relationship between theory and practice must be reaffirmed. Concepts like working-class education or women's education, which transcend age differences but reflect social reality, may have more to offer. Was the fact that children and adults could fruitfully learn together in the Owenite and Chartist movements entirely a result of the historical circumstances before the arrival of compulsory state education for children?

Many issues of policy and practice such as those raised in this book are usefully considered from this standpoint:

1   How *resources* are allocated for adult education cannot be separated from their allocation in education generally. It is not out of the question that an absurd situation could arise where state schools in predominantly working-class areas are starved of resources while adult literacy programmes are actually expanded (in some cases teachers who do nothing to campaign for their schools would be paid additional fees for teaching their 'failures' at night school). On the

other hand there may be good reason in some circumstances to expand further and adult education at the expense of schools.

2   The *institutional forms* of adult education are related to those of the school system in ways which need careful investigation as Keddie begins to show. Trenaman's famous phrase that adult education reinforces rather than remedies class differences in schooling provides a useful starting point. Yet there may be more opportunity to challenge those institutions when adult students are accepted as political actors in a way that children are not.

3   Then there is the *content* of education. This brings together two points I have already made: one about the importance of a willingness to be partisan but open to debate, and the other about a progressive critique of the Black Papers. I shall touch on the second here. In our efforts to overcome negative attitudes to schooling on the part of working-class adults we have stressed in recent years the value of informal approaches which link education closely to daily life and social or political activities, often calling this community education. This is only correct if it does not seek to justify any kind of activity whatsoever in educational terms merely because educational resources are involved. Bertrand Russell may well be right when he writes that education cannot be 'soft and easy and pleasant at every stage'. Working-class children or adults should not be sold short through misguided or mischievous attempts to make it so.

4   The only way to avoid this is to recognize the relationship between content and *process* in education. To emphasize the significance of subject matter and values in the content of adult education is not to regard the process as one of filling students with knowledge. It is to focus on *motivation* in education: what makes children or adults prepared to take the hard work. Freire's ideas are important here if they are not interpreted crudely. In short he emphasizes that individual development and collective consciousness go hand in hand when exploited and oppressed classes or groups take education seriously, as a liberating experience worth working hard at.

5   Finally there is the *relationship* between teacher (or other paid worker in education) and student, which can contain within it either a challenge or a reinforcement of prevailing class relations, institutional arrangements, and dominant educational processes. The age of students is a factor here but it is by no means the most important one in determining degrees of equality or hierarchy. The pitfalls are evident again in practice. Progressive educational attitudes about equality can easily lead to irresponsibility on the part

of those who are paid and expected to extend students, not merely to reassure them. The title of this book asks workers in adult education to make significant choices in each of these five areas. International comparison as well as historical study is valuable in understanding both the scope for action and the possibility of being sidetracked. They are all political choices. The most significant educational reform to be achieved remains that of ensuring that education can make a contribution to genuine advances by working-class men and women. In sum this will depend on their gaining substantial resources of time and money and on their influencing or controlling specific aspects of education in practice. In both cases the test of success will be who controls? and in whose interests?

Introduction

The apparently peculiar organization of adult education in Britain appears to many to be the consequence of being a small, haphazard and under-resourced service. [1] It accounts for only one per cent of local authority spending, and even with additional funds provided to Responsible Bodies by the Department of Education and Science, the overall picture is one of stringency. In 1974–75, for example, the total cost of all further and adult education provision, excluding on-the-job training, but including vocational courses and basic adult education, was £627 million. This was for a student population of 4 million. In the same period £700 million was spent on higher education for only 425,000 students — a difference of 10 to 1 in favour of those in higher education. [2]

The whole of adult education is consequently dominated by the constraints of resource allocation and the need to account for the money spent to those who provide it. The central organizing features are the centre and the class. As buildings, most of the centres are not specifically designed for adult education purposes, although most of them have a link with formal education provision of some kind. Enid and Edward Hutchinson talk of premises for adult education coming, 'by accident, seldom by design. Like the cast-off clothes of a long family . . . such buildings descend in order of educational priorities until, worn and out of date, they survive demolition to supplement, for adult students, their mainstay provision of nightly leavings of younger people's daytime schools and colleges'. [3] But although adult education often lodges temporarily in the premises of dayschools, community colleges and FE colleges, the commitment to an 'institutional base' for the purposes of class teaching is central to what is offered. Classes, with few exceptions, are topic or subject centred and operate on a fee-paying, enrolment economy, in which the range and viability is determined by the numbers of people registered. They are subject to occasional inspection by Her Majesty's Inspectors but standards vary, and in a fee-paying economy, numbers attending are often assumed to be more important than the quality of what is offered.

In bewailing the poverty of provision and the limited resources allocated to adult education, however, it's important to remember the social context in which adult education operates.

An examination of the social characteristics of the education system have largely been confined to the period of compulsory schooling. Over the last twenty years or so, a whole battery of reports and research programmes have produced a burgeoning literature dedicated to the exploration of the relationship between education and society. In the early years of research, sociologists were preoccupied with what Bernstein later referred to as 'in-put out-put problems', that is who gets into different parts of the system and what they come out with in the end, in terms of qualifications. [4] More recently, factors relating to the 'hidden curriculum' of schooling have come under close scrutiny. The business of socialization and acculturation, in which values and attitudes likely to further the social and economic interests of dominant groups in society, is now widely regarded as central to the process of schooling. [5] Bowles and Gintis depict schooling as a kind of 'training ground' for capitalism, in which new generations of workers are equipped with necessary skills, tuned into appropriate attitudes, fed with predetermined expectations and rehearsed in the relationships of authority and control which correspond to the economic, social and ideological relationships of production in the wider society. [6] A major characteristic of schooling is seen to be its reflection of the stratified nature of society and its consequent tendency to allocate pupils of 'measurably different abilities' into different schools, streams and curriculum options.

The major contribution made by the sociology of education over the last twenty years or so has been to challenge this notion of 'measured ability', to demonstrate the close connection between academic stratification and social stratification and to identify the sources of influence which inform both the formal and the hidden curriculum. It's now generally accepted by sociologists that in a variety of ways the operation of the education system serves to perpetuate an unequal and hierarchical society, and to reproduce actively the attitudinal and behavioural conditions necessary for its development in harmony with the vested interests of dominant groups.

So far, though, the analysis has concentrated on schooling. Most adult educationalists would argue that their practices are not equivalent to those of the schools and as such do not merit the same kind of scrutiny. But clearly this is not a view shared by the majority of the population. Could it be that those who have learned defeat early on in their school careers, and have come to regard education as an alienating experience, see adult education as merely the extension of this process?

The social context of adult education

The first thing to notice is that what is commonly referred to as 'adult education' is, in fact, only a small part of the post-school education available to adults. In terms of its relation to qualifications, its links with powerful academic interests and its ability to control and make available the knowledge required by prestigious elites, its contribution is marginal.

The provision of post-graduate studies and the organization and control of research by the universities is not regarded as 'adult education'. Similarly the array of professional qualifications available to lawyers, doctors, accountants and business managers, for example, all imply specialist and advanced study in keeping with the status and decision-making authority of present and future elites. But none of this comes under the conventional definition of adult education. Polytechnics and the existence of specialist colleges for art, drama and music provide yet another example. If it's true that the education system reflects in its sub-divisions the hierarchical nature of the wider society, it is undoubtedly the case that the kind of education for adults usually referred to as 'higher education' is where the influence and power lie. There is never any question of this version of education for adults being poorly served with resources or being regarded as marginal. In terms of this pecking order, the adult education we know — that which is provided by the responsible and voluntary bodies and the local education authorities — is small scale and second-rate in comparison. Its low position in the pecking order is in direct relation to its minimal contribution to conferring qualifications upon, and confirming the status of, significant social elites. In fact, as Enid and Edward Hutchinson point out, it is 'dominated by concepts of leisure time satisfactions', [7] and intrinsically valuable though these might be, they have a low currency value in a meritocratic education system servicing a work-orientated society.

It would be wrong to suggest that adult education is the 'poor cousin' who serves the interests of the poor, however. Its relationship to the institutions of higher education might seem analogous to the secondary modern's relationship to the grammar school, in terms of resources, prestige and influence, but there the analogy stops. Any suggestion that adult education is an alternative means of educational provision for the less educated is very far from true. In many ways it exists as a microcosm of the wider educational system, with the same inbuilt sense of hierarchy operating to consolidate the educational and social divisions pre-empted by schooling in a capitalist society.

The fact that, in the main, the products of adult education are consumed by a small and socially discreet section of the population, is well documented. [8] They attract those members of the middle and lower middle class who have already experienced a fair amount of 'educational success', who consider 'organized learning' to be a valuable and interesting endeavour and who are not principally motivated by vocational considerations. This ideal of 'education for its own sake' is one which the university tradition in adult education has deliberately cultivated. Its roots in academic scholarship and the patronage of the leisured and genteel classes in the nineteenth century [9] has contributed to the sense of detachment from contemporary society. Current defenders of this tradition still advocate it in preference to the 'practical instrumentalism' which they associate with more recent innovations like trade union studies and community education. [10] In the same tradition the contributors to the Russell Report (1973) claim that 'the value of adult education is not solely to be measured by direct increases in earning power or productive capacity or by any other materialistic yardstick, but by the quality of life it inspires in the individual and generates in the community at large'. [11]

Another characteristic of adult education is the demarcation between providers, both in what they offer and in whom they attract. In general terms, the university extra-mural tradition has grown out of intra-mural degree courses and the dissemination of academic knowledge in a manner associated with scholarship and sustained study. The Workers' Educational Association provision has in many respects become barely distinguishable from that promoted by the universities, despite its roots in workers' education and political and economic studies. [12] As a consequence, its students reflect the same social class and 'degree of schooling' as those who attend extra-mural classes, though it's generally claimed that 'WEA level work' provides only an 'introduction' to the academic humanities. Students who wish to deepen their understanding of the subject being studied would need the guidance of a university appointed tutor. [13]

Local authorities, on the other hand, provide educational activities which are more concerned with 'practical', 'recreational' and 'creative' subjects, rather than 'academic' studies, continuing the demarcation between 'high-status' and 'low-status' knowledge so familiar in the school curriculum. [14] LEA provision doesn't, on the whole, lead to any kind of advanced qualifications and is more closely identified with hobbies and leisure-time pursuits than the courses provided by the universities and the WEA. Whilst it might be expected that the provision of a fairly comprehensive range of offerings, depending on the size and status of the centre, could be expected to appeal to a cross section of the population, the social composition of LEA adult education classes is only slightly different from that of the universities and the WEA. Local authority students tend to be slightly older than Responsible Body students and lower-middle class as distinct from middle class in social standing. Women apparently outnumber men by about 3 to 1. [15]

Arguments concerned to account for the general 'non-participation' of working-class students in traditional adult education tend to concentrate on one of two explanations. The first is based on notions of educational, social and cultural deprivation. 'Non-participating' adults are claimed to have had unhappy memories of schooling which they associate with past failure and which makes them incapable of recognizing the value of what adult education has to offer. They are known to be more 'at home' with beer and bingo and if that is 'their considered choice' in a 'free society' it has to be respected. [16]

The other explanation takes a slightly less complacent and more self-critical look at the nature of what is offered. In its recommendations to the field, the Russell Committee noted that, 'less privileged social groups and those who had more restricted previous education [were] under-represented in adult education classes.' The Committee felt that part of the problem was 'the image' presented by adult education and the formal procedures that were regularly administered at the expense of the sensitivities of potentially reluctant students. 'Insistence upon regular meeting times, the routine of enrolment and registration of attendance, minimum numbers, the charging of fees in advance and formal teaching . . . often destroy any chance of successful penetration into these sections of the population.' [17]

Jenny Rogers and Brian Groombridge make the point that, 'at the most elementary level of organization, adult education filters and fails to be comprehensive in reach, simply because it is scheduled badly'. [18] The timing and siting of classes, the lack of crèche facilities, 'chaotic and insensitive procedures at enrolment time' and a cheeseparing attitude to resources, all contribute to deterring any but the most determined and confident from persevering.

The assumptions underpinning the approach of the New Communities Project in Leigh Park were very much influenced by these conventional wisdoms about the problem of 'non-participation'. [19] So far as the action-research team was concerned, the Russell Committee had

summed up rather neatly the problems [they] expected to face. It referred to 'people . . . hitherto untouched by adult education . . . discouraged from participating by their . . . circumstances, by unsuitable premises, by a sense of their own inadequacy, by fear of an unwelcoming bureaucracy in the administrative arrangements, or simply by the language we commonly use in describing the service' and it might have been added, the language and educated accent of many teachers. [20]

It's interesting to note that these two kinds of explanations are remarkably similar to those fashionable among educationalists in the 1960s in reference to 'the failure' of working-class children in the school system. Their 'solutions' were couched in terms of 'compensatory education', 'organizational reform' and a new commitment to 'curriculum relevance' — trends equally discernible in subsequent adult education initiatives. But I shall return to these explanations and solutions later to suggest that they are highly unsatisfactory. [21]

The extent to which adult education contributes to the transmission of values and attitudes which reflect the interests of dominant groups in society is a condition of adult education which is, as yet, under-researched and largely ignored by adult educators. Clearly the process of socialization and acculturation that happens in schools seems more significant because of the compulsory nature of schooling and the relative innocence and inexperience of the pupils. It might be argued that by the time children become adults, their initiation into conventional values and attitudes is complete, their role in the labour force — and all that that implies in terms of life-style and life chances — is determined, and their class character and condition are fixed. But, if indeed this were the case, the necessity for further confirmation of dominant attitudes and values would be unnecessary, and adult education could be genuinely disinterested in everything but its commitment to 'its traditional role of general cultural diffusion and personal development through studies on a broad prospective'. [22]

Of course education, or any other social activity for that matter, is less straightforward. In challenging the 'snobbism' that Colin Kirkwood detects in Lawson's critique of community education, he insists that Lawson apply 'the same kind of rigour to his own position'. [23] Kirkwood detects the kind of vagueness and arrogance which is motivated by the assumption that traditional adult education is somehow 'absolute' and 'god-given' and 'unsullied' by the prejudices and manipulations of men.

Bernstein has argued that subject loyalty (and the same could be said of educational loyalty) is systematically developed in pupils and students with each increase in their educational life, and then transmitted by them in turn, as teachers. The system is self-perpetuating. The more prolonged the experience, the more committed become the participants, and the more different they become from those who have not been admitted to the same systematic socialization. Part of the selective process is the development of careful screening procedures. All but a small minority are progressively weeded out along the way, since anything which is associated with social or economic prestige and value would lose its value by becoming generally available. A common language, shared experiences, implicit assumptions and agreed frames of reference indicate to those who have been initiated who belongs and who doesn't. [24] A consequence of all this is to attribute a 'sense of the sacred' to academic knowledge, something which Kirkwood, in his critique of Lawson, describes as an 'abstract essence'. In questioning 'What is this essence? What is this valuable culture that has to be diffused? Who makes it? And for whom is it important?', he asks the critical questions of all of those who would claim that adult education is a neutral activity.

So far as the LEA curriculum goes, not only does it represent 'low-status' knowledge by virtue of its association with non-academic, leisure-related hobbies and crafts, but its underlying 'concept of man' is that of 'homemaker', 'consumer' and 'well rounded individual', rather than 'scholar', 'political activist', 'trade union official' or 'victim of economic and cultural oppression'. In such circumstances the provision of classes in, for example, hostess cookery, beauty and skin care, dressmaking, interior design and yoga is as likely to encourage an implicit celebration of domesticity, quietism, consumerism and sexism as anything the most coercive instruction in passive citizenship could achieve.

The notion that any kind of education, however pure its motives or esoteric its subject matter, can ever be considered neutral is now a difficult position to maintain. In *Pedagogy of the Oppressed* Paulo Freire points out that

> there is no such thing as a neutral education process. Education either functions as an instrument which is used to facilitate the integration of generations into the logic of the present system and bring about conformity to it, or it becomes the 'practice of freedom', the means by which men and women deal critically and creatively with reality and discover how to participate in the transformation of their world. [25]

Gramsci, the Italian Marxist, develops a stage further Marx's view that the ruling ideas of any age are those of the ruling group. He uses the term 'cultural hegemony' to explain how 'their kind of ideas' are imposed upon the rest, the working class in particular, to prevent them from thinking for themselves. [26]

In both its form and content, in the assumptions which influence its providers and the criteria used to recruit its students, the practice of adult education has developed in historical circumstances governed by social, political and economic considerations closely related to the interests of dominant groups. The selection of liberal criteria for identifying content, prescribing objectives and deciding teaching methods, for example, represents as partial and political a commitment to a non-neutral process as that of Paulo Freire in Latin America or the staff and students who removed themselves from Ruskin College in 1909. [27] Even those not noted for their political radicalism have come to accept the essential accuracy of the argument. Paul Fordham in his article, 'The political context of adult education', agrees that although they may often be implicit and frequently go unrecognized, value judgements and a political dimension are inevitable in the planning and execution of all adult education programmes. [28]

There is one vital difference between the practice of adult

education and the practice of schooling, however, which needs to be stressed, for it is in this difference that the challenge to education and cultural hegemony can be mounted. Whilst 'adult education shares the overall insignificance of schooling, if it is to be judged in its capacity to promote major changes, it does not share its total insubordination to the dominant system of values. This is because it does not exist chiefly to measure and label people, and because its students are adults, i.e. citizens with political rights, and with experiences, which sometimes lead them to challenge or question inequality rather than legitimize it'. [29]

To examine these and other contradictions and to look beyond the commonly accepted and officially defined goals of adult education is a task which is long overdue. As Sallie Westwood points out in Chapter 1, adult education now needs to be re-examined with the insights provided by the sociology of education. This also means placing adult education firmly in the context of a stratified society and within the realities of political struggle. The collective argument presented here is that without such an understanding, and without such a class perspective, it will be impossible to radicalize adult education or to respond, with any degree of commitment, to the expansion of educational provision for working-class men and women.

Jane L. Thompson

University of Southampton
July 1979

Part One
Perspectives

1 Adult education and the sociology of education: an exploration

Sallie Westwood, Lecturer in Adult Education, University of Leicester

This paper takes as its central problem the theorization of the middle-class bias of adult education as a means of exploring the relationship between adult education and the sociology of education. The middle-class domination of adult education has a long history and has remained a source of debate and discussion to the present time. The premise upon which this paper is based is that unless we have a clear understanding and analysis of this middle-class bias we cannot begin to reconstruct or radicalize adult education.

The social class bias of adult education was statistically described in the National Institute of Adult Education Survey which showed clearly that the middle class is over-represented in all forms of adult education provision. [1] In addition, the survey demonstrated that the provision was itself stratified. Thus, the universities draw 92 per cent of their students from the A, B, and C1 categories and this representation of the A and B groupings lessens in the local authority sector. The conclusions of the survey are summed up by Fordham *et al.* in their recent book.

We began with the fact that students in adult education classes are increasingly drawn from the higher socio-economic groups and from groups with a background of full-time secondary or higher education. [2]

The fact that adult education is consistently biased towards the middle class requires that we re-evaluate current views of the field. It is suggested that adult education is distinctive and that its difference is defined by the diversity of forms present in adult education and the voluntary nature of the participation. This view leads to comments such as those made by Houghton, where he writes, 'At present in the post-industrial countries the adult education sector has a proliferation of courses and organizations which defy rational analysis.' [3] The following analysis seeks to oppose such a view.

An alternative but equally persuasive account of adult education is offered by the free-market view. This view suggests that adult education is an educational free market in which the provider is the entrepreneur and the public the consumers. This is clearly a mystification of the real situation: no free market exists where educational opportunities are differentially distributed and where the reasons for these inequalities are located in the class structure. Similarly, neither the entrepreneur nor the consumer is 'king' because the state at a national and local level intervenes and controls the flow of educational products. [4] The problems with this market view are similar to those within the economic model from which it is taken. The market view posits individual choice as a determining factor rather than the social conditions of existence of these 'choices'.

Neither of the above accounts or models of adult education offers the adult educator a basis for understanding the social-class bias of adult education; and here it is instructive to turn initially to the Alexander Report where it is stated that:

Adult education is part of the total educational system and is influenced by broadly the same factors as influence the rest of educational provision. In addition, the character of school education has a considerable influence on all post-school education as regards the foundations on which it has to build and gaps it may have to fill. [5]

The implications of this view are that any understanding of the nature and function of adult education must be set within the wider socio-economic structure and the relationship between this structure and the educational system taken as a whole. This suggests that an appropriate starting point for a theorization of the middle-class bias of adult education is a sociological one. To this end the remainder of the paper will be concerned with a presentation of some earlier and recent contributions to the field of the sociology of education and how these may usefully be appropriated for an understanding of adult education. However, this is not an analogy which is always accepted by adult educators. As Lowe has pointed out:

Seeing themselves as belonging to a hard school of pragmatists, realists one might say, many senior administrators are wary if not contemptuous of theorizing and hostile towards the aims of sociologists and psychologists and what they regard as the hocus-pocus of questionnaires and inquiries. Indeed, educators of adults in general have not yet perceived the relevance of the social sciences to their own work. [6]

I would suggest, however, that there are three major areas in which the sociology of education can contribute to our analysis of adult education. The first of these is the emphasis within the subject upon making education intelligible in relation to the wider socio-economic structure; secondly, children become adults and it is very clear that an adult's view of adult education is formulated in relation to his or her own school experiences; finally, all education must place itself in relation to cultural transmission. These areas of concern seem to suggest that the incorporation of adult education within the sociology of education is long overdue. Practitioners within the field already hold a variety of commonsense views which, I would argue, can be more easily codified in relation to a sociological understanding. Newman, for example, writing about one adult education centre notes the handicaps associated with the use of school buildings:

Using schools in the evenings does not always help. It requires faith on entering some adult education premises to believe that anything but a repetition of one's worst school experiences could ever take place in such surroundings. [7]

The message from this is clear but the reasons need further explanation; it is not simply the physical location of adult education that deters. It is, most importantly, the social location; that is, the social relationships of school and schooling that remain as part of the common stock of knowledge when education is remembered. It is the sociology of education that has tried to make intelligible the social relations of schooling.

The early sociology of education, as exemplified in the famous reader *Education, Economy and Society*, was based upon the 'technical function' view of education. [8] The basic premises of this view were located in the rapid technological changes apparent in the advanced industrial countries. The changes brought about through technology, it was argued, required an increasingly skilled and educated workforce to cope with rapid changes in the labour market. Education was given the central role of providing the skilled labour power by which technology could be translated into greater material wealth. It was, therefore, an *investment* area (as distinct from an area of consumption) in the key factor in the production process, labour. Clearly, this view still has a wide currency and is expressed in many of the arguments for continuing and recurrent education. It was used by the Alexander Report and can be seen as an underlying rationale for the recent discussion document on continuing education presented by the Advisory Council for Adult and Continuing Education. [9] Adult education has clearly been impressed by its basic premises and they have been incorporated into a general perspective on education and social change. Adult education like school education is presented as an area of investment.

However, to return to the early sociology of education, upon examination it was found that in Britain at least, the educational system was not functioning in an efficient manner in processing an educated and mobile workforce. As Floud and Halsey noted:

The truth is that the schools and universities function badly as selectors and promoters of talent. . . .

and further,

Schools and universities were not designed for the selection processes thrust upon them in a modern economy by the tightening bond of schooling and occupation, and hence social class, nor were they designed to act as agencies of social justice, distributing 'life chances' according to some meritocratic principle in face of the social claims of parents for their children. [10]

The evidence presented by the early work of Floud, Halsey and Martin emphasized the class bias of education in Britain. [11] Education could not promote talent or greater equality because it was itself stratified and unequal. But the mood of the time was optimistic and the demand for greater equality of opportunity for all children became the plank upon which a comprehensive educational system was based. The selection of children at eleven was considered not only divisive but economically unsound because it did not make the most efficient use of the nation's resources.

Randall Collins examined the technical function view of education and with the use of Berg's material was forced to conclude that education, and especially schools, had little impact upon technical skills. [12] Instead, he offered the view that: 'The main activity of schools is to teach particular status cultures, both in and outside the classroom.' [13] For Randall Collins schooling represented one aspect of the battle fought between status groups to control certain sections of the labour market. Status groups use academic qualifications as part of their struggle for control over certain occupations. Important to these struggles are the particular status cultures imparted within specific educational institutions. The analysis presented by Randall Collins anticipates later discussions on the hidden curriculum in schooling and the importance of the cultural components of education. However, by insisting upon a Weberian view of status groups rather than classes the analysis leads away from the crucial significance of the class structure. This failure is similar to that of the early sociologists of education; although they conceptualized the educational system they did not provide an adequate account of the framework within which it operates.

The analysis offered in the 1970s by the sociology of education, is in marked contrast to that of the 1960s and has its origins as much in the growing contradictions of capitalism as in academic disaffection from the dominant functionalist paradigm in sociology. The emphasis upon capitalism as defining the terrain of education, and thereby the struggles that take place within that terrain, is an important distinguishing feature of the more recent sociology of education. It begins with the understanding that capitalism is an economic system organized for the accumulation of profits which are concentrated in the hands of a few. Conflict and crises are inherent within such a system, but so too are the mechanisms by which the system is able to reproduce itself, both in a physical and in a social sense.

Capitalism must reproduce itself not simply in terms of the physical means of production, plant and equipment, but it must also reproduce that which is essential to the extraction of profit, labour power. At a physical level this is done through the wage system, but the ongoing nature of capitalism requires more than simple labour power; it requires an ordered labour force, one that is prepared to submit itself to the production process. Capitalism requires, therefore, a specific ideological climate which is located at the material level in education, the media, the trade unions and the institutions of the democratic process itself. All of these, but most especially education, have a vital role to play in the reproduction of capitalism.

These components of civil society become, for Althusser, Ideological State Apparatuses owing to the impact of the state on their formation. [14] The ISAs are essential to the reproduction of the capitalist mode of production because they reproduce for capital the existing social relations of production which encompass the class system and its antagonisms, and the sexual division of labour and its special place in the reproductive process.

The attention given to the process of social reproduction in the recent writings of Althusser, Bowles and Gintis and Bourdieu allows

us to see more clearly the role of education in relation to capitalism.
[15] It allows us to plot the fortunes not simply of classes, but of
classes in relation to the sexual division of labour and in relation to
the state. The early sociology of education ignored the role of the
state in relation to the nature and form of educational provision and
its processes. It could not do otherwise because it had not started
from capitalism but from a view of industrial society which
incorporated a pluralistic view of the distribution of power.
Similarly, it ignored the sexism of British education, a product of the
overriding concern with class inequality and, in addition, the sexism
of sociology itself. Recently, Rosemary Deem and Ann-Marie Wolpe
have made use of the work of Althusser and Bourdieu as a means of
analysing the sexist biases of the educational system. [16] Their work
has demonstrated how the sexual division of labour, with its inbuilt
inequalities, contributes to the process of social reproduction in an
essential way through the physical reproduction of labour pwoer and
its servicing and repair in the home by women. Domesticity is
important to the ongoing nature of the system as a whole. Schooling
has a vital role to play in the reproduction of the sexual division of
labour. Education imparts to children not, as we understand them,
conventional subjects and skills, but as Althusser notes:

besides these techniques and knowledges . . . children at school also learn the
'rules' of good behaviour, i.e. that attitude that should be observed by every
agent in the division of labour, according to the job he is 'destined' for; rules
of morality, civic and professional conscience, which actually means rules of
respect for the socio-technical division of labour and ultimately the rules of
the order established by class domination. [17]

Thus, for Althusser, schooling is ultimately a process that contributes
not towards knowledge in a pure sense, nor personal development, nor liberation but towards a quiescent work force. This
point is emphasized by Bowles and Gintis who, while ignoring the
role of the state as the facilitator of this process, describe a system of
correspondence similar to Althusser. Thus, Bowles and Gintis note:

The educational system serves — through the correspondence of its social
relations with those of economic life — to reproduce economic inequality
and to distort personal development. Thus under corporate capitalism, the
objectives of liberal educational reform are contradictory: it is precisely
because of its role as producer of an alienated and stratified labour force that
the educational system has developed its repressive and unequal
structure. [18]

The educational system reproduces workers for capitalism by its emphasis upon control, discipline and by teaching children the authority relations of the capitalist division of labour. Children learn early on in this process of schooling that they have no control over the manner in which they can organize their work, over the knowledge which they are required to acquire, and the way in which it is to be acquired. In the productive process as workers they will have no control over the pace of production, the goods that they produce, the setting in which they will work. In addition, as Bowles and Gintis point out, capital needs other forms of labour power and schooling provides more highly qualified labour power which is equally conscious of the social division of labour. [19] These products are the successes of the system, but they are drawn from a narrow social class which is enabled through the educational system to reproduce itself more effectively. [20]

If, as I have argued, it is essential to place adult education in relation to the educational system as a whole, how is the field to be understood in relation to the analysis of social reproduction? I would like to suggest that by taking account of the work of Althusser and Bowles and Gintis we are better able to understand the middle-class bias of adult education. [21] At one level this bias serves to reinforce the inequalities of the schooling system. Adult educators would argue that their practices are not equivalent to many of those of the schools but clearly, this is not a view shared by the majority of the population. From the work of Bowles and Gintis we can come to understand that those who have learned early on in their school careers, through the defeats of the classroom, that education is an alienating process regard adult education as an extension of this process. [22] Adult education has a social class bias born out of the defeats of school classrooms and its organization, in terms of classes, courses, teachers and its physical location within schools, colleges and universities represent to the majority of people a reproduction of school practices.

Along with schooling, Althusser's work includes the trade union structure within the ISAs but within adult education trade unionism and education come together in the trade union studies programme. This area offers an apparent contradiction to the overall view of schooling and the class bias of adult education because here the education is dominated by the working class. Althusser's view of this phenomenon, if it were to be consistent with his overall perspective, would suggest that the trade union studies programme was not organized upon a radical basis which would offer power to the trade unionist on the shop floor, but that it represented a more sophisticated incorporation that works clearly within the framework of capitalist relations of production and does not seek to challenge this framework. [23] This is a problem to which I shall return later in my discussion. For Althusser and Bowles and Gintis the contradiction is more apparent than real, for while there is no democratization of the workplace and no control by workers themselves over the productive process their education, as the education of future workers, must be schooling for social order and control.

If we turn to a different aspect of adult education, the Open University, the usefulness of the reproductive model is very clear. The Open University may be analysed in relation to the social relations of production under capitalism. Briefly, the centre controls knowledge and its production and consequently the nature of the teaching that takes place. In addition, the pace of work and form in which knowledge is presented is all carefully controlled from the centre. Courses are pre-packaged and they come through the door like commodities. To reinforce the production and transmission of knowledge there exists a large bureaucratic structure. The suggestion from this brief overview is that the Open University, situated as it is within a capitalist mode of production, must too become deformed, and with that it will encourage a mode of transmission of knowledge that is as alienating as the work process itself. Lack of control by the student over the curriculum and the pace of work contributes towards the alienating effects of the educational experience. Finally, the Open University is itself biased towards the middle classes. [24]

Although it can be shown that there is a correspondence between schooling and adult education, the hidden curriculum of adult education is less important because children have already been schooled when they arrive in our classes as adults. Similarly, we do not cater to all, but as this paper seeks to elucidate, to the few who represent the successes of the system and who because of this have little need of further inculcation into dominant modes of thinking. The working class stay away because they were early on alienated from schools and by that from education in a broader sense. But the mechanisms involved in this alienation are more subtle than the foregoing suggests and they require further elaboration. It is in this discussion that the work of Bourdieu is especially helpful.

The work of Bourdieu has given a new impetus to our understanding of the process of social reproduction, through his emphasis upon cultural reproduction. [25] Bourdieu takes as his starting point the proposition that within capitalism there exists, not simply a system of economic capital which defines the economic relations between classes, but also a system of cultural capital which is important to the symbolic relationships between classes. [26] Thus, each family passes on to their children not only economic capital, or the lack of it, but a certain cultural capital. Consequently, there are two forms of wealth in circulation, the one material, the other symbolic and it is the latter which is important in masking the naked exploitation of the capitalist system. Cultural capital is as unequally divided as private wealth. Although in an anthropological sense all classes and peoples have a culture, these cultures are not equally regarded, and under capitalism the dominant class has the power to enforce its definition of culture as universally valid. Thus, cultural production under the conditions of advanced capitalism is constrained because the dominant class impinges upon the creative project in multifarious ways. [27]

Schools have a vital role to play in transmitting a nation's cultural heritage; consequently what is taught in schools is regarded as valid and worthy of preserving. Cultural artefacts, knowledge and ways of transmitting knowledge and the values that surround skills such as literacy become consecrated and it is these cultural products which form the major part of schooling and its curriculum. This cultural heritage, notes Bourdieu, is offered to all equally but children coming into schools are not equal. They are already the recipients of social and cultural inequalities transmitted through the family. Consequently schools, by offering all children the same education regardless of their class origins, allow for the perpetuation of class inequalities. Bourdieu notes:

If, however, one takes socially conditioned inequalities with regard to schools and education seriously, one is obliged to conclude that the *formal* equity, which the whole educational system is subject to, is in reality unjust and that in any society which claims to have democratic ideals it protects privileges themselves rather than their open transmission. [28]

and continues:

In other words, by treating all pupils, however unequal they may be in reality, as equal in rights and duties, the educational system is led to give its *de facto* sanction to initial cultural inequalities. [29]

The school offers part of the stock of cultural capital to all, but only some of those to whom it is offered are capable of appropriating it and these are the children of the upper and middle classes. The ability to appropriate cultural capital in the form of school knowledge and beyond the school environment in the form of works of art, 'high' culture, and other valued cultural components is based upon a certain degree of cultural competence. This competence, as Murdock notes:

can be broken down into three basic components — knowledge about the legitimate stock of cultural capital, mastery of the intellectual and social skills surrounding its consumption and use, and the ability to deploy this knowledge and skill to advantage in social situations. [30]

Cultural competence offers the individual a system of related meanings and propositions by which the stock of cultural capital is made intelligible. It is a code or a grammar which allows cultural capital to be appropriated. In order to maximize upon this, cultural capital consists also in linguistic ability, in social networks and in knowledge of the nuances of certain sub-cultures which remain exclusive through the shared cultural system of their members.

The possession of a specific form of cultural competence allows those from the middle and upper classes to appropriate the culture of the school and thereby to accumulate cultural capital in the form of academic qualifications which have a specific market value. Academic qualifications have a direct bearing upon the rewards of work, intrinsic and extrinsic. But, as Bourdieu notes, they are a weaker currency than economic capital which is the determinant source of power and privilege. Academic qualifications may also be linked to other forms of cultural capital, social contacts, similar schools and university experiences which themselves offer sporting and social contacts which taken together form an elaborate network that can only be penetrated by a few.

Bourdieu's own analysis of the consumption of cultural products concentrated upon reading habits, the use of libraries, visits to the theatre and most importantly museums where there are no financial constraints upon consumption. [31] He found, predictably, that high educational qualifications were correlated with consumption in all the above areas. The professionals, having acquired high academic qualifications, prolonged training and specific occupational sub-cultures, were the groups with the highest level of cultural consumption within the areas specified. However, Bourdieu suggests that the owners of economic capital are becoming more concerned with the consumption of cultural products as a means to greater legitimation.

Bourdieu's work has important implications for the field of adult education. It offers an explanation of the middle-class bias of adult education in terms of cultural capital and cultural competence. The notion of competence is not new to adult education, a field in which, I would suggest, attention has consistently been given to the promotion of *individual* competence. In view of Bourdieu's analysis this individual notion of competence would seem to be partial and a more complete analysis of adult education is only possible once this becomes cultural competence. This is clearly linked to the work of Freire, who has noted the importance of the cultural component of educational transmission. [32] For Freire literacy is not simply a mechanical skill, but a symbolic skill which constitutes a cultural competence which provides a system for decoding signs. Such sign systems are essential elements of culture. Within conventional liberal adult education there is a clear stratification by the type of institution involved and the form of knowledge transmitted. University adult education offers classes in a wide variety of areas but these are taken up by a limited section of the population. It is this population who have the cultural competence necessary to decode the nature of the knowledge that is being offered, whether in the field of art, music or archaeology.

The critique presented by Bourdieu leads directly to an analysis of the curriculum as an aspect of cultural reproduction and this is no less important to adult education than to other sectors of the educational system. What is required is an analysis that looks at the cultural products transmitted within adult education and the consequences of this for cultural reproduction with its role in the reproduction of social inequalities.

I have already identified the reinforcing role of adult education and this can be seen in the curriculum. Mee and Wiltshire, for example, note:

Although there are marked differences in curriculum between different types of institutions, there is also a surprising consistency in the provision of a common core curriculum in institutions of all types. The impression is of a broad national consensus about what kinds of things adult education ought to offer, but we do not know what the processes are which determine and maintain this consensus or what the channels are through which they operate. [33]

My own exposition of Bourdieu's work would suggest that we have the tools with which to analyse the processes involved in producing and maintaining a consenus and that we need not be surprised by this effect. These effects are not the result of market choices where the consumer is king. They are part of the wider process of cultural reproduction.

In fact, the process is more complex than Bourdieu or Althusser have plotted. They have both concerned themselves with an analysis of the role of education in maintaining the relations of subordination and domination between classes. But there are problems with the concepts that they employ. The concepts of ideology and of culture are often ambiguous and used in a cavalier manner by both writers. Instead, we need to pose a conceptualization which brings both ideology and culture together while transcending the limitations of both. To this end we need to draw upon the work of Antonio Gramsci who has given us the concept of hegemony. [34] Raymond Williams, in his discussion of the concept and its usefulness, comments:

'Hegemony' goes beyond 'culture' (as previously defined), in its insistence on relating the 'whole social process' to specific distributions of power and influence. To say that 'men' define and shape their whole lives is true only in abstraction. In any actual society there are specific inequalities in means and therefore in capacity to realize this process. In a class society these are primarily inequalities between classes. Gramsci therefore introduced the necessary recognition of dominance and subordination in what has still, however, to be recognized as a whole process. [35]

Gramsci's work emphasized the role of ideological struggles within the revolutionary process because he understood that domination was as much a product of 'consensus' as it was of force or threat of physical coercion. His insights have become increasingly relevant under the conditions of advanced capitalism. Gramsci understood that those institutions beyond the productive process that were part of civil society had a crucial role to play in maintaining and perpetuating the existing order. Education, the media, the legal system and trade unionism are all forms of legitimation for the status quo.

Clearly, and he has acknowledged this, Althusser's ISAs owe much to Gramsci's concept of hegemonic control. [36] This is the process whereby those structures within the social formation that are outside the productive process have a central role in maintaining an economic system founded upon the exploitation of propertyless labour power. Advanced capitalism is a complex and sophisticated social formation that has used the organs of civil society very effectively in the service of the status quo. It is precisely because a consensus has been engendered that it is able to resist, incorporate and emasculate protest. Gramsci was anxious to point out that hegemonic control is a process which is not always unchallenged. It constantly faces challenges from different sections of society but these protests are often channelled through the mechanisms of hegemonic control. For example, trade unions have become enmeshed in a legal system that emphasizes individual rights and not collective ones; consequently the fundamental basis of trade unionism, its collectivism, is side-stepped by the law and the collective nature of the struggle is deflected.

Gramsci was clear that such control should be challenged and to this end he gave to education a very important role in challenging bourgeois hegemony. [37] He was particularly concerned with the role of adult education which he saw as political education. His model came from his work with the Factory Councils which had offered workers the possibility of control over the workplace and production. [38] Education for adults was securely located with struggles in the productive sphere and within the whole of working-class culture.

Adult education with its middle-class bias, its uniformity within a common core of the curriculum, I have suggested, has a reinforcing role. But in relation to the concept of hegemony it can be seen to have a much clearer role in maintaining the status quo, engendering a state of consensus and contributing positively to the mechanisms whereby hegemony is maintained. However, it is also in a position to mount a challenge to the accepted view of the world, at a minimum to question this legitimacy. One example which shows both the potential of adult education, and very clearly its setting within the state structure that creates and manages the consensus, is offered by Newman who traces the fortunes of a projected course called Gay Studies. [39] It was suggested to the sponsors of the course that it could be run as part of a liberal adult education programme, but the Inner London Education Authority stopped the course. The authority would not allow it to take place under their auspices, consequently bringing the power of the local state into full play. Ultimately it defined what would count as adult education and certainly Gay Studies in a heterosexual world would not.

There was a similar case, again in London, over a course in Marxist Economics which did run very successfully. Even though the subject was taught by an Oxford don the challenge to orthodoxy was not welcome. More often challenged, through Women's Studies courses, is the patriarchal nature of capitalism. In the universities it has been challenged by women in extra-mural departments who, despite the complaints that the subject has no pedigree, is biased and ideologically dubious, have succeeded in promoting in a very limited way the cause of Women's Studies. In all these cases there is a clear challenge to bourgeois hegemony. The point is that these courses have been offered through adult education. There is, therefore, the possibility of challenge and change within adult education. But it requires more than an attempt to establish courses that are unpopular with the local authority. In the field of trade union studies also the attempt has been made, as it is being made in Italy, to provide something more than a plain man's guide to industrial legislation and how to discipline persistently late workers. [40] In Italy the trade unions have abandoned this in favour of a genuinely participatory education which concentrates upon workers' control and an understanding of the role of labour power in capitalism.

If adult education is to maximize its potential for providing a counter hegemonic culture then it must re-appraise its purpose and methods. A start in this direction is to analyse the role of adult education in relation to advanced capitalism and to provide an answer to the clearly middle-class bias of the field.

As a conclusion to this exploration of the relationship between adult education and the sociology of education I would like to propose that adult education be re-conceptualized as a cultural field and one in which the cultural competence of the working class is as valid as that of the middle class. As Freire has clearly shown, adult educators must not colonize people, thereby making them inferior and by so doing devaluing their own cultural competence. In Gramsci's terminology this would be another example of hegemonic control. Instead, consistent with the view of adult education as a cultural field, adult educators must become, in Miliband's terms, 'cultural workers'. [41] This is the first step towards a redefinition of adult education and one which demands a new spirit of radicalism.

2 Adult education: an ideology of individualism

Nell Keddie, Senior Lecturer in Adult Education, Department of Extra-Mural Studies, University of London

Adult educators commonly claim a distinctive nature for their enterprise, implying that adult education [1] differs significantly from the rest of the educational system. This claim refers to its diversity of forms, its voluntary nature and its concern with meeting individual need through a student-centred curriculum. The current preoccupation with professionalization also emphasizes the claim that the education of adults requires distinctive teaching skills. I shall argue that within a sociological frame of reference it becomes apparent that adult education is more like the rest of the education system than unlike it, both its curriculum and its pedagogy, and I shall treat the claim to distinctiveness as an ideological claim which requires explanation.

I should stress that in raising questions about the beliefs of adult educators I am not questioning either the sincerity of those beliefs or the commitments of individuals. Ingleby argues that those involved in the 'people professions' may experience as a private or shared trouble the recognition that their role is 'to help people to lead better lives' within a political system which 'systematically limits the quality of their clients' lives'. He says:

it is implicit in their role in the social system that their energies will be devoted to adapting men to that system, instead of helping to adapt the system to human needs. It is the job itself, rather than the people who do it or the theories they inherit, that is by nature conservative. [2]

This is a problem for adult educators no less than for others engaged in educational work, although the individualistic ideology of adult education functions to obscure the contradictions inherent in the adult educator's role.

In suggesting that the claim to the distinctiveness of adult education be understood as an ideological claim, I am using the term ideology neither in a pejorative sense nor in its narrower meaning of political bias. I am following Harris's broader formulation that 'ideologies are not disguised descriptions of the world, but rather real descriptions of the world from a specific viewpoint, just as all descriptions of the world are from a particular point of view'. [3]

This means that different interest groups will see the world in different ways and the differences are likely to be explicable in terms of how a group locates itself within a social structure, what it takes as its main points of reference and what its relative power to negotiate its interests *vis-à-vis* other significant groups is likely to be. The ideology of adult education achieves for practitioners a promise to their clientele that their primary concern will be with students' needs and interests; and, equally important, it operates to combat the marginality of adult education to the education system and helps to confirm practitioners' professional identities.

This marginality is the result both of the non-statutory nature of adult education and of the low status of its non-vocational curriculum. Adult educators are continually confronted by the low priority which others accord to their activities and by the threat this holds for their professional identities. Insistence on the distinctive nature of adult education may be seen as a counterclaim which provides adult educators with a collective sense of their unique identity and establishes the value of their activities. Such counterclaims are common to the processes both of sectarianism and of professionalization and they frequently invoke a sense of unique mission for the group involved. [4] Historically, the mission of adult education was informed by a desire to reach those in society who had benefited least from the influence of education. Although this remains an element in the contemporary adult educator's ideology, the emphasis has shifted so that now it is more a matter of taking a better kind of education to those whose previous education has been misconceived. Thus, the value of student-centred learning in adult education is counterposed to the subject-centred learning of secondary schooling and the concept of individual need is counterposed to the accusation of the irrelevance of the school curriculum, although it is far from clear that these opposed concepts of educational theory lead to distinct and differentiated forms of practice. [5]

In advancing claims for adult education in ways which imply a rejection of traditional high-status subject-centred education, adult educators employ the same kind of status reversal that is found in other low-status areas of education. The ideology of adult education with its emphasis on student-centredness and the development of the whole person is strikingly similar to that of primary school teachers and of many remedial teachers in secondary schools. Both adult educators and primary teachers not only see education as person-centred rather than subject-centred, but also tend to value pedagogic skills above academic qualifications. The similarities between adult education and primary schooling indicate that adult education's claim to distinctiveness may be explained primarily by its status within the structure of the education system.

The emphasis on individual *need* in both adult and primary education blurs the competitive edge of the ideology of individual *achievement* which informs secondary and higher education. Nevertheless, adult education is oriented towards the same dominant or middle-class values that are reflected by the education system as a whole and are evidenced by its clientele. These values give particular social and political meanings to individualism which reflect the educational and cultural models of the elite. As Gelpi [6] notes, these models 'have often been passively accepted as models for the working class, even when its own social and political purposes have been very different from those of the elite.' The failure to recognize this leads to a notion of the learner as an 'abstract and universal individual' rather than as 'a person situated in a historical, social and existential context'. Formal educational structures are typically concerned with the 'social background' of students as an explanation of differential motivation. Thus the concept of disadvantage in adult education as in schooling, reflects a concern with helping individuals to adapt to dominant educational and cultural structures, but does not question the modes by which education controls differential access to knowledge and power.

Westwood and Griffin [7] demonstrate alternative modes of conceptualizing the relationship between education and society and between knowledge and power and move respectively towards concepts of cultural hegemony and lifelong education. In locating the dominant ideology of adult-education within a consensus model of society, I would argue that adult education is like, rather than unlike, the rest of the education system in its form of cultural reproduction, [8] and that the questions that have been raised about the curriculum of initial schooling can also appropriately be asked about the curriculum of adult education. However, because the claims to the distinctive nature of adult education lay stress on a person- or client-centred pedagogy, which is interlocked with the concept of a person- as opposed to a subject-centred curriculum, I shall first examine the claim of adult education to be client-centred and show how this is significantly akin to the child-centred ideology of the primary school.

Patterson's first chapter in *Values, Education and the Adult* opens by defining the author's area of concern:

It is significant that we distinguish adult education from other forms of educational provision by reference to the nature of its clients. Primary, secondary, further and higher education are differentiated from each other in terms of notional stages in the unfolding of the educational enterprise. Technical, physical, and moral education are differentiated from one another and from legal and medical education in terms of their distinctive contents and objectives. But, if nomenclature is any guide, the vast assortment of activities which are collectively styled 'adult education' derive whatever common character they have from the character of the clients, actual and potential, on whose behalf they are initiated. [9]

The author's intention here is to offer a definition of adult education which extends beyond its institutional meaning in order that he may discuss the distinctiveness of adult education in terms of the status of adulthood as opposed to childhood. Thus although he achieves his definition by distinguishing adult education as person-centred from other forms of education in terms of 'their distinctive contents and objectives' (for his second definition overlaps his first one of notional stages at all points), he actually pursues his discussion of the distinction in terms of how adulthood may be differentiated from childhood. That is, he changes his terms of reference from a distinction between forms of education defined by reference to subject (as contents and objectives) and to client, to a distinction based on differentiating between different clients — adults and children.

Although Patterson wishes to make a formal distinction between adult education and other forms of education in terms of the former's reference to the nature of its clients, it is perhaps more significant that in practice there is remarkable similarity between the ways in which adult educators and primary school teachers construct their student-centred and child-centred ideologies respectively. [10] Both express a primary concern with the needs of the individual student and see as a primary task of education the promotion of personal growth through a curriculum that is student- rather than subject-centred. Both refer to behaviourist developmental psychologies to explain the nature of human learning. The psychology of child development and the psychology of human ageing are similarly concerned with a notion of normal development and maturation in terms of the emotional, physical, social and cognitive processes which supposedly obtain to different stages of the human lifecycle and their relevance for identifying the interests and capabilities of the learner at successive stages.

I have already noted that both adult and primary education occupy low-status positions in the education system as a whole and have suggested that this is in part a response to the subject- or discipline-centred ideology of the high-status elitist tradition of higher education and the academic streams of secondary schools. In its pure form education which is subject-centred subjugates the 'needs' of the student to the demands of the discipline. The learning situation is necessarily teacher-centred insofar as the authority of the subject is vested in the teacher. Syllabuses are determined not by reference to students' supposed or expressed interests but by reference to what they need to know to progress within the discipline at any given stage, that is, by reference to the internal logic of the subject. The accusation that much of secondary schooling is academic and therefore irrelevant to pupils' interests is necessarily true because the notion of relevance within the academic curriculum is contexted within that curriculum itself. At any stage learning a subject will ideally build on what has gone before and prepare for what lies ahead. A course of study at 'O' level is less likely to be determined by a consideration of the needs and interests of those who will leave school at its conclusion, than by a consideration of what those who will proceed to 'A' level courses will need to know.

In this context it becomes clear that the low status of both adult and primary education is determined by the distance of both from the major processes of certification and, as far as adult education is concerned, it is not its non-vocational nature only which makes it vulnerable (since most education in schools and universities cannot be accounted strictly vocational in the sense of providing a direct training for a specific job), but that no value is set upon it in the academic marketplace. In high-status subject-centred areas of the education system, the teacher's professional identity is primarily located within a subject area or discipline which has itself been studied at a high or relatively high level and status distinctions are based on the level at which the subject is taught. The higher the level at which it is taught the less will a teacher need to be concerned about the capabilities of the students since their ability to gain admission to the course is evidence of their competence. In both primary and adult education (with the exception of the relatively small amount of provision made by extra-mural departments where teachers take university standards and therefore their subject specialisms as their main point of reference) the status attached to being a teacher of a subject is relatively low and the nature of the student body much more diverse in terms of the interests and competence of the students. Thus, although teachers still teach subjects, their professional commitment is reversed so that their identity is located primarily in their pedagogic expertise as a concern with students' needs.

It must be stressed here that we are talking about the dominant ideological emphases between groups of teachers differently located in the hierarchical structure of the educational system. It is not suggested that teachers in the academic streams of secondary schools and in higher education are not concerned about how they teach or about their students, nor that primary school teachers and adult educators are unconcerned about their subjects or incompetent in the teaching of them. Nor is it suggested that these different ideological emphases differentiate practice in significant ways, since evidence pointing one way or the other is lacking. Rather it is important to understand what structural constraints within the educational system may account for the particular kinds of claims that adult educators make, in order to understand their professional commitments. For although the commitment to student-centredness can also be accounted for by reference to the voluntary attendance of students and a concern to be open to the demands of those who come to classes this does not in itself explain why, for example, the notion of response to demand should be linked with a concern about individual need and growth. Nor, given the forms demand might take, does it explain how the curriculum of adult education should, as Mee and Wiltshire's analysis suggests, [11] be so limited in its range or so uniformly provided, nor does it explain why adult education succeeds in attracting students from some sections of the middle classes and hardly at all from the working classes. To explore these issues further we can return to the notion of student-centredness which primary and adult education hold in common and examine some of the problems which arise from the interdependent concepts of person and curriculum that it encapsulates.

In the first place it appears to be liable to a number of contradictions of which the most obvious kind is manifested in the common practice of encouraging tutors to draw up a syllabus in consultation with students whom they will not meet until the beginning of the course, having already required the same tutors to produce a detailed course outline several months beforehand. What this points to, however, is a much more fundamental problem of how what counts as student-centred learning or a student-centred curriculum is determined. Who decides what students shall learn and how they will learn it. In a recent paper, Griffin [12] drew out the ideologies of continuing and recurrent education to suggest that in their most extreme forms they are polarized so that in the concept of continuing education decisions about both content and method lie with the teacher whereas in the concept of recurrent education the autonomy of the student is absolute and the teacher becomes virtually redundant. While in practice some kind of middle ground may be negotiated, the polarized model suggests that the notion of student-centredness will be delimited with respect to the student's autonomy if the teacher is to retain a professional role and identity.

A recent study of the infant classroom by King indicates how in the primary school context the concept of the child-centred curriculum is mediated in practice by the teacher's concept of what children are and ought to be, which in turn determines and legitimates the curriculum of the infant classroom. In particular he identified in the teachers' ideologies a belief in childhood innocence, which enabled teachers to decide what kind of knowledge could be admitted to the classroom and what could not. This delimited another aspect of the primary teacher's ideology, that children learn most when learning is based on their interests. By this means children's interest in the popular culture mediated through television, for example, is defined out of the classroom while stories about witches are allowed in. Thus, although infant teachers espouse a concept of good practice based on learning relevant to children's interests, they also defined the curriculum by approving some interests and censoring others. King also found that children who came from middle-class homes were most likely to evince an interest in those things of which teachers approved. This meant that for working-class children, whose imaginative life was expressed in images drawn from popular culture, there was a discontinuity between the life of home and the school which did not exist for middle-class children. In this respect the alienation which working-class students express towards school in the later years of secondary schooling may be supposed to be a feature of their school experience from the first.

King also comments on the child-centred ideology of individualism:

There was little individualism in what children were manifestly taught or learnt. There was only one acceptable answer to a sum, and only one meaning to an arrangement of letters when reading or writing. When painting, doing craft work, projects, and 'free writing', there was some scope for individual expression, but . . . this was constrained by the teachers' action in accord with their ideologies of development and innocence, and the observance of conventional reality. . . .

Individualism was mainly found in the typifications of individual children. . . . Individual typifications were used to make particular explanations of the behaviour, progress, and peer-group relations of each child. These definitions had real consequences in the form of actions on the part of the teacher which attempted to bring about conformity. The 'shy' were 'brought out' and the 'boisterous' 'calmed down' in an attempt to bring both closer to a teacher's definition of what a child should be. Thus an ironic consequence of defining children as individuals were attempts to reduce individuality. [13]

The notion of individualism was also informed by theories of child development which defined an image of the 'normal' child at any stage and to which middle-class children were most likely to conform. The failure of working-class children to conform in their behaviour to the desired image was not seen as a manifestation of individuality but was attributed to deficiencies in their home backgrounds.

While we may not expect a substantive fit between the practices of infant teachers and adult educators, King's empirical investigation of the infant teacher's ideology in practice suggests there is a need to look at the very similar ideology of adult education in terms of how it may legitimate similar educational processes. What King's analysis points to most strongly is that a person-centred ideology may express an alternative mode of control from that exercised through a subject-centred curriculum. The teacher's ideology is used, in practice, to achieve children's conformity to an image of what children ought to be, and both the behaviour of the children and the content of their education is constrained by the teacher's definition of the child. I shall suggest that we have to understand the implications of King's analysis for the ideology and practice of adult education in different ways, according to whether we are concerned with 'normal' students in 'mainstream provision' or 'disadvantaged' students in 'special provision'.

King's analysis and data support those of other investigators [14] which indicate that the main task of primary education is to achieve a commitment in the very young to the processes of schooling as they are perceived by educators who have themselves been socialized into the norms of the dominant culture, and that they are most successful with pupils whose families are already located in that culture. Those pupils whose commitment to educational achievement is most successfully managed by the teacher (and an important element in that commitment is the acceptance of the teacher's authority to determine the nature and assessment of educational tasks) are those who also succeed in their secondary school careers. Among them are the majority of those who become both teachers and students in adult education and share as part of their common previous educational experience the norms and expectations of the processes and purposes of education, including how the relationship between student and teacher will be managed. On the whole the docility and deference of adult students is more remarkable than their willingness to question either the administrative processes they are subjected to or the nature of the learning situation. [15] Although adult education is provided on the basis of a response to demand, demand more often appears to be a passive rather than an active quality and voting with one's feet more common than any attempt to change the situation.

This is itself sufficient reason to question whether adult education has a distinctive form since it is more likely that it attracts the students it does because it confirms their established notions about the nature and purposes of education. In this respect such things as a relative informality in the teacher-student relationship, respect for the interests of individual students and a concern with a pleasant learning environment are a necessary recognition of adult status and the voluntary nature of attendance, but do not in themselves indicate that the forms or practices of adult education differ from those of initial schooling or of higher education. If the nature of initial schooling is held responsible [16] for the reluctance of working-class adults to use the adult education service, then it must also in some measure account for its appeal to middle-class adults. It is at least worth exploring this possibility because if there is evidence to support it we should have to ask whether the claims of adult education to be a distinctive educational form tend to promote practices which hinder rather than help it to become a resource for the whole community. And if it is most appropriate to see adult education as an extension of the forms of compulsory schooling rather than a distinctive educational form, then the concessions made to the adult status of the students are marginal compared to the reproduction of more fundamental processes.

An examination of the 'mainstream' curriculum of adult education tends to confirm this. Given the imaginable variety of courses of study that might be demanded by adults, there is a remarkable uniformity about the curriculum of adult education which needs to be explained and studies of the genesis of the typical provision now offered by local authorities are lacking. Mee and Wiltshire comment:

Although there are marked differences in the curriculum between different types of institutions, there is also a surprising consistency in the provision of a common core curriculum in institutions of all types. The impression is of a broad national consensus, but we do not know what the processes are which determine and maintain this consensus or what the channels are through which they operate. [17]

One feature of Mee and Wiltshire's data that is of particular significance is that indicated by the opening clause of the first sentence above, which suggests that although provision is seen as a response to demand, different institutional settings 'create' different emphases in demand. This suggests that adult education must in part, at least, be understood as operating a provider's model and is less constrained by the demands of the local community than is sometimes supposed. At the same time it is likely that we are dealing here with shifts of emphasis and the uniformity of the core curriculum has to be explained by reference to other factors.

Given the client or student-centred ideology of adult education it may be noted that not only is the core mainstream curriculum highly subject specific but that the content of courses within a given subject appears to be surprisingly similar. This suggests that we need to explain how, as in the infant classroom, individualism tends to produce uniformity rather than diversity. First, it is relevant to note that the notion of individuality as a desirable personality goal is not universal, but is culturally specific and tends to be found in those cultures where high status is obtained by competitive individual achievement. Nor is it valued equally by all groups within our society. The force of the research which has attempted to distinguish between middle and working-class cultures has stressed that while the middle class are, like the schools, oriented towards the value of individual achievement, working-class culture places emphasis on collective values which have been held to account for the failure of working-class children in school in a variety of ways. [18]

As King's analysis suggests, however, it would be wrong to suppose that the practice or expression of individuality is free floating. How individuality may be expressed will depend on social settings so that in some a socially recognized expression of individuality may be the wearing of a colourful tie or the decision to study astronomy when all one's friends choose dressmaking. Such expressions of individuality are not only socially determined but to step over the limits may court disapproval and rejection. The social art is to know what counts as an approved expression of individuality in any given social situation.

If we apply this analysis of the relationship between the ideology of individualism and the means by which it is socially determined and delimited to explain the uniformity of a curriculum which is supposed to express a response to individual need and interest, one or two possibilities present themselves. Leisure is socially sanctioned as an appropriate arena of individual expression where an individual can develop interests and personal qualities that may be inhibited in the work context and, here again, it is relevant that leisure styles show patterns of conformity within different social groups. It may well be that attendance at adult education classes needs to be understood as a subcultural leisure style within the wider social groupings in which attendance is normally shown. [19] That is, although organizers recognize in practice that a particular subject or group of subjects may attract students from a particular group distinguishable by age, sex, social status, etc., there is a tendency to treat both the programme and the student body as homogeneous, whereas the patterns of use which determine and maintain the core curriculum may be susceptible to much finer analysis.

One cultural pattern of use which stands out and for which some explanation may be attempted is the greater appeal of adult education for women than men and the number of courses that come under the general heading of 'women's interests'. Here, at least for women whose employment is wholly in the home, adult education classes may be less an opportunity to develop leisure interests as such, and more often be seen as an opportunity to restate their sense of themselves as individuals against the demand to service the needs of others that are made on them in the home. [20] At the same time it would appear that the subjects women are most likely to study are those which support their roles as managers in the home [21] rather than open up new roles for them. [22] It is not only more economical to make rather than to buy clothes for the family, but many of these subjects provide for the socially sanctioned ways in which women, especially middle-class women, can express individuality in managing and servicing the home, through the special dinner party recipe or the colour blends of the furnishings or the arrangement of flowers. In this respect the mainstream curriculum of local authority provision not only underpins the status quo and services the traditional roles of women, but it is uniquely geared to meet the notions of individualism which those roles require and which are pre-scribed by the narrow margins of fashion and 'good taste'. The distance of adult education from the processes of certification allows a curriculum sufficiently flexible to be relevant to individual students' needs and interests since the degree of choice that may be relevant, once one has joined a woodwork class, may be whether to learn how to make joints through making a ladder or a bookcase, or once one has joined a class on nineteenth-century literature, whether to read Dickens or George Eliot. [23]

There is no suggestion in the attempted analysis above that it is adequate or complete. What is suggested is that the individualistic and student-centred ideology of adult education has to be analysed and investigated in terms of its significance in supporting some cultural styles and not others. The likelihood is that these can be identified far more precisely than they so far have been. Indeed, it may be said that the rhetoric of individualism obscures the way in which terms like 'individual need' and 'student centred' are socially constituted and located in ways that make adult education more readily available to certain social groups.

I suggested earlier that the way these terms are used with reference to 'mainstream provision' differed significantly from the way they are used to legitimate 'special provision' for the 'disadvantaged' and it is the latter I now want to explore.

Some measure of the commitment of adult education to a form of education informed by the norms of the dominant educational ideology is the strength of feeling with which 'mainstream provision' has been defended against encroachment on its resources in the name of provision for the disadvantaged. We may note here that the notion of special provision for the disadvantaged has led adult education increasingly to mirror the differentiated curriculum of secondary schooling where there is a clear distinction between the academic curriculum leading to 'O' and 'A' levels, the less academic curriculum leading to 'O' level and CSE and the remedial curriculum for the less able. As with the school curriculum there is a correspondence with the social class index, with a marked number of students in occupational categories A and B in the academic provision made by extra-mural departments and a predominance of those in C1 in local authority classes. How far provision for the disadvantaged has actually recruited from unskilled and semi-skilled occupations and from the unemployed and how far it is atypical of those 'socially deprived' groups it is intended to reach is not clear, but the NIAE report on literacy provision suggests that certainly at the start of the literacy campaign those who came forward 'were not necessarily representative of the total population of sub-literate adults'. [24]

Although it is not clear substantively who those who use the special provision for the disadvantaged are, and whether they do represent a social group which can be clearly defined, the introduction of the concept of disadvantage into adult education has been of considerable significance because it has tested the claims of adult education to be a distinctive form of education available to the whole community, and because it has highlighted ideological conflict within adult education. [25]

The concept of cultural disadvantage or deprivation posits a culture of poverty which runs alongside the mainstream culture. This is a theory of social pathology which explains social problems as a malfunctioning of the socio-economic system, where social ills are manifested in those individuals or groups who are most vulnerable and who suffer multiple deprivation: low income, unemployment, poor housing, low educational standards, etc. What this kind of explanation achieves, in practice, is a severing of the connection between the political nature of *social* problems and the *individual* who presents problems which, if they are severe enough, or sufficiently troublesome to others, will be dealt with as individual problems by the social worker, the police, the remedial teacher, or another of those whom Everett Hughes called the 'dirty workers' of our society, meaning they do its dirty work for it.

If we look at the way in which the ideology of individualism has been used in formulating a policy for special provision for the disadvantaged we see it conspicuously avoids any mention of social class and that the concept is contexted, as in initial schooling, within a social pathology which separates the problems presented by individuals from the social and political order which creates these problems. For if the obverse to educational success is educational failure, so the obverse to individual achievement is the individualization of failure. This was apparent in the policy of the BBC literacy campaign in which the tutors' handbook, which was an initial training manual for a considerable number of new tutors, failed to context illiteracy in the massive failure of schools to improve the life chances of the majority of working-class pupils. Instead, illiteracy was explained by reference to individual circumstances such as absence from school, a particular teacher and so on. This individualistic formulation has been challenged by the more radical theory and practice of many literacy workers since [26], but it has recently been restated in far more elaborate terms in the report on adult basic education published by the Advisory Council for Adult and Continuing Education. [27]

Although the report is nominally about a wider idea of basic education (to include, for example, pre-retirement courses), its main preoccupation is with remedial programmes. It locates the need for such programmes not in the failure of the school system but in poor schools and truancy and in what appears to be a theory of endemic late development:

if all children attended school regularly, and if all school education were of high quality, the need for adult basic education would not disappear. There are many people whose need for learning emerges only in the practicalities of life and who discover that in that context they can learn effectively. (para 11) [27]

The reference to the 'practicalities of life' suggests that schools may pay too little attention to these and that the school curriculum lacks relevance. The curriculum which is proposed by the report is, however, very similar in its underlying principles to the curriculum offered to many of the 'less able' pupils in their latter years of secondary schooling, that is, a combination of remedial literacy and number skills with a strong emphasis on subjects and topics that are drawn from the 'life contexts' to which the report refers. As many of the earlier Schools Council curriculum projects for the less academic pupils and ROSLA schemes show, together with, for example, the Humanities Curriculum Project, the thinking about the curriculum for the less able secondary school pupil has moved away from strong subject boundaries towards a more integrated curriculum which is held to be more relevant to pupils' interests, at least as relevance is imputed by educators. Another feature of these programmes has been their concern with moral and social education and with attitude formation. [28] The report expresses a similar concern in its proposals for the basic education of adults and is in this respect an extension of the education offered to less able pupils in secondary schools.

Its curriculum proposals are based on inter-connected assumptions: that an adult who seeks help with learning to read is almost by definition deficient in many other respects (this is not assumed about an adult who wants to learn car maintenance or to paint); and that anyone in need of basic education is in need of the *same* basic education. Thus, although the basic education curriculum it proposes is supposed to be based on 'individual needs' and to be 'student-centred' it is so only within very narrow limits. These limits are the educator's definition of 'needs'.

If we look at the report's strategy for deciding what needs individuals will have we see how it arrives at its curriculum proposals. Paragraphs 5 and 6 read:

We can, however, indicate the groups and types of people likely to be affected, whilst emphasizing that we are concerned all the time with individuals and individual needs. Most are likely to be found in one or more of the following categories:

   those living in socially deprived communities
   members of ethnic minorities, including recent immigrants
   the unemployed
   the physically and mentally handicapped
   special age groups such as young single parents, older workers facing redundancy, pre- and post-retirement groups
   those in and released from penal establishments.

Not everyone in any of these categories is in need of basic education nor is it claimed that education can solve all social ills. But it can put people in the way of perceiving them more clearly and making their contribution, either in social or in personal terms, towards a solution. To deny such educational opportunity is to add despair to deprivation.

There is a significant shift here from the idea of a 'group' to the idea of a 'category'.

Groups are about the shared circumstances and experiences which give a shape and meaning to individual lives. While people identify with a group through common experiences and interests, categories are used to classify people and to fit them into an administrative structure. Such structures tend to express the purposes of those who devise them and do not necessarily reflect the needs of those they are intended to serve, and the shift achieves a severing between the nature and causes of 'social ills' and the individual problems of those who are most vulnerable to them.

Paragraphs 7 and 8 argue the need for basic education within a social pathology model and a fear of political disaffection:

However successful people may have been in the past in adapting to deprivation and tolerating their lot, the social and economic trends of the day are making that response even less feasible. Disadvantage and alienation grow in the wake of inner-city decline, of rural isolation, of structural unemployment and the break-up of traditional home-and-work relationships, and the increasing complexity of administration even in those services designed to give help.

It is essential that basic education should be available wherever needed to counter the loss of personal dignity, the waste of human resource and the vulnerability to political extremism that hopeless unemployment can bring.

This list of social ills is not contexted within any analysis of the crisis of capitalism and therefore the nature of the 'contribution' the individual can make towards their solution must be adduced from the kind of 'basic education' which is proposed.

The contexts of meaning offered are the contexts of the student's own life. But these also represent an educator's view since there can be few people (in need of basic education or not) who think about their lives in terms like these: work, home and family, the stages of adult life, leisure and citizenship.

These are not life contexts, but they are (for the educators of the report) ways of defining the curriculum of basic education in terms of a potential student's deficiencies. If we look at these contexts in detail we can see that by specifying what the student might 'need' to learn they also specify what the student can be expected to lack, for example:

ii) Home and family, including an understanding of family relationships, as well as problems of housing, of family planning, of domestic economy, of family health and diet, and some knowledge of the available welfare services.
iv) Leisure, including participation and responsible spectatorship in sport; outlets for any creative urge and potential; hobbies and cultural activities; home and foreign travel.
v) Citizenship, both in terms of responsibility towards society and also in terms of understanding and safeguarding civil rights and freedom.

The notion of responsibility is much more conspicuous in the report than the notion of rights and there is an overt concern with developing attitudes in students which will make them more accessible to every kind of managerial and bureaucratic form of control, as is clear from its definition of the 'coping' skills the individual needs:

Knowledge of the main government and social service agencies. Observing the law; handling and completing forms; dealing with local authority services and departments; using the postal, library, and citizen advisory services.

Work related knowledge. Applying for jobs; personal presentation; dealing with superiors; income tax and national insurance; trade union participation; basic understanding of industrial economics, including the economic facts of industrial and social life, wealth creation, and productivity and profitability; the needs and aims of industry and public and social services; rights and responsibilities under employment legislation; superannuation.

The economic 'facts' of industrial and social life are defined in terms of 'productivity and profitability'. What the 'needs' of the social services might be — apart from the need to have clients — is less clear.

The report's references to the individual needs of the student produce a picture of the student as illiterate — with a need 'to speak so that others understand what is said', innumerate, incompetent in family relationships and in handling money, ignorant or careless of the law, quite possibly irresponsible in leisure and in need of instruction about the responsibilities of a worker and a citizen. What emerges is a classic picture of under-socialization which is not, and could not, be supported by reference to evidence. The curriculum is laid out in terms of specific skills without any reference to an educational process through which students might gain some wider and relevant understanding of the social and political institutions and structures which these curriculum areas are actually about. There is no sign anywhere in the report that it has followed its own aim to 'put people in the way of perceiving social ills more clearly'.

In its intention to counter the damage done to the individual lives of those whose needs the social and political order most fails to meet, the report produces education as social work in a way that justifies Ingleby's contention that 'welfare services' are

. . . a system set up *alongside* existing society, rather than part of it, whose task is to repair the damage done to human beings by the way of life the social system entails for them: its function thus being inevitably corrective, rather than preventative. [29]

However unwittingly, this concept of basic education is premised on bad faith, because the 'problem' of the welfare services is managing the demand for scarce resources. As we move towards 'structural unemployment' every individual whose basic education achieves a job means another individual without one. Likewise the shortage of good housing stock means that some achieve better housing at the expense of others. If all were to try to use the welfare services as they have a right to, need could not be met from available resources. For the individual, basic education may offer rewards, for the disadvantaged as a group it offers very little that can ameliorate the circumstances of individual lives or the conditions which produce them.

The report, *A Strategy for the Basic Education of Adults*, exemplifies the most extreme example we have seen so far of the way that a concept of individual need and student-centredness are used to legitimate an ideological commitment by adult education to the status quo. It makes it clear that needs are prescriptively defined by the educator in terms of the educator's perception of those needs, a perception which derives from a concept of disadvantage which seeks to remedy social problems through the imputed inadequacies of individuals.

Willis, in a recent empirical study of secondary schooling, notes that the education system creates those very problems which it then tries to solve because failure is built into the system as the necessary obverse of success:

It is in the school with its basic teaching paradigm that those attitudes needed for *individual* success are presented as necessary in *general*. The contradiction is never admitted that not all can succeed, and that there is no point for the unsuccessful in following prescriptions for success — hard work, diligence, conformism, accepting knowledge as an equivalent of real value. There is a generalization in school from an individualistic logic to a group logic without recognition of the very different nature and level of abstraction of the latter. [30]

In so far as adult education programmes for the disadvantaged are aimed at ameliorating the supposed deficiencies of individuals, Willis' analysis of secondary schooling is likely to apply equally to adult education:

. . . the logic of class or group interests is different from the logic of individual interests. To the individual working-class person mobility in this society may mean something. Some working-class individuals do 'make it' and any particular individual may hope to be one of them. To the class or group at its own proper level, however, mobility means nothing at all. The only true mobility at this level would be the destruction of the whole class society.

Conformism may hold a certain logic for the individual then, but for the class it holds no rewards: it is to give up all possibilities of independence for nothing but an illusory ideal of classlessness. The individual might be convinced by education's apparent résumé of what is supposed to happen in society — advance through effort for all who try — but the counter-school culture 'knows' much better than the state and its agencies what to expect — elitist exclusion of the mass through spurious recourse to merit. The counter-school culture and other working class cultural forms contain elements towards a profound critique of the dominant ideology of individualism in our society.

The force of Willis's study, and of others which point in the same direction, is that adult educators need to find more adequate reasons than 'a lack of confidence to come forward' or a generalized disapproval of school education to explain the lack of take-up of the educational opportunities in adult education among working-class adults. The individualism of adult education itself and a curriculum which reflects middle-class life-styles may be a sufficient deterrent in themselves.

The main argument of this paper has been that if we examine the ideology of adult education there is reason to question whether its claims to distinctiveness can be maintained since it is apparent that both in its curriculum and its pedagogy it is appropriately seen as an extension of initial schooling not only in how it legitimates its practices but, so far as one can see, in substance also. Insofar as it is moving towards a more highly differentiated curriculum, it is becoming more and not less like the educational hierarchy in providing a stratified curriculum for a stratified society. In this sense education's problems are society's problems. Whether adult education can radicalize the nature of its enterprise depends on whether it is willing to examine its practices critically. That is, change will depend on seeing that the 'problems' lie within the nature of the provision adult education makes and not in those who do not avail themselves of the resources it offers. The enormous and undoubted commitment of adult educators to reach a wider population will continue to be misplaced, if the commitment to meeting individual need is understood and contexted only within the cultural bias of individual achievement and middle-class life-styles, and if the only alternative is predicated upon the individualization of failure. The issue is not whether individuals have needs nor whether they should be met but how those needs are socially and politically constituted and understood, how they are articulated and whose voice is heard. Adult education responds to the collective voice of individualism, but it has in a large measure failed to identify or to identify with the needs of those who reject the premises on which individualism is based.

Acknowledgements

The critique of the report, *A Strategy for the Basic Education of Adults*, appeared in a slightly different form in *Political Papers,* no. 5. *Political Papers* are published at and available from the City Lit., Stukeley Street, Drury Lane, London, WC1.

While I am wholly responsible for the way I have presented the issues and for the conclusions I have drawn, I am indebted to many seminars and discussions in which some of the issues raised here have been debated. In particular, and without thereby committing them to my views, I should like to thank Stephen Parrott and all other colleagues who as students and tutors constitute the present Diploma in Adult Education course of the University of London Extra-Mural Department, for their help in unravelling the problems this paper addresses.

3 The theory of community education and its relation to adult education

Colin Fletcher, Senior Research Officer, Department of Adult Education, University of Nottingham

The topic of community education so moves adult educators that they rarely analyse what it means and usually react strongly because of what it means to them. The dominant view is that community education is both an 'enemy within' and a 'lost cause'; it may be a fresh departure but the voyagers are lost, not to say doomed, and could take the ship down with them.

Reviewing a recent contribution to *Studies in Adult Education*, the editor of *Adult Education* wrote:

a very timely article . . . which expresses lucidly the doubts which many must feel about the current fashion for community education and the real danger that funds will be transferred to this highly labour intensive area of work away from traditional adult education programmes. [1]

Sometimes, though, adult educators feel that although community education is different from traditional adult education and probably a threat to its security, it nevertheless has 'something to say'. Thus, the third group of priorities raised by the North West Adult Education Conference in 1978 was:

a) Community Education should be perceived as relevant to individual needs and should offer the possibility of change through the immediacy of coping with the problem. If related largely to 'disadvantaged' areas, does it have any relevance for the traditional adult education student?
b) Community implies a sharing of interests as well as a sharing of geography and so community education ought to encompass both.
c) Changes are needed in the formal administrative structures to allow for development in this field.
d) All teachers should have as part of their professional training some aspects of adult learning and teaching. [2]

In this attempt to be fair, accommodative and clear about the limitations of community education the participants have indicated three themes said to be aspects of community education. They viewed it as problem-centred and dealing with the disadvantaged; locally based and informal or inexpert or at least not necessarily grounded in educational theory and practice.

These points are interesting precisely because they skirt a subject as if to contain it and so the meaning of the subject remains largely implicit. This is to be expected when authors have a much clearer view of traditional adult education and are convinced by personal experience that this tradition is worth perpetuating and developing from within.

The theory of community education is therefore necessary for a number of reasons. First, it is worth exploring for its own sake. Second, it will permit theoretical criticism rather than practical criticisms such as 'we can't afford it' or 'it will take money away from what we need to do'. Third, if the following theoretical arrangement is correct then certain errors have crept into the discussion. The errors are most important at this time; community education is all too rapidly becoming a type of education appropriate to a type of people as distinct from 'derived from a theory' and so a full educational perspective.

The purpose of this paper can now be summarized:

1   To advance a theory of community education.
2   To point out errors in some beliefs about community education.
3   To evaluate the hostile criticism as well as those writings full of hope, for they show the way in which the working class are both discussed and not discussed in adult education.
4   Finally one contemporary question is considered, namely whether extra-mural work could be a model for intra-mural work in universities in the 1980s.

The theory of community education

Nobody is entitled just to write a theory; they have first to state what they mean by theory. The technical meaning of theory in the social sciences is the one taken here; that there are at least two independent premises from which primary deductions can be made; and then secondary deductions can be made by relating primary deductions. [3] A premise is a statement at a relatively high level of abstraction which is held to be true. A deduction is the drawing out of implications of this premise so that it can be observed in the realm of human action.

premise so that it can be observed in the realm of human action.

Deductions are made, too, by taking the implications of two or more premises together. And so theories are often illustrated with lines between premises and deductions, between first principles and their dependent related procedures. Theories are apparently simple because they can be expressed in a few words or in a diagram. A closer look, though, reveals concepts and phrases which mean many things.

The theory to be outlined here is not original in the sense that I have dreamed it up but rather it is the result of my search for the themes of past and present practice. Thus, the theory has a number of sources of inspiration, though not all of them have equal significance. Having put the theory together, the premises are as follows:

1   The community has its needs and common causes and is the maker of its own culture. This is a new premise, one which stands in opposition to the Renaissance view of knowledge. In the latter ideas exist independently of, and outside, people. The more ideas they have the more knowledgeable they are and the civilizing process is that of putting the ignorant sufficiently close to the knowledgeable.

The new premise says that culture is an active, shared component of life. It does not exist independently of its creators and its creation depends very much upon the problems people face and their celebration of their own causes.

2   Educational resources are to be dedicated to the articulation of needs and common causes. Articulation does not mean mobilization or publicity; it means the making of clear, distinct connections. It means joining ideas and analysis and being disposed to seek for needs rather than wait for demands. The resources are those of capital, plant, land, equipment and people. Each of these resource areas is substantial in itself and could be broken down into many further parts. For example the premise does not say 'teaching to be devoted . . . .' because it is held that the theory of community education is rather more than a prescription for good professional practice. In effect, this second premise might be called the curriculum or 'what is to be done' premise and is closely related with the third 'how is it to be done' premise.

3   Education is an activity in which we alternate between the roles of student, teacher and person. The roles are not occupied separately but in interdependence; this means being sympathetic to the other person, playing another part and believing in the purpose and principle of alternation. This means not wanting to be distant and absorbed in oneself, not believing that some types of people will never

be able to lead and other types will never be able to follow. This implies trust, co-operation, joint achievement, a mature and equal relationship. Being a student or a teacher is not a preserve or a protectorate — not if persons are taking turns.

The premises obviously depend heavily upon the meanings of their key words; less obviously perhaps, they are also part of broader theories of human development where even a brief glimpse can catch sight of a broad vista. T. R. Young defines community by what might be called both its actions and its essences:

The world in which human beings have a social (i.e. intended/reified) relation to each other. In a community all persons have standing. Standing entails the right and responsibility to produce culture in its manifold forms. A person shares community with another when the person cannot disengage from his social relationship with the other. A good test for (and consequence of) this is if a person can ignore another person's trouble then those two don't share community . . . . 'Community' is the translation of the German word 'Gemeinschaft'. To say that an organisation or society has community is to say that it is non-alienating, and somehow in tune with the conditions by which humans create themselves as human beings. [5]

Holly puts the resources issue as an individual matter and yet prepares the ground for its collective purpose:

Properly understood, education is the social organization of human learning; this learning being itself a reflexive process involving the individual psyche in relationship with the surrounding natural and social world. [6]

If, then, the social organization is put to work at the fulcrum of the reflexive process it is to be situated at the point where individuals are making culture — where they are improving their own conditions together. Culture is only produced, as distinct from reproduced, when different efforts with the same problems or the same efforts with different problems emerge. Education then has the choice to be part of the solution or part of the problem. The question, in relation to the articulation of common causes, is 'whose resources are they?' The theory does not appear to anticipate conflict with the community but implies that if resources are not currently dedicated it must be because an employer does not wish it to be so. In effect, the second premise rests upon partisanship as a manifest function and a break between agent and employer as an implicit condition. [7] This, of course, is not a problem in respect of whether the education will 'work' but of whether it will be allowed to work and at this point we must observe that there are both liberal and liberating interpretations of the second premise, that there are two streams of thought and action springing from this common source. In fact, the liberal and liberating meanings can be found throughout education; liberal assumes that the person is 'free' and should be yet freer and more enlightened whilst liberating assumes bondage and the setting free of whole classes of persons.

The third premise is avowedly revolutionary for education because the 'person' is seen as a whole being whilst pupil and teacher are seen as partial and institutional roles. Without doubt persons are either children or adults and in all but the most enlightened of thought; children are simply less than adult and represent a condition into which adults can unfortunately regress. [8] Nevertheless, thinking in terms of a school perhaps, T. R. Young goes some way towards describing what a fully developed alternation between roles would mean:

a form of education in which cumulative capacities are developed and critical use of them encouraged in a classroom and out within the framework of community. The line between teacher and pupil is eliminated and co-operation rather than competition marks the progress of the class. [9]

Such a premise may be debated, particularly by those who regard teaching as the professional spreading of *their* enlightenment of self-expression. But they may be surprised to learn that the advocate of such ideas was not Marx but George Herbert Mead — a man who believed in pragmatism and evolution. [10] His subtle theory of social development holds that we learn through those we know of those beyond ourselves and when we 'take the role of the other' we learn more about ourselves as well as about others.

The three premises can be summarized and related to deductions (see the diagram on page 70):

1   The educational centre should serve both as a place that people can visit in order to make use of resources and as a place from which the educationalists leave in order to establish what resources are required and where they are needed most. Thus, a primary deduction from the first two premises is that what both teacher and student are to concentrate upon together is how the centre provides for the periphery, and how the periphery puts its expectations clearly to the centre. The corollary of this is that activity has no *a priori* location and takes place wherever it is most convenient and most required.

2   A primary deduction from premises 1 and 2 is probably more

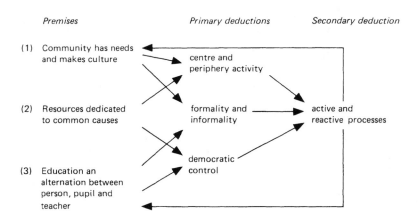

| Premises | Primary deductions | Secondary deduction |

(1) Community has needs and makes culture

centre and periphery activity

(2) Resources dedicated to common causes

formality and informality

active and reactive processes

democratic control

(3) Education an alternation between person, pupil and teacher

The theory of community education

obvious; it is that of democratic control. In fact, the deduction is simply that of democracy as distinct from democratic control. In the relationship between executive and electorate, the one does not necessarily represent the other.

3   The secondary deductions have often been seen as if they were premises for community education, whilst in the light of the theory advanced here, social action and social reaction are an outcome of initial premises as distinct from specific intentions. The distinction between action and reaction is largely technical; action is intended to imply innovation and something coming from a need or demand expressed from within, whilst reaction is intended to be a response to change, externally stimulated change.

4   Clearly the question raised is what do people need to know? Questions are asked backwards; once one knows what has happened or could happen the issue is how to find out and where to find out.

5   A secondary issue is also to learn the languages used by others to discuss oneself and one's community. Meanwhile the theoretical question which focuses upon pedagogy is not what do people need to know but how do people learn? The answer to this question appears to have gone further than people learning by doing; the answer lies at

the point where people commit themselves to improving their own circumstances. At this point people learn theory *and* skills; knowledge is useful precisely because without it there is either negligible action or a near inevitability of failure.

The theory and some misconceptions

No matter how a theory is expressed it always remains hard to grasp its real meaning and full implications. Errors also come from misunderstanding or outright mischief and whatever the motives it becomes difficult for all but a few 'insiders' to follow the lines of argument.

Such problems are probably compounded by the kind of theory to which the theory of community education is most closely related. It is a theory authenticated by practice — by doing. It is not a scientific theory which is more or less right regardless of observer; it is a social scientific theory which guides human action and is guided by it. [11] Community education is defined by critical social theory which is a kind of thinking which empirical thinkers, Bacon and David Hume, might not have recognized but one which Locke and Rousseau could have readily engaged in. [12] It is true, however, that critical social theory is nowhere near as widely taught as it could be and that most of those with some understanding are self-taught. As with other misconceptions, therefore, the purpose of this section is not to apportion blame but to separate the theory from that which it is not, to situate the theory as clearly as possible.

The theory does lend itself to a variety of definitions (or more properly descriptions). The definition of community education could be:

Community education is a process of commitment to the education and leisure of all ages through local participation in setting priorities, sharing resources and the study of circumstances. Thus, the community and its educational provisions qualify and enhance each other.

This definition shows that community education does not derive from an adult educational theory but an educational theory which also applies to adult education; the theory equally applies to secondary education and to the voluntary sector. That which adult education practitioners have therefore chosen to make their own is often a matter of convenience; convenient because as adult educators they have the possibility of community education. Further, there is nothing in the theory which says that it is solely for the working class. Keith Jackson has rightly pointed out that the theory of community education applies just as readily to commuter suburbs as it does to inner-city ghettos. [13] It is not therefore an outcome of the theory that community education is said to be for and of the working class, it is the outcome of an additional premise about what constitutes valid personal action [14] and also what constitutes effective social change. And so, the distinction between the liberal and liberating interpretations rests not upon subverting the premises of community education but upon adding further premises which then qualify the *kind* of community and so the *kind* of personal and social action. The liberal interpretation confronts a range of real hurdles and particularly the problems associated with being a part-time service. The liberal interpretation has had, in fact, considerable appeal to local education authorities [15] whilst the liberating interpretation has found support in the Workers' Educational Association and university extra-mural departments. The common ground of these two interpretations is the need for changes in emphasis and larger aims. The common interpretation is quite rightly, as far as the theory prescribes, action and advocacy. The interpretations could be said to be between realism and utopianism. [16] The liberal and liberating interpretations actually require separate treatment if the concern lies with the consequences of their actions. Thus, there are two misconceptions surrounding the question of 'whose community?' The first is that the liberal and liberating interpretations can be treated as being entirely the same and the second is that they are entirely different.

Neither is there an element in the theory which specifies that it should be for or devoted solely to 'deprived groups'; this misunderstanding would seem to depend upon a view of the particular relevance and particular effectiveness of styles of education with certain types of people. [17] Freire, for example, is writing of education as 'dialogical' both between teacher and student and topic and troubles:

The heart of Freire's message is universal: in his pedagogy, the process of learning becomes a radical way of being more fully human through critical involvement with others in improving social conditions. [18]

In fact, Keith Jackson, who has come closer than most to basing his evaluation upon a sound analysis has observed that 'deprived groups' are not compatible with the theory:

The 'old', the 'young', 'the disabled', council tenants, slum dwellers cease to be stereotyped categories and become people with views about how they want to be treated. [19]

Community education is in no sense intrinsically the cause of evangelical activists or parachuted experts dropping silently down upon an unsuspecting community. There is no reason why the educators should not be 'born and bred' local people.

Informality and outreach activity have already been seen as stemming from those premises. A common error, though, is to interpret these aspects as ends when in point of fact they are means. When they become ends, in theory at least, community education can become a spectator sport for precisely those who are responsible for its process.

The word process is most important; community education is not a policy or set of procedures. The word process means that community education is literally in the process of clarifying itself at the same time as demonstrating the relevance of the theory. That which is produced by the process is therefore the programme. Yet more broadly still it can be said that a mechanical theory produces the notion of policy and procedure whilst an organic theory produces the notions of processes and programmes. [20] A process is a dedication and a programme is a limited commitment to be criticized in the light of that process. A policy is a clearly set list of objectives and a procedure is the optimal expectation of the way in which these objectives are to be achieved. It may be that traditional adult education began as a process but it is hard to accept that it is not now a set policy with routine procedures.

The error, therefore, in the final analysis is to use the criteria of one kind of theory to criticize another; a theory is best criticized in its own terms even if it does mean learning the theory first and thereby giving it a measure of credibility. As the theory of community education requires the commitment to a process then no programme is ultimately defensible, there is no security in parts when the whole is a critical and democratic response. The micro-political aspect of this must be confronted for either the adult student is subordinate or equal and the relationship in which both teacher and learner are involved is an actual moving from the former to the latter. The error as a whole is to assume that community education is more than a commitment to a process, that it has fixed goals. There may be achievements but they could equally be called by-products, or milestones passed by some individuals upon a road taken for and by large groups in the community:

As far as individuals are concerned success can be reckoned (though hardly measured) in terms of extension of vocabulary, increase in social ability, acquisition of communication skills, acceptance of the notion of cause and effect and of the notion of evidence and other intangibles; but in the most important sense success will depend on the extent to which adult education contributes to the process of social change. [21]

Aspects of the case against community education

Criticism covers the range of response from thorough and reasoned doubt in a theory's own terms to shrill notes of heartfelt hostility. K. H. Lawson, [22] for example, has taken community education to task 'because of its values'. Just what does this mean? It could mean that adult education in the traditional sense is value free, whilst community education is value laden. [23] It might also mean that the values of adult education are not compatible with those of community education, or it may mean that the values of community education are suspect. Dr Lawson's criticism would seem to spread across all three possibilities; what he really dislikes is the relationship between community education and community development. He thinks that community educators engage in persuasion, that their involvement is a subtle form of social control, and that the biases which they show are like those of self-appointed leaders of lemmings. Clearly, Dr Lawson is not concerned with the theory but with the practice; he finds it possible to describe community education activity as 'practical instrumentalism' and although this remains undefined it does appear to be a suspect if not sinister activity.

Dr Lawson's criticism is that community education is a means to dubious ends and the ends are dubious because of an implicit belief that 'society is in danger'. [24] Dr Lawson, in effect, responds entirely to the link between community education and community development, that is to the liberating as distinct from liberal interpretation. He does not confront the theoretical premises, perhaps because he does not believe that they actually exist. This is after all a surprisingly common perspective; it is an everyday truth that if one does not like another's actions then one doubts his/her reasons for them — or even that formal reasons could possibly exist. In this way community education has suffered already through lack of *direct* criticism. Instead there are small bands of antagonists or protagonists from both the political left and right. Consciousness certainly as a collective product is not an issue for writers such as Lawson, his ends or values for adult education are 'cultural diffusion and personal development'. [25]

Criticism from the left is based upon dynamic premises. British society is morally bankrupt, in a state of chronic economic crisis, at the brink of imminent change and confronted daily by the need for radical transformation to social ownership of all social products whether they be material or cultural. For thinkers in this vein whilst the premises of community education may be unobjectionable the practices are most certainly those of either naive or cynical error. For critics of the left, community education represents all that is wrong in reform movements: paternalism; patronage; tokenism; parochialism; even the catch-all, crime of deviationism. Although these criticisms are not yet in written form they can be sensed as if felt by community educators; they are aware that the view that community education is excessively labour intensive is held for different reasons by critics of both the left and the right. For the right it is a case of cost whilst for the left it is a case of mistaken cause. Thus, the theory of collective action that depends upon notions of class consciousness is held to be in opposition to notions of community consciousness; some would even go so far as to claim that community consciousness is a form of false class consciousness.

In this way critics of both left and right deny the validity of basing educational work upon the notion of community. In their different ways they are making a claim that community is an illusory concept, a web of all that is weird in the world. Consequently all critics begin, not with the premises of community education but with doubts upon the notion of community.

So far, however, social science-based criticism has not made any real headway, at least with adult educators. The practice is to deplore the proliferation of definitions and to suggest that in the absence of easy agreement there is no perceptible way forward. This tactic, of course, ignores a wealth of work in community studies and in the sociology of communities. [26] It is true that almost the opposite condition actually applies, community studies are one of the best developed areas of the social sciences as a whole, and they contain much of the best work. [27] Criteria have been advanced elsewhere which are, at least arguably, groupings of conditions distilled from some of this better work. [28]

The point being made here is nevertheless of a different order; left, right and scientific centre combine their critical forces on the front of suggesting that community defies definition; that the absence of a coherent definition wilfully misleads local people and takes place through the activities of a few naive malcontents 'subverting the system' without having a trace of decent doubt. [29]

But it's difficult to see what the fuss is all about. To be sure works cannot be cited to prove that such thoughts are thought. (Largely because astute critics sense some vitality and success and so exercise a measure of public caution.) The full blast has yet to be felt, too, because most critics are aware both that there are advantages in using the term 'community education' and that liberating activity is not one which they would happily and openly oppose.

This then is the crunch of the criticism of community education to date; a loose alliance of left, right and centre, who do not like it, know in their bones that they will never like it and put the onus upon community educators to explain themselves as programme activities whilst denying that there could be anything like an acceptable process. Perhaps the muted nature of this criticism has actually helped the development of community education so far, certainly it has not prevented advocates working out their ideas.

What are the advocates saying?

It must be understood that many of the arguments in favour of community education are immediately recognizable as extensive criticisms of other forms of adult education, criticisms which span from exhausted enthusiasm to the collapse of original purpose. But tempting though it may be to counterpoint community education with traditional adult education, an attack on one form is hardly a defence of another and what is noticeable in community education writings is self-criticism as well as eloquent argument. [30]

The first proposition has to do with the desire for community among all classes in Britain. [31] Colin Kirkwood put it thus:

there is a profound, spontaneous desire for what we might call organic community among people of all classes in Britain. The word community is popular because through it people can express this yearning for communion with each other. It is a yearning for social wholeness, a mutuality, an inter-relatedness, as opposed to the alienated, fragmented, antagonistic social world of daily experience. Linked with this desire for warm relatedness is the desire of stability. [32]

Here then is the first problem realized and recognized by community educators, that there are deep and definite divisions within communities when the term is used to describe a long-established place. But it can also refer to a different kind of relatedness, that which is co-operative and egalitarian and it is this organic meaning which is preferred and consequently used. [33]

The second judgement is that there should be a dialogue to discover and pursue interests and concerns. Thus, the content is jointly defined, the adult educator also learns. [34] Unfortunately this aspect of the argument is all too often expressed ambiguously whilst, in fact, there are three distinct parts to it. The first element is that adult education is not a separate solitary service but rather one of a number of services. Brian Stewart puts this (as he puts all his points), in the form of a rhetorical question. Here though, it suits the tone of this paper to note that he calls on adult educators to:

gain access to and the acceptance of community groupings . . . involve ourselves with the work of voluntary agencies . . . strike constructive and fruitful alliances with colleagues in the related fields of health and housing. [35]

adult educators will themselves learn a great deal from association with such programmes. [36]

Not least because:

adult education must be seen . . . as an integral part of a whole series of activities which are community based and concerned with the total community. [37]

This position must not be seen as one of empire-building or a takeover-bid or mimicry but rather that of wanting a comprehensive community service in which adult education is a knowledgeable and active part. [38] Not the least among the reasons for this is to retain control over the programme for a broad base in a strong defence against any pressure to contract provision and narrow its bands. Put as first principles this aspect becomes clearly combative:

Build a broad base of planning on goals and needs recognized by participants. The programme must never become a tool of the administration, priesthood, top management, etc. . . . Establish a climate free from fear and harmful tension. . . . Let participants share in programme development, feedback and evaluation. . . . Adapt programmes to the unique features of each institution. [39]

This 'becoming more like a social worker' is not quite so crudely put; the argument is that adult education has something to give and take. With those involved in community development it is a question of appropriate skills: '. . . both could profit considerably if the relationship were fully explored'. [40] Or more contentiously: '. . . adult educators will provide a better service if they adopt some of the skills of the community worker'. [41]

Obviously these advocates *believe* in adult education and have high hopes for it, perhaps it resembles a permanently frontier activity: discovering, developing and rediscovering without too great a concern for establishments, privileges and home comforts. Perhaps too, the adult educator surges towards frontiers because of the value he or she places upon education:

Every adult educationalist is an agent of change and is committed to social change in so far as he works for the dissemination of educational values. [42]

And if there are to be two camps, the traditional 'hawks' and the progressive 'doves' then:

Everything we do should have an educational objective and every activity we offer should contain a significant element of progressive education. [43]

Progressive in this context refers to content as well as form. What emerges is that community education is innovative adult education:

by innovative adult education I mean such work as women's studies, trade union studies, local newspapers, parents' discussion of and involvement in their children's education, participatory education taking off from issues like play, roads, housing, community councils, vandalism, race, oral history, the writing of poetry, short stories, and reminiscences by people who have learned through the processes of traditional school education that they are incapable of such creativity. [44]

But if the metaphor of frontier is to have much value, we should be explicit about the country or continent of which we speak, for then it becomes clear that there are boundaries and landlocked territories avoided, as it were, because of their difficult terrain. This is hardly satisfactory and so an argument for community education is that it moves closer to the total programme — to there being 'something for everybody'. [45] This total programme really does have formidable obstacles — at times the terrain is virtually impassable without special equipment: 'half the population is inhibited by attitudes that are deeply rooted in social circumstances and earlier education'. [46]

Thus what is being done has to be part of how it is being done — recruitment is more effective through social and kin ties than it is through formal means. [47] The class will be held together by its collective achievements and traditional aims, such as essay writing, are not necessarily neglected:

Learning will take place through action, through writing letters, organizing petitions and surveys, meeting officials and councillors and arranging social and other activities, as well as through group discussion. Incidentally, there has been no problem in obtaining written work in this kind of adult education group. [48]

This shared action though marks a frontier for the tutor as much as the student; neither has necessarily spent much time on each other's territory. That which helps more than anything is the tutor's flexibility — the preparedness not rigidly to take adult education in a particular direction but to mix freely with fellow mortals:

Tutors must accept that one activity will flow into another and must be willing to become involved in other activities connected with the group, e.g: helping with a Christmas pantomime or organizing a bazaar. [49]

It is just at this point that the advocates of community education feel at their weakest and their strongest, they are aware that only the initiated can see the educational aspect of selling jumble; only they can see what common purpose has been established and what common ground now exists for discussions upon trust; the poor, other people's waste and clothing a family in cast-offs:

Individuals who were *submerged* in reality, merely *feeling* their needs, *emerge* from reality and perceive the *causes* of their needs. In this way they can go beyond the level of real consciousness to that of potential consciousness much more rapidly. [50]

And so private troubles can be seen as social problems because it is *how* things fit together that often eludes people, they often have the picture and the individual pieces:

Many recent innovative forms of adult education take as their starting point matters of immediate interest or concern to participants. They need not, however, remain locked in practical particularity, but can, and often do, branch out into matters of general significance and multiple inter-connectedness.

At no time do advocates spur adult educators into conflict with authorities. This is consistent with the view that the educators and social workers should work together rather than be locked in jealousies meaningless to their 'clients'. Nevertheless, adult educators are likely to get 'drawn into' political controversy and it is surprising that there is little comment upon this. [51]

Why these conflicts become so important is because they occur with sections of the community for whom education as a personal experience was often damaging or simply distant and for whom education represents authority. The argument has, however, taken two distinct lines, and sometimes it is difficult to recognize that they derive from the same source.

The first says that there are many for whom adult education could be irrelevant without special effort whilst the second says that without being reached by such provision distance is compounded by yet another disadvantage. Thus, there should be a special effort made for those for whom no special effort has been made previously.

These two themes, that of a sector of the population and that of positive discrimination, refer directly to principles of social justice. The values are egalitarian in origin and intention and inspire more conflict and reaction when they set out to regard others as equal and oppressed rather than different and confused. Advocates, therefore, tend to pursue their chosen alternative despite real and intensive social conflicts; it would now seem appropriate for them to share some of their knowledge in this respect. Perhaps this has not been done simply because those who act prefer others to write and analyse and leave only cryptic messages themselves.

One such project was that of Phil Collins from a street based tenants' and residents' group in Havant, Hampshire. It is clear that engagement *in* community education is advocacy *in action* and that it produces self and process criticism.

The street based group is based around a facilitator/co-ordinator who lives in the street or neighbourhood and meetings take place in the home of one of the members. Crudely, street based groups are about providing educational opportunity for adults who would not normally use Higher/Further and Adult education provision. In this particular setting it was envisaged that the group situation would act as a bridge to further education participation.

Advantages: of the groups were that they were held in a familiar and informal setting and eradicated problems such as: travelling, punctuality, finance and regular attendance.

Drawbacks: were limited space, the insularity of the group and the temporary nature of the group (funded as an experimental project).

Results: led to community involvement, greater confidence among members, and take up of formal education course.

Lasting benefits: an increase in members' ability to take advantage of wider activities and an ability to cope with everyday problems.

Discussion points: usefulness of groups, lack of intermediate link between group and formal education. [52]

The advocates are actually asking their case to be heard against the sounds of a creaking service, [53] it is not the society which is in danger but the service:

We are not yet developing a social conscience and . . . unless we change, a service which is potentially enormously valuable to the community and to society as a whole . . . is in imminent danger of perishing. [54]

Keith Jackson concludes his argument for a closer relationship between adult education and community development with the view that there would be 'advantages to the quality — substantial and reciprocal — a new life'. [55]

Nevertheless, it is absolutely crucial to realize that liberal and liberating views are working towards different kinds of services or institutions. The liberal argument would seem to centre upon the community school or at the very least a combined youth and adult education service:

The school of the future — not that one can sit down and paint its portrait — will certainly be a community school. It will provide more and more flexible learning opportunities for all children, young people and adults. Boundaries between types of education will merge and a unity based upon the needs of a community will be at least a possibility. The community college in concept and practice helps to map that future. [56]

In contrast the liberating view is essentially a response to the majority class *in its own terms*, there is no suggestion of taking school, college or university out to the people. Instead there is a 'huge need and potential for adult education provision for working-class communities if the adult education movement in this country is prepared to remove its shackles and adopt a radically new approach'. [57]

The relevance of community education to university extra-mural education

The liberating interpretation of community education has considerable implications for an extra-mural department, just as the liberal interpretation has major consequences for the LEAs and WEA. In the latter group few LEAs have not established or experimented with community education, and they have found the strengthening of the institutions, the enlivening of the staff, and the involvement of local groups most gratifying. [58]

The question here is the response of the extra-mural department; for the university department functions both as a full university member in the sense of research and as a marginal in the sense of its teaching. Clearly community education could not be a model for the universities intra-murally without the transformation of the universities themselves. Where, however, the extra-mural department can play its part is in the co-ordination of research in relation to local knowledge, in its preparedness to devote teams or task forces to particular communities, in its support of in-service training of community educators [59] and so its support for LEAs and WEAs. In the process, of course, the work of the extra-mural department would remain as experimental and risky as it ever was.

Yet the salience of this essay can be easily missed because of this concluding section's title. The essay could have been addressed to the 'English question'; upon change in English education through *ad hoc* activities; upon social class as the analytical framework to which community education properly applies, and to the ritual of resistance through which English institutions pass whilst they delay, and at the same time shape, the incorporation of novel forms.

In any event it remains a task for the university departments to examine and publicize the theory of community education, particularly in the form of reflection upon its purposes and practices. Most departments have made some kind of move in this direction, that which is needed is quite simply impetus.[60] It has been the purpose of this paper to propose a theory of community education whilst recognizing the danger that a dynamic theory of community education may be developing at precisely the moment when institutions are most resistant to structural change.

4 Adult education and the disadvantaged

Jane L. Thompson, Lecturer in Community Education,
University of Southampton

The rediscovery of poverty and the concept of deprivation

The poor, it is said, are always with us, but it is only recently that they
have become fashionable. In the wake of Macmillan's 'you've-never-
had-it-so-good' Britain and the liberal polemicism of Kennedy's
campaigning America, Britain in the 1960s 'rediscovered' poverty.

The first soundings of alarm came from a number of commissions
of inquiry set up by the government to consider London's housing
(Milner and Holland), children and young people (Ingleby), primary
education (Plowden), the personal social services (Seebohm), and
people and planning (Skeffington). One after the other the reports
told the same sad story of bad housing, urban decay, educational
disaster areas, unacceptable levels of poverty — in a phrase 'urban
deprivation'.

The discovery of the problem of urban deprivation led in rapid
succession to a vocabulary of complementary diseases — 'areas of
special need', 'pockets of deprivation', 'twilight zones', 'priority
areas', etc. Their inhabitants were variously referred to as 'the
disadvantaged', 'the under-privileged', the 'culturally'
'environmentally' 'linguistically' and 'educationally deprived', 'the
needy', 'the maladjusted' and 'the handicapped'. As Rutter and
Madge point out, deprivation became one of the most overworked
words in the English language. [1] Bowlby had used it earlier to refer
to lack of mother love. [2] Casler saw it as a lack of sensory
stimulation. [3] Runciman discussed deprivation in terms of financial
and material resources. [4] And Eckland and Kent defined it in terms
of deviation from what is considered to be normal and appropriate by
dominant groups in society. [5] In the same vein Ginsberg and others
discounted the whole notion of deprivation as a myth based on
middle-class misconceptions about poor people. [6]

One of the effects of the over-use of words like deprivation and disadvantage has been the tendency to use them as a form of shorthand, lumping together a wide range of precariously related and generally denigratory tendencies into a common stereotype. Maternal deprivation, for example, 'has been used to cover almost every kind of undesirable interaction between mother and child — rejection, hostility, cruelty, over-indulgence, repressive control, lack of affection and the like.' [7] In fact, 'the words almost function as a pejorative test in which each reads into the concept his own biases and prejudices.' [8] All of this could well be dismissed as 'academic semantics' were it not for the fact that behind the labels, the over-simplification and the stigma are people who, for whatever reason, continue to experience various forms of personal and social hardship.

In 1972, Sir Keith Joseph, then Secretary of State for Social Services, voiced what, in the circumstances, was considered to be a logical appraisal of the deprivation/disadvantage debate. He asked, 'Why is it, in spite of long periods of full employment and relative prosperity and the improvement of community services since the Second World War, deprivation and problems of maladjustment so conspicuously persist?' He was referring by deprivation to those 'circumstances which prevent people developing to nearer their potential — physically, emotionally and intellectually' and which reveal themselves in 'poverty, in emotional impoverishment, in personality disorder, in poor educational attainment, in depression and despair'. His conclusion was simple — in the majority of cases, the symptoms of the disease deprivation were endemic in the poor and transmitted from one generation to the next in a 'cycle of deprivation' exacerbated by the feckless, apathetic and dis-organized behaviour of those involved. He has of course gone on to clarify his association of deprivation with a form of personal pathology, transmitted from one generation to the next, and to recommend that every effort should be made to prevent those concerned from reproducing themselves in such irresponsibly large numbers. Needless to say the logic and persuasion of Sir Keith Joseph's view of a 'cycle of transmitted deprivation' has come under strong fire, not only because of its racist undertones, but because it seems to link poverty with maladjustment. Nonetheless, the insinuation that poverty and deprivation are a direct consequence of personally derived inadequacy still underpins a good deal of the continuing debate about deprivation and disadvantage.

An additional consequence has been the extent to which the

government has felt compelled to intervene and be seen to be responding positively to the recommendations made by commissions, academics and social planners. The introduction of Urban Aid, the setting up of the National Community Development Project and the identification of five Educational Priority Areas were the most famous of a number of projects designed to

provide for the care of our citizens who live in the poorest parts of our cities and towns . . . to arrest, in so far as it is possible by financial means, and reverse the downward spiral which afflicts so many of these areas (and in which) there is a deadly quagmire of need and apathy. [9]

The CDP was described as

a neighbourhood-based experiment aimed at finding new ways of meeting the needs of people living in areas of high social deprivation . . . by bringing together the work of the social services under the leadership of a special project team and also by tapping resources of self-help and mutal help which may exist among the people in the neighbourhoods. [10]

About the same time as the Urban Aid Programme was being set up, the DES announced that an action research project based on five areas of educational priority was to be undertaken. The scheme was part of the national programme of EPAs promoted by the Plowden Report. The DES decided on five special project areas identified in terms of their proportion of low income, low-status families, poor amenities in the home, high demand for free school meals and large numbers of children with language problems. The purpose of the projects was to offer 'positive discrimination' in an attempt to compensate for the inadequacy of the children's home background and in an attempt to make them more susceptible to the benefits of education.

In all of these initiatives there were related and important assumptions motivating the interventions. The final report of the Coventry CDP identified them as:

1 Disadvantaged areas are a minor blot on the urban landscape.
2 The problem can be blamed partly on the apathy or abnormality of local residents and partly on the incompetence of local government.
3 The solutions lie in self-help and more active participation by local people and more sensitive services and better communication and co-ordination on the part of the local authority.
4 Solutions can be found at very little extra cost and that a carrot and stick approach by central government can spur the local authorities to do things better in the future. [11]

All of the initiatives were littered with the language of 'project' and 'experiment', emphasizing the essentially temporary and tokenistic nature of their provision. And despite a good deal of public relations propaganda about 'positive discrimination' they operated on an incredibly small budget. The whole Urban Aid Programme (of which the CDP formed only a small part) represented only one twentieth of one per cent of total public spending, and only one tenth of one per cent of total social service spending. Moreover the Urban Aid Programme was not additional money. It was deducted from the total rate support grant generally available for local authority spending. The EPA project lasted three years between 1968 and 1971 and cost the DES and the SSRC a mere £175,000.

The co-ordination of local authority services was seen as another important feature of strategies designed to relieve poverty and disadvantage. Seebohm had promoted the idea of a generic approach to provision in the personal social services. Better co-operation at local level between those of the various 'caring professions' and local authorities was seen as a good way of streamlining provision and concentrating resources. 'Participation' was another key word, designed to challenge the latent apathy of the poor and galvanize them into constructive self-help activities.

It's hardly surprising that in this climate of opinion, the conscience of adult education was stirred into action, and the relevance of existing adult education provision was called into question.

Adult education and the disadvantaged

In 1973 the Russell Committee published its Plan for Development in adult education. The fact that this report represented only one of four major collections of information, reviews of provision and recommendations about policy in adult education this century, has made it of critical importance to all those involved in adult education. [12] During the preceding twenty years or so adult education seemed to many of those engaged in it to have lost some of its earlier momentum. [13] Although the 1944 Education Act had been quite specific about the duties of local education authorities with regard to primary, secondary and further education, it didn't actually mention adult education by name. All of this contributed to the sense of insecurity and insignificance which many people felt about adult education and why the policy statements made by Russell were seized upon with such eagerness and gratitude.

As part of the preparation for its general report, the Russell Committee called for an inquiry to be carried out by Peter Clyne, directed by Henry Arthur Jones, based at the University of Leicester, and funded by the DES, to provide information about 'the education of the handicapped, and especially the informal educative influences upon him.' [14] Those involved began with the assumption that access to adult education was generally and widely available to the 'normal' population although its quality and quantity might vary in different places.

The test of disadvantage then was to identify factors *in the individual or in his personal circumstances* that would prevent him from participating in whatever the quality of the local provision of classes. The factors lie in three main areas: physical and mental handicap, which may be temporary or permanent; social disadvantage, which would include geographical isolation as well as poverty of life in areas of multiple deprivation; and educational disadvantage, which would include illiteracy, linguistic problems such as those of immigrants or the born deaf, or *a residual hostility to the whole idea of education.* [my italics] [15]

As in all the other circumstances discussed above, the notion of disadvantage was uncritically related to a wide range of physical and personal defects and social conditions in which diverse groups were linked together, and by which complex social, economic and political manifestations of inequality went unchallenged. The consequence was to reduce them all into a single uncomplicated category — 'the disadvantaged'.

The language of 'personal deficit', 'affliction' and the need for 'treatment' to 'rehabilitate' the 'malfunctioning' adult into 'normal' society runs like a medical checklist through the literature. The tone is one of mission and concern for the less fortunate, in areas in which the 'distinctions between therapeutic, educational and welfare needs become very difficult to establish'. [16]

The results of Clyne's inquiries became central to the recommendations of the Russell Report. The thinking behind them is more elaborately revealed in his book, *The Disadvantaged Adult.* The thrust of his argument is to present the view that adult education 'is a community service which can effectively bridge the gap between education and the social services'. Adult education is about aiding 'the individual towards self-fulfilment, self-confidence and a more capable involvement in [his] family and community'. 'Adult education must be concerned with people as human beings and not primarily as drivers, shop assistants, office workers or executives.' It must provide a 'tool to enable individuals to live their lives in a more informed and contented way as members of the community'.

'But on the fringes of adult education are the millions of men and women who, because of physical or mental disability or social or cultural disadvantage, do not, and cannot, participate in the general programme of adult education.' 'Many of [their] problems can be traced back to, and explained by, the home or the neighbourhood environment.' These are the 'Newsom adults', the 'unclubbables' and the 'drop outs' 'who have failed to understand, maintain contact with, or become involved in the rapidly changing technological society'. In such circumstances 'there is ample evidence of a cumulative deficit — the passing on from one generation to the next the disadvantages of poverty, unemployment, poor schools, etc.', of problems of 'inadequate vocabulary and the inability to articulate', and the 'many symptoms of individual, family and community malfunctioning'.

In such circumstances, Clyne concludes that 'disadvantage and degradation will increase if left unattended'. The intervention of adult education in close co-operation with the social services and community workers is the solution. Adult education can and must provide 'a compensatory and remedial education service' designed to help the disadvantaged 'improve their physical and mental welfare' so that they can achieve 'personal fulfilment, social usefulness and contentment as members of a community [with] the ability to contribute to, rather than take from, the national wealth'. [17]

The Russell Report's attention to the educational needs of the disadvantaged is clearly a testimony to the influence of Henry Arthur Jones and Peter Clyne. The committee's recommendations to the WEA that it should become increasingly responsible for work with the disadvantaged, and to the service generally, that it should attempt to co-operate much more closely with the social services and voluntary agencies, have become important guidelines. [18] The impetus given to creating posts of special responsibility for 'organizing the disadvantaged' and the recognition that 'community education' had a part to play, has encouraged — if it needed any more encouragement — yet more support for the 'community solution' to problems of structural poverty.

The outcomes of the committee's recommendations have been two-fold. The reaction of those persuaded by their logic has been to proliferate a whole range of new initiatives, everything from the

National Literacy Campaign and its more recent offspring Basic Education [19] to a multitude of small-scale, localized projects designed to meet the challenge of 'Russell category work'.

The other outcome has been to see the recommendations almost totally ignored, not because of their dubious custodialism, but by the dead weight of institutional complacency, fearful of such developments in case they divert limited educational resources towards community education and other innovatory projects and 'away from the more traditional role' of adult education when 'it is by no means established that community education is a desirable or viable replacement'. [20] Wiltshire and Mee are fearful that traditional provision, attracting as it does lower-middle and middle-class students on the one hand, and offset by a shift of resources towards the disadvantaged on the other hand, will neglect the vast majority of the population in the middle which adult education ought to be serving. [21] (It's astonishing how in this respect — as with the CDPs and the EPAs referred to earlier — exaggerated claims about positive discrimination have led many to believe that vast sums of money are being squandered on the essentially feckless and have confirmed 'the bottomless pit' hypothesis. [22] But in fact, as A. H. Halsey has frequently pointed out, considering the enormity of the problems encountered the magnitude of the aims outlined and the height of the expectations raised, the amounts of money actually forthcoming have been minuscule.)

Much more significant than either of these reactions to Russell has been the general acceptance of the assumptions upon which the committee based its assessment of disadvantage. This generally uncritical view of pathological and personalized explanations of disadvantage has served, as it did in explanations of the failure of working-class children in the school system, and the half-hearted response of successive governments to urban deprivation, to divert attention away from a more fundamental examination of the structural causes of poverty, inequality and educational divisiveness in our society.

However unsatisfactory it might appear to be, the notion of disadvantage has many strengths when it comes to educational and governmental intervention. Because it's a term used to refer to a 'multitude of sins', so far as policy makers are concerned, it has the capacity to appeal to a wide range of people with varied and conflicting ideologies. To social and political liberals it indicates the need for initiatives based on optimistic progressivism and couched in terms of 'compensatory education' and 'positive discrimination' in favour of 'deprived groups'. Even to political and social conservatives, educational provision for the disadvantaged has the attraction of being cheap and conciliatory and intended to transform the feckless and potentially disruptive into more responsible citizens. Such expectations are of course not new. Education has frequently been seen as the popular solution to social and political ills. [23] Christopher Jencks commenting on the American 'war on poverty' during the Kennedy/Johnson era — a campaign that did much to influence the thinking and practice in Britain — has suggested that its intention was essentially conservative in that it aimed to educate the poor to change their 'wrong skills, places of residence, personality traits and fertility patterns and to provide "character building" in lower-middle class virtues'. [24] So far as middle-class America was concerned the belief was that if 'they' were just more like 'us' everything would be all right. [25]

In recent years this view of cultural deprivation and disadvantage has come under fierce attack in both America and Britain. Friedman in America [26] and Bernstein in Britain [27] have both argued that cultural deprivation is an inaccurate term, in that no one can be deprived of a culture which every individual possesses, however different it may be from mainstream culture. [28] Kenneth Clark has argued that the labelling of people as deprived and disadvantaged is used as a kind of alibi to cover up the deficiencies of the education system. [29] Bernstein makes the same point when he says 'how can we talk of offering compensatory education to [people] who in the first place have not, as yet, been offered an adequate educational environment?' The concept of compensatory education 'serves to direct attention away from the internal organization of the educational [system] and focuses attention on families . . . [who] are regarded as deficit systems.' [30]

William Ryan suggests that the ideology of deprivation and disadvantage 'makes it seem that unemployment, poverty, poor education and slum conditions *result* from family breakdown, cultural deprivation and a lack of acculturation'. [31] To sustain the ideology, it is necessary to engage in the popular sport of 'savage discovery', and to fit the theory savages are being discovered all over the place. 'The all-time favourite savage in America is the promiscuous mother who produces a litter of illegitimate brats' in order to benefit from welfare subsidies. The British equivalent would no doubt be the 'isolated' and 'apathetic' residents of vast council estates, prisoners' wives, ethnic minorities and single parents, all identified by their 'obvious inadequacy' and beloved by those engaged in basic education and Russell category work.

In many respects the definitions of disadvantage used by adult educators reflect the worst aspects of individualistic and pathological explanations of inequality and are quite uncritical of the fact that these are principally cultural definitions. Even the references to the physically and mentally handicapped consistently fail to distinguish between physical disabilities and culturally defined handicaps, so that they too become gross oversimplifications of complex inter-relationships and are reduced to clinical categories of people exhibiting 'special needs' and requiring 'special provision'. [32]

In their investigations designed to examine the labelling of negro underachievement in America as pathological, Stephen and Joan Baratz were forced to conclude that 'the social pathology model has led social scientists to establish programmes to prevent deficits which are simply not there'. [33] Negro behaviour, according to their research findings, was not deficit but different. The differentiation arose because of socio-economic circumstances in which certain forms of cultural behaviour were rated differently to others, and in which the behaviour patterns of the poor and powerless were considered to be inferior. The corollary to this assessment, of course, is the assumption that those who are not generally labelled disadvantaged, namely the middle class, exhibit behaviour patterns that are measurably superior. But as Keddie points out, 'models of the good home, etc., when critically examined, are likely to rely on moral imperatives that derive from culture bound experiences which are presented as given', and determined within the context of a mainstream culture which celebrates the middle-class view of normality and reality. [34]

Bernstein also sees explanations of deprivation and disadvantage as being fixed by a particular view of working-class culture. The problem lies in the extent to which definitions of disadvantage are imposed upon one group by another more powerful group. Cole and Bruner make the same point, but in a slightly different context:

Cultural deprivation represents a special case of cultural difference which arises when an individual is faced with demands to perform in a manner inconsistent with his past [cultural] experience. In the present social context of the USA [and this is also true of the UK] the great power of the middle class has rendered differences into deficits because middle-class behaviour is the yardstick of success. [35]

The point of all this is not to suggest that disadvantage does not exist. In structural terms, inequality of opportunity, of influence, of social and political power and of economic resources are clearly embedded in the class system. It is the use of the term to stand for 'personal deficiency' which has to be questioned. The great value of the arguments presented to challenge deficit and pathological explantions of disadvantage has been to attack the assumptions on which they are based, their tendency to associate maladjustment with poverty and to hold vast sections of the population personally responsible for their own misfortunes.

The contribution of writers like Keddie and the others has been 'a useful reminder in a literate society that the illiterate are not inferior beings and that they may [actually] be rejecting the skills of literacy as part of a rejection of other aspects of mainstream culture'. [36] Because they have not as yet responded to adult education initiatives 'does not mean that they are educationally sub-normal or inadequate as people; many are intellectual and highly articulate, often with well developed practical and social skills'. [37] And the notion that cultural deficit is essentially the creation of those adhering to the values of mainstream culture is an important antidote to the rooting of 'disadvantage' in explanations of deviance. But merely to replace theories of cultural deficit with theories of cultural difference, and to suggest that in a pluralistic kind of way, a variety of conditions are equally valid, underestimates the social and economic context within which equality and inequality operate.

The liberal solution

An additional problem so far as adult education is concerned, however, is the essentially liberal persuasion that underlies its philosophy, and which makes a social analysis based on notions of cultural hegemony and structural inequality exceedingly rare.

The associations tied up with the term 'liberal' go much deeper than its more usual party-political meaning might suggest. It began as a 'specific social distinction, to refer to a class of free men as distinct from others who were not free'. [38] It came into the English language in the fourteenth century, and when it was used to refer to the 'liberal arts' at that time, it was used with social class connotations.

The 'liberal arts' were the skills and pursuits appropriate, as we should now say, to men of independent means and assured social position, as distinct from other [mechanical] skills and pursuits appropriate to a lower class. [39]

In the eighteenth and nineteenth centuries the term gathered dilettante connotations and the sense of 'open minded' and 'unorthodox' views which has since led to its disfavour with those of more conservative persuasion. But socialists, and particularly Marxists, have been even more critical. From their perspective, liberal ideas seem essentially weak and sentimental and consistently reluctant to take account of the hard realities of social and economic divisions in society. Certainly in its historical context, liberalism has been 'a doctrine based on individualist theories of man and society' and as such 'in fundamental conflict, not only with socialist but [also] with social theories'. [40] The further observation that liberalism is the philosophy most commonly associated with the views of dominant groups in bourgeois society underlines the contradictions between its 'liberating' and 'limiting' ideas of human behaviour — that people should be free to do what they want, unimpeded by too much state interference, just so long as their behaviour doesn't challenge the prevailing distribution of power and influence. In capitalist terms, therefore, liberalism is essentially a doctrine of 'possessive individualism'. [41]

Adult education with its roots firmly in the nineteenth century, has been part of the trend associated with the progressive enlightenment of an industrial society. Partly initiated by philanthropists, industrialists and liberal academics as a way of civilizing the masses, and partly struggled for by those who regarded it as a tool of self-improvement it has become both the means of self-fulfilment, and like education generally, a source of enlightenment and reason, dedicated to the development of useful and contented citizens. From the liberal standpoint, adult education can both enhance the quality of individual life and disseminate useful and socially valued knowledge to a limitless range of people, so long as they recognize its intrinsic value. As Bowles and Gintis point out, the liberal view of education creates a belief that education provides the means of furthering personal benefit and fulfilment, whilst at the same time promoting social justice, equality and the integration of the diverse interests of different groups in society. [42]

The assumptions underlying the New Communities Project in Leigh Park in Hampshire, for example, were a celebration of the liberal view of man in society. [43] The action research team based in a predominantly working-class neighbourhood was clear that 'class solidarity' with the local people would be 'self defeating, unnecessary and perhaps distorting. . . . If the whole of our cultural heritage should be available to the working class, then education for individual self discovery and self development' should be the starting point. The team's conclusions were that if education 'begins where people are' and aims to 'encourage growth in human personality, character and creativity' and provides space in which to develop 'greater confidence in their own ability and potential' then 'trends in adult education during this century (towards the monopolization of provision by middle-class groups) will be arrested and the balance of opportunity may swing to a more central position.'

This sense of optimistic progressivism has been a feature of liberal adult education since its inception. It provided the enthusiasm which once established and developed tutorial classes and identified a curriculum considered to represent the highest and most worthy forms of thought then known to man. It has informed and fostered the national literacy campaign, and the sentiments for notions of continuing education, community education and life-long learning.

During the last ten years or so, however, there has been a fair amount of criticism of the liberal position — largely in terms of its naivety and lack of critical social awareness. In America writers like Illich, Reimer, Postman and Weingartner, among others, have challenged the whole notion of education as an enlightened and liberating experience. The brunt of their critique is made against the alienating procedures of schooling, but it is the process of manufactured education which they are criticizing, and as such, much of what they say is equally applicable to adult education. Pre-packaged courses and inflexible procedures bedevil much of the provision and despite the rhetoric of 'student-centredness', in a fee-paying, enrolment economy, they are readily reduced to statistics. In its recent report, *A Strategy for the Basic Education of Adults*, the committee set up by the Advisory Council for Adult and Continuing Education and chaired by Henry Arthur Jones chose surprisingly mechanistic language to describe a procedure in which:

a tutor or organizer is likely to spend several hours *on* an intending student *(case discussion* with the *referring agent, diagnostic* and advisory interviews with *briefing* the prospective tutor) before the student becomes, if he ever does, a *statistic on an enrolment card.* [my italics] [44]

For the deschoolers educational institutions are essentially repressive organizations which peddle a commodity-based view of knowledge, and which measure success and failure in terms of procedures and values which are meaningless to the vast majority of potential students. As such their claims about 'concern for the individual' appear to be particularly hypocritical.

A rather different kind of challenge to liberal ideas in education has come from social economists like Bowles and Gintis, who argue that even in its own terms, liberalism has not fulfilled the expectations which it has created. Their examples of the bankruptcy of American attempts to combat social and educational disadvantage can be paralleled by similar futilities in Britain. Despite Urban Aid, community education, community development, positive discrimination in Educational Priority Areas, the national literacy campaign and a proliferation of long-term and short-term action-research projects, all designed to provide new opportunities for the disadvantaged, there is no evidence to suggest that the poverty we rediscovered in the 1960s, and which we have now added to by structural unemployment, has in any way subsided. In retrospect, most of these initiatives seem to have been essentially the piecemeal and pragmatic responses to externally defined local problems, and sustained briefly by virtue of the inordinate energy of exceptional and highly motivated individuals. Experts with minimal resources found that their ability to effect change was limited. So long as they were there, however, the appearance of 'something being done' was sufficient to harness the enthusiasm of new recruits to the liberal cause.

Unfortunately, as in America, there is now some suggestion that the liberal reform bubble has burst. In political as much as in intellectual circles, the current mood is one of retrenchment.' [45] But the weakness of liberalism generally, and liberal views about educational needs, is more fundamental than the 'temporary setback' accounted for by a change of government or the 'short term effects' of an international recession.

As Bowles and Gintis point out, the central weakness of the liberal view of education and society is that it leaves unquestioned the economic and political structure in society, in which the creation of disadvantage occurs, and in which educational reforms are expected to operate. In a society like Britain, the existence of a capitalist economy, the social class divisions created as a consequence of it, and the contribution made to its preservation and reproduction by the education system, render liberal aspirations based on 'spiritual fulfilment', 'personhood' [46] and 'social integration' impossible to achieve. The likelihood of conditions like these, whatever they actually mean, becoming generally accepted, seems totally unrealistic when they are examined in terms of an education system which exists to deny anything but marginal modifications in the prevailing distribution of resources in society. The liberal hope of changing the context and process of education to make it more responsive to the needs of the disadvantaged is a vain one without corresponding and significant changes in the organization and control of economic life.

The suggestion that adult education should tackle this problem alone is, of course, rarely advocated. But the view that adult education can play a corrective role in co-operation with other professional and voluntary agencies is a familiar plank in the liberal platform. So far as education for the disadvantaged is concerned, Russell gave the seal of approval to inter-agency co-operation as a key strategy in its development, and much discussion about the 'grey area' between education and social work has informed a good deal of recent thinking on the matter. [47]

But of course the contradictions affecting the liberal position in education are just as apparent in the other, so-called 'caring professions' of social, health and welfare services. Their responsibilities demand that they address themselves to relieving the deprivation, alienation and inequalities which accompany the prevailing economic practice of capitalism, dedicating themselves to the general enhancement of human development and fulfilment. The extent to which members of the welfare professions deliberately conspire with others to perpetuate false expectations is, of course, not the charge being made. But by subscribing to the collective delusion of short-sighted liberal optimism, they leave unquestioned the deep-rooted political and economic structures which make their aims impossible to achieve.

In addition, their naivety and energy serve as excellent methods of social control. Their benevolence and sense of vocation encourage them to work harder than they are paid to do, and their reputation for being 'good people' neutralizes the hostility of their 'clients' and renders objectionable, subversive, or jaundiced the challenges of their critics.

Their achievement is to socialize their clients into what Smith and Harris refer to as 'ideologies of need'. Rather like a self-fulfilling prophecy, they create 'states of awareness' from which people develop both the symptoms and the frames of reference which make the diagnoses of their deviant behaviour seem perfectly plausible. [48]

Illich argues that the capacity of 'welfare bureaucracies (to) claim a professional, political and financial manipulation over the social imagination, to define the needs and problems of the clients, and to set the standards of what is valuable and feasible' makes them 'addictive'. [49] Their language and quasi-medical terminology not only mystifies their expertise but reinforces their authority as agents of social control.

In comparison to all the literature dedicated to the rehabilitation of social deviants, it is refreshing to read Jenny Headlam Wells's contention that 'a person's *failure* to "adjust" to disability may be interpreted as a positive sign, indicating a refusal to accept the patronizing, infantilizing and passive role that our society tends to ascribe to the disabled.' [50] But her opinion is the exception rather than the rule.

It would be unusual to expect the welfare professions and the work they do to be anything other than reformist, however. In many cases their origins are recent. They lack the corporate identity and exclusivity of the older professions, but by the careful expansion of training and professionalization over the last thirty years or so, they have steadily extended their realm of influence, until together, they have become increasingly responsible for the assessment and treatment of behaviour in many areas of social life.

These are groups who have acquired social legitimacy as 'experts', and in the process of their professionalization, they have become adopted as professional experts by the state and local government, operating from a respected and privileged social position. A good deal of authority is accredited to their judgements, so that collectively they are encouraged to identify and service the needs of an entire population according to *their* interpretations of reality. Economic and political questions are translated into individual and technical problems, and as such, they have disguised the extent to which they are engaged in a highly important and supremely political range of activities.

For adult education to combine with these agencies in the identification of needs and the provision of programmes for those considered to be disadvantaged, there is a real danger that welfare therapy and the central ideology which typifies its professional position, will emerge as the predominant characteristic of educational programmes — programmes which should be essentially different kinds of activities. Clearly, then, in an attempt to assess the initiatives intended to respond to the needs of the disadvantaged, it is important to be clear that there are different ideological assumptions at work and different explanations of the causes and characteristics of disadvantage. Inevitably both of these cultural pre-conditions influence the aims and objectives, the curriculum and pedagogy and the evaluation of the activities which are offered.

In this respect Colin Fletcher's distinction between liberal and liberating interpretations of community education is crucial [51] as is Thomas La Belle's distinction between a 'deprivation-development' and a 'dependency-liberation' classification of education and social change in the Third World. [52] La Belle is referring to strategies of development in developing countries. He contrasts interpretations of society which equate educational disadvantage with pathological explanations of human deficit (i.e. deprivation) and those which explain disadvantage as a consequence of structural inequalities that keep powerless groups in a state of dependency on the economic and cultural decisions made by ruling groups. Strategies to deal with deprivation, in La Belle's first typology, employ remediation, compensatory education, training and behaviour modification (development). Those which seek to challenge and transform the relationship of dependency described in his second model are those which set out to enhance the authority and power of the disadvantaged in relation to the dominant group. To promote liberation in fact. But 'liberation' may seem a bit strong when transferred to the British context of adult education. Freire's equally committed language of 'conscientization' and the like is more palatable — largely, I suspect, because his views have become a part of the content of the academic study of adult education, much as the ideas of Illich and the deschoolers became part of the curriculum of every respectably progressive teacher-training establishment in the early 1970s. So long as their ideas seem to be interesting, but of no direct relevance to educational practice in this country, they can be incorporated in the curriculum, and discussed in abstraction, without seriously challenging the behaviour and practice of the institutions involved.

But La Belle's notion of liberation is an important one to take up within the context of British adult education because there *is* a different set of assumptions and explanations about what adult education should be about in relation to the disadvantaged. It is largely a minority view, for obvious reasons, but it's a view which needs to be put with increasing vigour if educational opportunities for working-class men and women are to advance much further.

Adult education and the working class

Critical educational theorists of all types — from Althusser to Bowles and Gintis — have agreed that education is one of the most important (if not the most important) institution by which ruling groups, in western society, establish and maintain their hegemony and reproduce the conditions of capitalist production.

The problem is to relate the theoretical arguments of Althusser, Gramsci, Bowles and Gintis, Freire, the deschoolers and all the rest to understanding everyday educational experience, and especially adult education in which the legacy of unquestioned liberalism is perhaps most complacent. To begin with, none of these theorists is British. Their theories were developed in different cultural, historical and social circumstances. In reaching Britain they have become separated from their original political contexts. The links between these theoretical perspectives and British educational practice still have to be made.

A second problem relates to the demarcation between theory and practice in British adult education. Colin Kirkwood argues that:

practitioners are out in the field, taken up with teaching (if they are lucky), organizing and administrating the provision. Most theorists, on the other hand, live and work in academic worlds remote from those of fieldwork practice. Much British adult education theory is bland, latinate, unilluminating. For insight and regeneration of the world of practice it substitutes . . . rationales for the existing pattern of practice. When fieldworkers enter the debate, it is not to contribute at a conceptual or theoretical level but merely to give accounts of their practice. [53]

Keith Jackson makes a similar point in his scepticism about a good many action research projects which so frequently provide a 'post-hoc eulogy of whatever happened to happen' without much attention to theory. [54]

A third problem is the contradictory tendencies of those political groups in Britain which exist to represent working-class interests.

Historically the British working class has been at the forefront of the struggle for state education — ever since the Knowledge Chartists argued that education could be an important counter to the raw exploitation of working-class children by an unrestrained labour market. [55]

The Labour movement, the Labour Party and the Communist Party have all seen education as a potential weapon with which to resist the exploitation of workers by employers. All of the developments in state education during the last hundred years or so have been to some extent the consequence of pressure for equality of educational opportunity for working-class people demanded by their representatives. The tension between the provision of education by the state as a means of social differentiation and control, as against the demand for education by the working class as a way of transforming its situation, has been a continuing conflict both in schooling and in the provision of adult education. Corrigan and Frith describe the history of British education as:

a reluctant bourgeoisie slowly yielding to socialist and working-class demands for general schooling, secondary education for all, the expansion of higher education, comprehensive schools and the raising of the school leaving age. [56]

But all of these developments, as we have seen, distract attention from deeper considerations about the role of education. Within the general expansion of educational opportunity, and the shift towards more comprehensive provision at all levels, rarely have questions been raised by the working class or its representatives about the content or control of these facilities.

The critical arguments advanced by the theorists about the education system and its relation to society are all part of a genuine attempt to change that society. But the difficulty is one of relating the theory to everyday practice, and one of relating changes in educational institutions to the class struggle generally, especially within the context of social and ideological structures which are very powerful and highly resistant to change.

The libertarian solution of the deschoolers is to disestablish the professions and deinstitutionalize society on behalf of individual freedom. But this much vaunted individualism does not have much relevance to the conditions of the working class generally and, as some would argue, makes it 'more akin to the right wing, *laissez-faire* approach of the "educational voucher" Tories'. [57]

The Midwinter solution, based on recommendations about curriculum relevance, enjoyed initial support in the late 1960s and early 1970s because it appeared to celebrate cultural difference as a positive alternative to the denigratory notions of cultural deficit. The same call for relevance has been a popular feature of adult education developments in working-class areas and with groups considered to be socially disadvantaged. But the identification of relevance as an objective begs the important question of whose definition is being advanced? Critics of the relevancy and relativist view of knowledge warn of the danger of locking working-class people into a limited and parochial view of the world, and depriving them of the forms of knowledge they need if they are to transform their social and economic situations [58] Martin Yarnit, from a totally different political perspective, has the same reservations about Midwinter's restrictive use of the concept of social relevance. [59] Traditional knowledge is not 'of itself ' repressive; it is made to be repressive through the processes of certification, specialization, monopolization and control used by ruling groups in society, seeking to maintain their cultural hegemony over the others.

To limit access to this heritage on the grounds that its relevance to working-class men and women is not immediately apparent is, in effect, to perpetuate the system which creates this irrelevancy. It is to concede defeat without even attempting to win: it is to institutionalize the exploitation and alienation experienced by the working class as consumers as well as producers, in the cultural and educational sphere. [60]

A fourth problem is that, just as an increasing number of working-class children respond to their schooling with apathy, boredom, indiscipline and truancy, working-class men and women seem to be visibly unattracted to adult education for the countless reasons that prevent it being seen as useful, interesting or exciting to them. Their apparent resistance lends great weight to the views which depict their 'indifference', 'residual hostility to education' and general lack of appreciation of the 'finer things of life' as symptomatic of their 'cultural deficiency'. But again, as Keith Jackson and Bob Ashcroft point out, because the ruling class has profound cultural supremacy,

in addition to control over the means of production and its accompanying coercive apparatus, the dominant class [also] exercises crucial control over the apparatus of cultural dissemination (institutions of learning, the arts, the mass media) *in short over all those means through which social consciousness could be effectively created.* Without resorting to the contentious notion of false consciousness, ruling class cultural hegemony can be seen as giving the working class *no effective choice between alternatives.* Without wishing to question the consumption choices themselves, of material goods and leisure pursuits by the working class . . . [it is important] to question *the milieu in which these choices are made.* This milieu is essentially one of constraint and manipulation [which] emerges from a social structure which in the most extreme form limits the options open to the working class and expands those open to the middle class. [my emphases] [61]

In such circumstances, the relative disinterest shown by working-class men and women to adult education, working-class politics, literature and social history, for example, compared to their concern for other commercial and leisure pursuits, is a measure of the success of the ruling class's contribution to the creation of working-class counter-consciousness.

Frith and Corrigan's conclusion is that

state education is a good thing as a source of skills necessary for the working class to resist the brutalizing effects of the market; state education is a bad thing as an instrument of bourgeois domination . . . these contradictions reflect the contradictions within capitalism itself . . . in the long run the contradictions will only be solved by the transformation of capitalist relations in general, but the immediate problem of educational policy is a tactical one: how can educational systems become a part of the struggle for socialism? [62]

So far as working-class adult education is concerned, does the politics of education mean gaining control of existing institutions on behalf of working-class students in the universities, the WEA and local authority classes? Or does it mean creating independent socialist institutions as the Plebs League tried to do in 1909, and more recently, the Southern Region Trade Union Information and Research Unit has tried to do in reaction to the industrial studies policies of Southampton University? [63]

Underlying all of these questions is the problem of the relationship between education and society and the extent to which significant changes in the provision of education can be achieved without major social and economic changes in the wider society. Paradoxically, though, it is precisely because the education system is a reflection of the vested interests, social values and economic concerns of dominant groups in capitalist society that it provides the setting in which the contradictions of the class struggle can be made explicit. The conflicts and struggles apparent within the education system reflect the conflicts and struggles of the wider society. By exposing these and re-examining them in political terms, it is possible to make clear to the teachers, tutors and students involved, the implications of the process and procedures in which they are caught up. Conscientization is a crucial first step. The fusion of critical awareness, social action and reflection upon action through praxis is consequently an important socialist response to the issues raised in this paper so far.

No wonder it is a minority view! It's a response in favour of the definition of 'disadvantage' being made in class terms, the provision of educational activities which take seriously the social condition and educational development of working-class men and women, and a political commitment to their class interests as concerns which are very different to middle-class interests. This means placing adult education for the working class very specifically in the wider context of political struggle, and to ensure, as the students of Barbiana demanded, that educational means are never isolated from political ends. [64]

Illustrations of this kind of adult education for working-class men and women in contemporary Britain are, for obvious reasons, not easy to find. But for those who are attempting to relate their practice to a realistic assessment of the structural repercussions of a class-based society, the work of Tom Lovett in Northern Ireland, and in a different context, Keith Jackson and his colleagues in Liverpool, has obviously been an important influence. [65]

Like many activists, Jackson's writing has not always kept pace with his activities, and it is to the earlier articles produced with Bob Ashcroft, and to relatively obscure conference papers, that we must turn for inspiration. To repeat Jackson and Ashcroft's commitment to a clear theoretical framework as a guide to practice, and their recognition of the specific values and interests which education serves in society, would be to reinforce the arguments already outlined in this paper. Their important additional contributions to the debate are in three main areas.

The first seems to me to be the fearless and specific use of class terminology in relation to adult students and educational practice. There are parts of the country — and Southampton is one of them — where the definition of 'working class' is seen as both pejorative and divisive. It is also, paradoxically, seen by many to be both patronizing and irrelevant in terms of adult education provision. For Jackson and Ashcroft there are no such problems — nor for the students referred to by David Evans and Martin Yarnit either, I suspect. [66] But whilst the softer south disguises some of the more visible manifestations of class difference and class inequality, the relative mal-distribution of resources is no less true in areas like these. The resistance to attempts to make them explicit and part of the process of education and conscientization is strong in an area which has been sheltered to some extent from the worst excesses of industrial and economic dislocation. Relative affluence has allowed the conviction that 'we are all middle class now' to dig deeper into the social fabric, and to distract both the middle and working class from many of the face-to-face realities of urban decay and structural unemployment. But whilst Leigh Park, central Southampton or down-town Portsmouth might seem like 'paradise' compared to Scotland Road, many of the houses still have black damp, there are still minimal social amenities, high rates of youth unemployment and a local stigma attached to living there. Their residents are still those who are most vulnerable to economic crisis and least well served by the education, health and welfare services, and their adult residents are just as unlikely as working-class men and women anywhere to find their way into adult education classes which reflect any understanding or concern about their situation.

However unpalatable it may be to some people, the concept of social class is a much more appropriate one in which to discuss educational opportunities than those of 'personhood', 'disadvantage' or 'deprivation', precisely because it places the discussion firmly in the context of a stratified society in which middle-class interests determine the parameters within which the education system operates. It also allows the application of terms commonly understood in 'sociological' as distinct from 'social problem' analysis to be used.

Jackson has distinguished between two broad definitions of working class. [67] The first definition concentrates on

an aggregate of low status individuals . . . whose low status is defined by social and economic criteria: employment (or lack of it), income, educational background, job opportunities, general access to resources indicated by area of residence, ability to choose residence, lifestyle, etc.

The majority of the various groups already referred to as 'disadvantaged' in liberal terminology would come within this definition of working class.

The second definition is of a group who share the social and economic conditions described above but who have a 'degree of consciousness' about their position. In this sense the concept working class takes on more active and positive connotations. Jackson describes this understanding of being working class as one of 'being involved in a social, economic and political relationship, varying according to personality and experience. It entails belonging to a social class not a category'. Each of these definitions has different implications for educational action, thus Jackson and Ashcroft's second contribution is to challenge their potential divisiveness, especially when they are further qualified by notions of 'working-class affluence' and the 'culture of deprivation'. They argue quite rightly that 'the similarities between the social experiences of the "deprived" and "affluent" working class are much more important than the differences'. To concentrate on 'the deprived', however half hearted and ineffective that concentration turns out to be, puts the emphasis on neighbourhood consciousness rather than class consciousness. It sets one neighbourhood against the other in competition for scarce resources and one deprived group's 'positive discrimination' becomes another's 'economic restriction'. It replaces the strength of class consciousness and the recognition of class conflict by the less abrasive and more malleable notion of 'community development'. It helps explain why affluent workers in less critically deprived areas feel little or no allegiance with working people in other areas. And why the desperation of poverty, unemployment and poor housing conditions can easily be converted into the acceptance of racialist and materialistic propaganda — the effective modern solution to the old concern to 'divide and rule'. The concept of deprivation or disadvantage, therefore, is not appropriate unless it is extended to cover the position of the whole working class, whether poor or not, and used to demonstrate the links between their common powerlessness in comparison to others in contemporary society.

Their third contribution is the emphasis on work with activists and the recognition that well-informed, politically conscious and influential activists have a much greater social and political influence among their neighbours and workmates than others working from a strictly educational base. The account of the 'Second Chance to Learn' course in Chapter 9 describes developments which are to some extent the consequence of having taken the decision to work with activists as far as possible in Liverpool. In these terms even small resources put into trade union education or educational work with 'natural' as distinct from 'elected' leaders can have a much more important multiplier effect than the same resources used in the school system. And if the definition of 'skill' and 'resource' is wide enough to encompass other forms of working-class cultural expression, then broadsheets, drama, radio, TV and poetry, for example, can all be used to reflect and inform working-class action. [68]

Central to all of this, of course, is the element of equality and common interest implicit in the term 'solidarity'. It is this demonstration of 'solidarity' that is so frequently missing from philosophies of adult education which 'treat' students as 'disadvantaged', philosophies which imply that there are two clear sides to the relationship. 'Those with the needs, mindless incompetents, on the one hand, and the need-meeters on the other, perceptive, enquiring, responsible, able to take a broad view and make prescriptions'. [69] Rather, the relationship between teachers and students should be built upon the demonstration of solidarity and on principles of equality and genuine mutual respect.

In practice all of this means believing that education is a dialogue in which the teachers must be as ready to learn as the potential students. The point is well made in Paul Thompson's book, *The Voice of the Past*, in which he describes the oral historian of working-class history as one coming to listen,

to sit at the feet of others who, because they come from a different social class, or are less educated, or older, know more about something. The reconstruction of history itself becomes a much more widely collaborative process, in which 'non-professionals' must play a crucial part. [70]

In education the dialogue should begin with the issues chosen by the student and not the teacher. Since 'education for its own sake' is rarely a luxury that working-class men and women can afford, these issues will be largely instrumental — concerned with welfare rights, employment, housing, etc. The responsibility of the teacher is to try to develop the discussion beyond the boundaries of the already known, and into the area of the unknown, which still has to be discovered, understood, mastered and controlled by the students. This will mean making the kind of intellectual demands upon working-class men and women that are properly made on all students.

By comparison, the limitations built into the notions of 'functional literacy', 'role education', 'coping skills' and 'basic education' generally all serve to reinforce the restricted expectations that teachers frequently have of those labelled 'disadvantaged'. The limited expectations are reinforced by the psychological explanations which underlie them and which assume that the motivation to learn is personal. As Freire, Bowles and Gintis, the deschoolers and the others have demonstrated, however, low motivation and lack of achievement are closely related to the alienating experiences of the educational system dominated by hierarchical social relations. If the educational process is based on a mutual dialogue which sets out to incorporate the class interests of working people into its operations, then the opportunities to learn become quite different and are based on a different set of relationships and assumptions. If, as Keith Jackson and Bob Ashcroft argue, education is 'directly concerned with consciousnesss and awareness in class terms, the form of the educational dialogue can closely relate motivation, the concept of learning and its cultural matrix'. [71] Although uncommon in Britain, this is essentially the approach which has been used with some success in Latin America.

The use of 'social class' as distinct from 'disadvantage' as the conceptual base from which to operate poses a number of problems for those engaged in adult education, however, just as it did for those employed by the Home Office and local authorities in the CDPs. It's difficult to imagine any circumstances in which this kind of work could ever become a regular part of conventional adult education.

Those of us involved have obviously learned by experience where the institutional boundaries lie. Clearly there is no problem, or very little problem, expressing solidarity with illiterates, the handicapped, the elderly, or in developing community links with a mothers and toddlers group or a parent-teacher association. But when a group, conscious of its working-class interests, wishes to use the normal democratic procedures in society and bring them into the curriculum of adult education, then there are problems. Such boundaries mark out quite clearly the real limitations on the popular rhetoric of 'relevance' and 'responding to felt needs' so beloved by adult education practitioners.

The counter-arguments employed by our colleagues are well known. They point to the elitism of the Ruskin-type tradition, which they argue elevates bright working-class people into the middle class and away from their roots. And clearly they are right. Some working-class adults will use education as a means of escaping from the social and economic limitations of their previous experience. But 'learning' as such does not necessarily need to be a synonym for self-improvement. If education is initially related to 'consciousness', then learning becomes a 'social' as distinct from a purely 'personal' activity. For other critics, education for social awareness is 'a recipe for resentment' and 'a formula for frustration'. It is considered wrong to 'raise people's expectations' when nothing can be changed. This argument also hits home. Those who are made aware of their impotence by education are clearly in a difficult position. The prevailing social structure would also be better served if they were left in ignorance. But if working-class men and women come to see more clearly, and to understand the extent and the range of the restrictions imposed upon them, then they are in a better position to do something about them. Critical awareness is the essential prerequisite for the determined action necessary to alter such restrictions.

In either argument the liberal tradition in adult education ideas finds its justification for keeping things much as they are. But if inequality is indeed the social context in which education operates, then to do nothing, or to resort to pious declarations of concern for the 'hidden and largely defeated population whom life has taught to keep their heads down and not expect much' [72] is to perpetuate the system which orchestrates their defeat.

The third counter-argument is simple. It is that views like these are held by 'politically motivated activists', 'committed to creating class conflict' where it does not exist and relentlessly ignoring 'the freedom of individuals' to 'live as they choose'. But of course the simple is also the simplistic. The commitment to working-class adult education, and the recognition of conditions which positively reinforce working-class culture on the one hand, and negatively restrict working-class opportunities on the other, is not a stand any of those involved in such practice would wish to deny. More serious is the denial of the ideology which is not made explicit in the philosophy and practice of adult education generally, and adult education for the disadvantaged in particular. It is this 'hidden' ideology which really imposes on working-class men and women; perpetually determining, and yet repeatedly disclaiming any responsibility for, their defeat.

5 Independence and incorporation: the Labour College movement and the Workers' Educational Association before the Second World War

Geoff Brown, Resident Tutor, Department of Adult Education, University of Nottingham

There have been two major organizations devoted to working-class adult education in this century: the Workers' Educational Association and the Labour College movement. [1] By the 1930s the WEA had each year something like 60,000 mainly working-class students on a wide range of courses, though with those in Economics, Politics and related subjects predominating. About 20 per cent of the students were in tutorial classes (three-year advanced courses), provided jointly with universities. Most of the classes received some state financial aid via the Board of Education. The Labour College movement had about 30,000 students at the peak of its success in the mid 1920s, but declined thereafter: in 1937–38, for instance, there were just over 13,000 students in 728 classes. [2] The Labour College movement prided itself on being, necessarily, independent of both the universities and the state. The core of its teaching was, according to the secretary of the National Council of Labour Colleges, 'Marxian economics and history interpreted by the materialistic conception of history'. [3] Whereas the WEA was accused by the Labour College movement of teaching 'bourgeois social science', and of being incorporated into the status quo.

After the Second World War both organizations altered considerably. The WEA grew fast in student numbers, and after a great deal of heart searching about the fact that it was no longer predominantly supported by working-class people interested in the social sciences, became essentially a general provider of leisure education for people from all, but mainly higher, social classes. The NCLC by this time provided an educational service for members of the trade unions affiliated to it, with postal courses being particularly important. A great emphasis was placed, from the time of the first majority Labour government, on subjects which were regarded as functional to the position of labour in the 'new world' — courses on Britain's economic problems, local and national government, secretaryship and chairmanship, and even Work Study and Industrial Management became common. The Labour College movement was a very different organization from what it had been in its heroic days before the First World War and into the 1920s. There had been a sharp battle between the Left and the Right in the NCLC in the late 1920s and early 1930s with the Left wing leaving. Its strongest institutional supporter, the South Wales Miners' Federation, disaffiliated at this time, and by 1930, for example, the profoundly anti-Communist National Union of General and Municipal Workers felt safe in significantly increasing its financial contribution to it. [4] In the 1950s and 1960s the NCLC maintained a merely superficial allegiance to 'Marxism', and in general gave uncritical support to the Labour Party, and by then co-operation with people from the WEA and the Universities was quite common. In 1964 the NCLC was closed down and merged into the TUC's education department.

Both the WEA and the Labour College movement had, in the years in which the Labour Party seriously challenged and increasingly replaced the Liberal Party as an alternative ruling party, been responsible for the education of many working-class incumbents of public and political office and for the training of many trade union officials and active Co-operators. [5] On the available evidence neither side can, without resort to mutually damaging and teleological balance sheets, claim in reality to have produced more 'loyal' servants of the working-class movement than the other. The position put for Llanelli by a Labour College stalwart, James Griffiths, can be generalized: 'the WEA and the Labour College classes have trained successive generations of leaders for the trade union and Labour movements'. [6]

With the revival of interest in working-class adult education in the 1970s, not least in the WEA itself, there is a natural desire to locate theory and practice within the history of the WEA and of the Labour College movement. Does either of them offer models which might be replicated? What is to be the nature of the new provision for working-class adult education?

How is it to be mounted? What should its objectives be? What should its content be? What should its relationship be to other institutions? The history of the WEA and the NCLC particularly up to the Second World War, and the debate between the two organizations offer some guidance, both negative and positive. It is the primary purpose of this paper to explore this history with a view to providing this. Such an exercise is long overdue, since in some quarters the Labour College movement has been virtually ignored or at best belittled. In other quarters, the Labour College movement has been praised uncritically and the WEA attacked unfairly. [7] These histories are merely reflective of the polemical antagonism between the two organizations up to the Second World War, where each side caricatured the other, to legitimate its own approach. The reality of the WEA and the reality of the Labour College movement have thus been obscured; the closeness between the two organizations on some points has been ignored; and no one has seriously drawn out from the history of both those policies and practices which might be appropriate to the real world of working-class adult education today.

The WEA — guilt by association?

The Central Labour College was established in 1909, in the aftermath of the strike of that year at Ruskin College. The immediate cause of the strike was the dismissal of the Principal, a socialist: a decision which a large section of the students found intolerable. For the strikers the Principal's dismissal highlighted the fears they already had about the college not being a 'true Labour college', about its coming increasingly under the control of Oxford University and within the grip of non-socialist academics. Former students of Ruskin had already started the Plebs League, through which they began to agitate against the involvement of the university in working-class education and in favour of socialist education. The publication, a year previously, of the famous report *Oxford and Working-Class Education* had done much to inflame these fears. In order to extract resources from the university, and ultimately it was hoped from the Board of Education, the Oxford Report had played strongly on contemporary ruling class fears (it was only two years since the General Election of 1906) about 'changes which are taking place in the constitution of English society and in the distribution of political power'. The universities, it was stated, should aspire through university/WEA tutorial classes to continue to exercise their traditional privilege of training men for 'all departments of political life and public administration. ... The Trade Union secretary and the "Labour member" need an Oxford education as much, and will use it to as good ends, as the civil servant or the barrister.' [8] At the conference in Oxford in the summer of 1907 which had led to the Report views of this sort had already been put forward, as had the criticisms of them around which the Labour College movement emerged. Noah Ablett, a South Wales miner representing the Ruskin College Marxian Society, had shocked the assembled dignitaries from the University Extension movement by saying that the trade unionists he represented viewed the proposed developments with suspicion. 'They wonder', he said, 'why the Universities have suddenly come down to help the workers to emancipate themselves.' [9]

Ablett's view, of course, was that the universities through the WEA were trying to head off and confuse the Labour movement, not to serve or assist it in its historically determined task. Sentiments of this sort were to characterize the relationship between the Labour College movement and the WEA for many years.

Scarcely an issue of *Plebs* appeared between 1909 and the mid 1920s without it containing at least one attack on the WEA. For the most part these attacks were unwarranted: the WEA was financed by capitalists, its constitution favoured social harmony and industrial peace, most of its students got jobs behind the counter in Labour Exchanges, and they were allegedly mainly middle class and unconnected with the working-class movement. The most serious charge related to the WEA's receipt of some of its finance from the state. Following some of the more generalized and functionalist formulations of Marx and Engels about the state, and anticipating Lenin's undifferentiated and reductionist view in *The State and Revolution*, the Labour College movement asserted that the state was 'an organ of *class* rule, an organ for the *oppression* of one class by another'. [10] This crude approach involved a substantial under-estimation of the nature of bourgeois democracy, of the role of the Labour movement in forcing its concession, and an underestimation of the reforms which had been and might be extracted from the capitalist state. [11] But because the state was regarded merely as an organ of class rule and oppression, and it received some of its finance from it, the WEA was assumed automatically to be a tool of that state. An editorial in *Plebs* in May 1913 said of the WEA that:

The master class is using it as an indirect method of continuing their domination of the forces of labour: 'divide and conquer' has been replaced by 'devise and conquer' via the WEA and kindred bodies.

The Labour College case against the WEA on this point essentially rests on guilt by association, and on the simplistic view that the aspirations of the ruling class for 'social control' via the WEA could, in reality, be brought about. But in order not to repeat the unsuccessful experience of the University Extension movement with regard to working-class people, even these elements had to concede democratic rights to WEA students over content, teachers and teaching methods, and organization. As the Guild Communist and Labour College supporter, William Mellor, acknowledged in 1920, although the WEA officially knew nothing of the class struggle,

> fortunately for the WEA its constitution leaves to the students a great amount of liberty. . . . It is, indeed, just in those places where the official view has least hold that the WEA succeeds in securing the support of the working classes, and thereby in becoming an efficient instrument of working-class education. Places like the West Riding of Yorkshire, for instance, have managed to evade most of the regulations designed to keep the WEA in the straight path, and the workers do control their own education. [12]

Although the WEA in Yorkshire was outstanding in this respect, the position was, in fact, similar in most WEA districts in the 1920s and 1930s. [13] It was easy for the Labour College movement to criticize the WEA on the basis of the latter's 'head-office' pronouncements and on the statements of some of its ruling class supporters, but this was not a realistic assessment of the work of the WEA at the level of the branches and the classes, where there is much evidence (as will be shown later) that the students did not share these ideas.

In another respect the Labour College analysis was naive, as G. D. H. Cole in 1924 pointed out in one of his many reasoned and patient defences of the WEA. If one rejected state aid to education as a sham, one would also have to, surely, reject such things as Workmen's Compensation legislation, Housing Acts and Factory Acts on the same grounds — ignoring, incidentally, Marx's own enthusiasm for the latter as constituting a triumph of the Political Economy of Labour over the Political Economy of Capital. Cole mischievously asked, that since it had been the recent Labour Government which had increased the grants to the WEA, whether the NCLC regarded this as 'a deep capitalist move'? [14] The WEA, especially after the Board of Education Adult Education Regulations of 1924, received substantial aid to its teaching costs both from the board and from local education authorities. It did, however, on principle raise the rest of its funds from its own resources in order to retain its independence. After 1924 WEA districts, along with universities and some other organizations, were regarded as 'Responsible Bodies'. The state, generally assured that the WEA was a suitable organization for the promotion of adult education, exercised only a fairly loose control over the WEA's work, mostly through inspection of classes. It did, however, keep files on 'Political bias of the WEA'. Such things apart, acceptance of state aid by the WEA did not involve any fundamental compromise of its independence, either in what it taught or how it taught it. The same applied to the relationship with local authorities. Occasionally there were attempts by Conservative-controlled councils to discipline the WEA, but the latter always resisted such attempts. In 1923, for instance, E. Gitsham, a WEA organizing tutor in the East Riding of Yorkshire was accused of making 'indiscreet remarks' and advocating 'socialism'. At a county council meeting a Colonel Saltmarshe said that Gitsham had suggested that a time would come 'when all workers would be paid alike'. The county council, disliking this sentiment, threatened to withdraw its £75 per year grant to the WEA if Gitsham was not dismissed. The WEA rejected this advice out of hand, saying that it would raise the £75 from its own supporters, with the result that the county council eventually backed down. [15] In 1932, when a Conservative-Liberal alliance temporarily captured control of the Sheffield City Council from the Labour Party (of whose councillors twenty-two were at that time former WEA students) [16], the WEA was stripped of its grant — a fact which merely makes the point about the generally politically progressive posture of WEA students.

Although the Labour College movement had a theoretical opposition to state and local authority financial aid, this policy was in some respects more a product of necessity rather than choice. And that necessity was then enshrined as a virtue, and used to amplify the theoretical stance. The Labour College movement primarily looked to the Labour movement for its finance — most notably to the South Wales Miners' Federation and the National Union of Railwaymen, but also to many other affiliated unions. Although the movement was, therefore, independent of the state, it was not independent of all external agencies. Consequently the dilution of the NCLC's politics from the late 1920s was partly brought about by the movement's need to keep its new right wing union patrons happy. It is quite arguable that in this respect the NCLC was under more severe constraints about the content of its education than was the WEA. One of the contradictions of the bourgeois democratic state is that, despite its ultimate orientation to capitalism and the ruling class, it has to make some concessions even to institutions, such as the WEA, with which it might not be entirely happy. Certainly it cannot be claimed that the sources of some of the WEA's finance led its members to be any less involved in the working-class movement, or any less assertive of the interests of their class.

The NCLC in its report for 1925 scorned the WEA and Ruskin College for the fact that 'they receive large subsidies from Capitalist State funds.' This did not, however, prevent the local Labour Colleges in areas where the Labour Party had control of the local education authority from asking for, and sometimes getting, grants from the LEA. This happened, for example, in 1925 itself in Barrow-in-Furness, and in Carmarthenshire in 1935. In both cases the Board of Education intervened and closed the classes. The NCLC commented of the Carmarthenshire case that the incident conveyed two warnings:

first, that the Capitalist State is not likely to subsidise education for emancipation, and second, that the NCLC's policy of keeping the classes and tutors entirely under working-class control is the only satisfactory policy for the working-class movement. [17]

There was though, as the occasion for the previous statement makes clear, nothing wrong in trying to get aid from the state. One of the leading figures in the earlier years of the Labour College movement, Mark Starr, asked in *Plebs* in November 1917, 'Why not get your classes run by the Education Authority, the County Council or the state?' His conclusion was that circumstances altered cases and that 'Plebeians' should make use of classes in social science run by 'the Co-operative Union, the Urban District or County Council, propagandist Socialist parties, or even the WEA, in order to push the need for independence in that branch of knowledge.'

The WEA had support from the state, the local authorities and the universities without, I feel, it seriously compromising the content or outcome of its work. The NCLC's intransigence over content — the thing which denied it state aid — would only have been entirely admirable if this produced an approach to teaching in working-class adult education which was superior to that of the WEA. In this next section I want to explore the approaches to teaching of the two organizations.

Teaching approaches

The WEA believed strongly that its students should make up their own minds after an examination of a wide range of conflicting evidence and interpretation, and had much proof that students had this ability. At a tutors' conference in 1938, H. L. Beales gave one example of this phenomenon. At the end of a session a few years previously he was told by one member of the class that he had become convinced 'rather against his wish, of the necessity of socialism', whereas another student in the same class told him that 'socialism was all rot!' Beales commented that he had been doing his best 'to let the facts speak for themselves. I had not shirked direct questions, but I had not knowingly weighted the scales or indulged my convictions, uncertainties or prejudices.' [18]

This approach to teaching is entirely compatible with student democracy. It is no weakness to explore questions in a many-sided way and, given the complexity of the issues about which students wish to be informed, it is an approach which is essential if genuine understanding is to be reached. Many students, for example, went to classes, both with the WEA and the NCLC, in the 1930s to discover the causes of and possible solutions to unemployment. A fault with the Labour College approach, and one which it shared with elements in the socialist movement generally, was to say, in effect, that capitalism caused unemployment and that socialism would solve it. Although this may well be true, it is surely inadequate, as an outstanding WEA tutor Barbara Wootton put it in 1934, 'to answer every question and dispose of every criticism by a "reference to the abolition of the capitalist system".' [19] Such a response gives people very little real purchase on events and it does not help them to make a realistic intervention in the debate about unemployment. In this way the WEA approach to complex issues was in advance of the Labour College approach, but the WEA approach, handled badly, had a major defect. After a course of the WEA type, some students, primarily seeking solutions, could be further away from their original intention and might complain that their studies 'did not get them anywhere'. The Socratic approach adopted in WEA teaching — 'on the one hand this, on the other hand that', might tend to be extremely non-committal, and could degenerate into what Wootton called 'unconstructive teaching'. The ultra-scepticism of the WEA's Socratic tradition might mean that the original practical and constructive approach gets forgotten, the vital drive is lost, and the only tangible and lasting gift that the expert leaves with his students is inoculation with the Socratic tradition.

Wootton proposed that classes should, having looked at many sides of a subject, then commit themselves to conclusions. She did not want to start with conclusions, since that would ignore the virtues of the WEA tradition. These virtues were, firstly, that there was a distinction between education and propaganda, and, secondly, that it warned students off 'facile solutions' and trained them to think for themselves. She had no quarrel with a sceptical tradition, 'but I do quarrel with a sceptical tradition which is sceptical and nothing else.' [20]

Decisiveness and commitment was without doubt a great attraction for students in Labour College classes. John Brown, a former seaman and tramp who had previously attended university evening classes in Newcastle, who started to attend NCLC classes in the late 1920s was very struck by their refreshing directness: 'This was something different to a university class!' [21] Brown though had experienced both approaches and therefore was able beneficially to draw on them in his own thought and practice. This seems to be striking proof of the point made by an Education Commission of the Bradford ILP in the early 1930s which suggested that:

The ideal education for a worker is first a Labour College course, and then as a corrective a Workers' Educational tutorial course, say in economics, to instil a shade of modest doubt, to suggest alternatives and generally to mellow the whole attitude. [22]

This transition from Labour College to WEA classes in fact happened quite frequently. It is documented as having taken place, for instance, in the Rossendale Valley (where by the early 1930s there was no longer any Labour College provision), and in many parts of South Wales. In one case in South Wales a WEA tutor in philosophy found her class full of students of Joseph Dietzgen, the philosopher of proletarian logic much favoured by the Labour College. [23] J. Dover Wilson, His Majesty's Inspector for Adult Classes in Yorkshire in the early 1920s, positively valued the collision between the two approaches. He recalled in his autobiography that:

... it was not uncommon to find a member of the Labour College, a Marxist rival of the WEA, in one of their classes. And I was always pleased when it happened, since he with his rather crude Marxism was apt to call the class back to fundamentals. He acted like garlic in the salad. [24]

Without the presence of students who had a background in the
Labour College movement or in socialist education of some sort, a
WEA class *might* degenerate into an educational process in which the
tutor was regarded with too much deference. This seems to have been
the case in a WEA class in political philosophy with Professor J. L.
Stocks as the tutor in Rochdale in 1932–3. One of the students, a
greaser in a cotton mill, recalled that:

I absorbed all that I could from my tutor, and as I sat listening to his wise and
so charmingly delivered talks, I earnestly hoped that the day might come
when I should be as cultured, as wise, and as gentle as he.

Stocks, incidentally, was precisely one of those tutors who tended to
be too Socratic, and who complained in 1936 that his students were
often 'too much interested in the conclusion of the argument, too
little interested in the methods and considerations by which the
conclusion is reached'. [25]

Normally, however, the discussion periods which followed
exposition from tutors in WEA classes were combative occasions. In
the report of the first major inspection of tutorial classes by the Board
of Education before the First World War, HMI Headlam and
Professor L. T. Hobhouse noted that in the discussions views were
exchanged between tutors and students 'with great frankness and
simplicity' and that controversial subjects were 'frequently raised by
one member or another of the class, and sometimes pursued with
considerable vigour and plainness of expression'. One can almost
note a sense of regret on the part of Headlam and Hobhouse about
the nature of the discussions, but we need not share it. Rather we
should see the vigour and range of discussions in WEA classes as their
saving grace. It might also serve to disabuse people of the absurd
notion that WEA classes were exercises in the 'brainwashing' of
WEA students into the acceptance of views and interpretations which
did not tally with their experience and their existing interpretations of
social reality. Headlam and Hobhouse wrote of class discussions that
if the class contained a group of students 'who have formed strong
opinions of their own, they are apt to take up the whole time with a
vigorous "heckling" of the lecturer on any point where he may
happen to have run across their views'. [26] The testimony of an
ironmoulder who was a member of the Salford Tutorial Class
between 1911 and 1914 bears out the reality of the liveliness of the
discussion period in WEA classes. He writes that the tutor had to put
up with 'storms and reproaches' and 'long-winded criticisms'. He and

his fellow students also took their new knowledge, sifted as it was through their own political stances, into the working-class movement, the workshops and to street corner meetings. One of their tutors is recorded as having interspersed his remarks with such statements as 'Now don't let me hear any of you speaking at the street corner in Manchester say this or that, unless you fully understand this or that'. [27]

Nor did this sort of thing die out in the 1920s and 1930s — if anything it intensified after the WEA (both independently and through its trade union wing, the Workers' Educational Trade Union Committee) turned its attention more explicitly to the labour movement from the end of the war. [28] The Board of Education's *Report on Adult Education in Yorkshire* of 1928 made the point that WEA classes were still mainly made up of people who had strong political motives and who were drawn from organizations in the working-class movement. WEA classes were:

. . . almost entirely composed of persons who are already asociated together in groups or are ready to fall into such groups whose basis and bond of union is not purely cultural or intellectual.

Discussion remained an equally prominent feature of the conduct of the classes, and appeared to the Board of Education to have been so politically orientated that it began to have reservations about the method often adopted:

Catechetical and dialectical methods, however, have their limitations. . . . An unskilful dialectic is irritating and futile, and occasionally tutors have neglected systematic presentation and exposition in favour of discussion, possibly under the influence of a false derivation of the word education. Discussion is always a feature of these classes, but its value is overrated when irrelevancies are unchecked and it is allowed to degenerate into mere expressions of opinion unsupported by evidence or reason. [29]

There is even one piece of evidence which suggests that the discussion periods in WEA classes were so potent that tutors were sometimes converted to views which they had not previously held. John Thomas, the first secretary of the WEA in Wales but who by the time of writing (1922) was South Wales Miners' Federation Agent in the Anthracite coalfield and the tutor of a class at Ystalyfera, suggested that in spite of the WEA's own stance 'because of its very Socratic method of teaching, with question and answer, between student and teacher, particularly in the second hour' the WEA class was 'a disseminating ground for Marxian teachings to be discussed, if not actually spread.' Although most of the tutors were not Marxists, the left wing students in the class, well read in the Marxist classics, were apparently unable to:

... resist an opportunity to discuss very ably, certain Marxian doctrines. ... In fact, so effective has been the criticism of some of these students in classes, in Economics and some Social subjects that the tutor himself has been forced to hold a Marxian outlook, as opposed to the Marshallian outlook. [30]

Discussion, then, was one of the central pedagogic devices in WEA classes. Another was that tutors should look at questions from a wide range of viewpoints. An illustration which typifies the WEA approach can be found in the subjects being studied at the WEA's Durham Summer School in 1934 as a response to student interest in the problem of unemployment. The subjects included: economic planning in the USSR and in the USA, and a comparative study of the economic principles of capitalism, the corporate state, and socialism and communism. [31] Neither the Oxford Report of 1908 in its model syllabus for economics classes nor the non-socialist founder and first general secretary of the WEA, Albert Mansbridge, had in any way proscribed the use of Marxist texts, though they were, of course, to be used alongside more orthodox works. Mansbridge wrote in 1913 that a tutorial class in economics should have 'access to the opinions of all economic writers, the orthodox equally with the unorthodox. No class, for example, can afford to disregard either Marshall or Marx.' [32] At a conference of tutorial class tutors in 1922 it was stated that any class which failed to consider Marx and the Materialist Conception of History was a failure. [33] And at a similar conference three years earlier G. D. H. Cole spoke on 'The place of Marx in economic teaching', and argued that all teachers of economics should 'know Marx well, not only in order to agree with him or to refute him, but in order that they might be able to approach economic [sic] teaching from the right point of view.'

Cole on that occasion addressed himself explicitly to the difference which was supposed to exist between the WEA and the Labour College movement, and noted, quite fairly, that the Labour College's Marxism was primarily industrial in outlook and that it was based very largely on the labour theory of value. Cole, convincingly to my mind, argued that the labour theory of value was not the real strength of Marxism (it was, he said, neither true nor untrue, but was merely 'useful as a means of criticizing other economic theories of value').

The real strength of Marxism arose from 'the historic elements in the theory', and clearly, given the WEA's very strong emphasis on economic history and its leading role in the development of the subject in Britain, [34] its work in this respect was exemplary. The attraction of the Marxian theory of value for such groups as the Labour College was that it seemed to give a scientific sanction for the rest of Marxian economics. As Cole pointed out, in reality it did nothing of the kind, 'but it acquired an artificial importance in their eyes in part because it was difficult, and because within the circle of its own assumptions it was watertight'. [35]

Given willingly self-imposed limitations of this sort, the work of the Labour College movement was in many respects remarkable. Worker-teachers of singular dedication taught difficult and abstract material, sometimes very imaginatively, to people of little educational attainment. The Labour College movement relied on the resources of its own membership for successive cohorts of tutors, especially through its use, up until its closure in 1929, of the residential Central Labour College as a kind of staff college. [36] Its journal, *Plebs*, contained well-written articles on a wide range of theoretical, as well as day-to-day agitational, matters. It produced a small flow of its own short text-books, some, like Noah Ablett's *Easy Outlines of Economics*, being of high quality. In its strongholds in South Wales, the North East of England, Lancashire and in the Glasgow area, it made a lasting contribution to the education of at least a generation of labour movement activists.

In spite of the heterodox nature of the content of its teaching (Marx on economics, Engels on primitive societies, Dietzgen on philosophy), its teaching methods were in some respects highly orthodox. Although courses were usually shorter than those of the WEA, regular reading and essay writing was required of students, and exposition from the tutor formed a central part of the class. Indeed, the latter seems to have had a greater place in a Labour College education than was the case with the WEA. The unfamiliarity of the content, and the deep-seated belief in the complete correctness of it, meant that many of the students were almost totally subservient to their tutors. Even one of the Labour College's most outstanding (and at that time most militant) members, Frank Hodges, conceded faults of this sort in the approach to teaching. It was, in fact, the 'only criticism' he could find of the work of the Labour College:

that the average student himself, not having the leisure to fully study and understand the historical and economic laws which create our modern social system, is prone to accept, without examination, the remedy his own tutor prescribes for the speedy abolition of the present social and industrial conditions. [37]

Dogmatism and extreme generalization seem to have been a fault of all but the best tutors. One former member complained in 1926 of 'crudity of their outlook', and another complained:

... they have a fixed position for everything. Their dogmatic emphasis would outdo any irish Catholic when he is postulating his certainty of Holy Michael.
.... Their lectures are parrot-like and have mathematical precision. ... History is just to emphasize the obvious fact that the 'haves' some time ago didled the 'have nots'. ... [38]

J. F. Horrabin, a key figure in the Labour College movement and then the editor of *Plebs*, in 1926 rejected such charges of the pumping of dogmas into passive students. His case, interestingly, was based on a recognition of the importance of discussion as a preventative of this — the same thing being, as I have argued, an important defence of the despised WEA approach! Horrabin wrote that:

The discussion which forms the most important part of the work of the Labour College class is a pretty good safeguard against the pumping process, and at the same time an effective means for the encouragement of individual minds. [39]

In the tutors' exposition, however, no presentation of alternative views was thought either necessary or desirable. It had been argued right from the start of the movement in the famous pamphlet *The Burning Question of Education* produced shortly after the Ruskin Strike, that such an approach would have been 'suicidal' for a Labour College, and the view of a former Ruskin student was quoted with approval:

It is well to understand your opponent's position, but surely it is more important to understand your own. The working-class student has no time to listen to elaborate apologies made on behalf of the oppressing class. ... What he requires is a knowledge of the social forces operating in society, and how best they can be utilized for the benefit of the people, while it may be as well for him to know the other side of the case in the field of Political Economy, it is essential he should know his own side. [40]

The implication of this is clear: 'knowing the other side of the case' could easily become an optional and dispensable extra. The really able Labour College supporter might, however, make the effort, and his Marxism, if it stood the test of exposure to uncomfortable and opposed points of view, would truly be strengthened and would itself be a product of dialectical method. Noah Ablett was one who successfully followed such a path, as a reading of his *Easy Outlines of Economics* — with its dialogues between 'Marginal Bill and Marxian Socialist' on 'The Theory of Marginal Utility vs. The Marxian Theory of Value' (where Böhm-Bawark as well as Marshall are taken on), and on 'Capital, Labour-Power, and Surplus Value' — makes abundantly clear. [41] As Ablett himself once said, quoting Dietzgen, 'In order to throw a man out of the temple you must first of all embrace him.' Although such as Ablett adopted this approach, for most it was clearly too close for comfort to the best WEA practice. One suspects that normal Labour College practice was more nearly summed up by Joe Walker of Leeds in the same (February 1917) issue of *Plebs* when he wrote:

The WEA policy is no use when you want to tell workers *why* and how they are robbed and kept with their noses to the grindstone. It's no use wasting valuable time going from Leeds to Liverpool to get to London.

Walker's attack on the WEA was characteristic of the Labour College movement, though it was rather on the mild side. The Labour College movement maintained a pretty constant barrage of attacks against it, and paradoxically these became more extreme precisely at those moments when the WEA increased its orientation towards the Labour movement: for instance in the 1920s during the period of, eventually abortive, discussion for trade union educational unity. As G. D. H. Cole, the key figure on the WEA side in these negotiations put it in the Winter 1923 issue of *The Highway*:

Most Plebs Leaguers thoroughly enjoy doing battle with the WEA, and representing it as a disguised capitalist agency,

and in response:

Some WEA'ers enjoy denouncing the wickedness of the Plebs League as a perverter of the mind, teaching the workers, not to think freely for themselves, but to imbibe certain doctrinaire opinions supposed to be a guarantee of rectitude in the class struggle.

In a stream of articles in *The Highway* and *The Student's Bulletin*, Cole attempted to deal systematically with the Labour College's often unwarranted slurs on the WEA. The attacks did, however, have at least one salutary effect on the WEA. As one American observer put it, it led it 'to define its purpose, to reiterate its allegiance to working-class principles in stronger and stronger terms'. [42] Cole was the driving force behind this development: he sought constantly to integrate the WEA into the Labour movement, and to detach it from the worst aspects of its links with universities. He never denounced the Labour College movement, regarding its approach as a legitimate one though he constantly sought to make a distinction between propaganda, and education. 'In political and industrial work,' he said, 'I am a propagandist seeking to persuade others to my opinion, in education I am a midwife, trying to help them to bring their own ideas to birth.' This did not mean that Cole, nor many another WEA tutor, accepted the notion of 'impartiality', for in the *Student's Bulletin* in April 1925 he wrote:

. . . we must clear our minds of the cant of impartiality and academic superiority. There is no such thing as an impartial teacher. Every teacher is bound to teach the facts by the light of his interpretation of them. Nor can a good teacher honestly suppress his own interpretation, or keep it in the background. If he does that, he submits coloured facts — facts coloured by his own interpretation — without confessing the colour. He deceives his students — which is dishonest. Let us be as partial as we like to our own views, provided we expound as faithfully as we can the views of others.

In conclusion

This approach, the best practice of many of the WEA's tutors, is surely the one to adopt in working-class adult education today since it is based both on an unpatronizing assessment of the abilities of working-class students themselves and also on a recognition of the diversity of points of view, even within the Labour movement. This approach is also what ultimately secured the resources of the state for WEA work, and denied it to the Labour College movement. There can be no objection whatsoever to the Labour movement providing and paying for its own educational and propagandist services, and one hopes that it will increasingly do this. But surely it is both unwise and unnecessary to ignore the possibilities of using the resources of the state. The TUC has been able to get financial assistance for the 'non-political' parts of its educational programme in the past few years, without it involving any dilution of its normal content. In this way the Labour Government of 1974–9 effectively gave the TUC education department Responsible Body status for its courses, and this clearly has been an advance for the Labour movement. Given the important recent reorientation of the WEA to working-class adult education, not only in industrial studies but also in political education, its potential, given the paramount importance of adequacy of resources, is considerable. To argue that only provision of education by the Labour movement itself is of any use, on the grounds that only it can have an adequate degree of commitment is not proven by the past and present practice of at least some elements in the WEA. In addition, the WEA's tradition of democratic control by students, if applied through 'Industrial Branches', would mean that a vital ingredient of working-class adult education absent in TUC provision would re-emerge. [43] Provision by the Labour movement itself might also, if the history of the Labour College movement is anything to go by, fail to produce the sort of strengths required to deal with complex problems. Just how much of a compromise is it to reject dogmatism and the oversimplification of difficult and contentious issues?

Part Two
Selected studies

6 Reform and reaction — the Workers' Educational Association post-Russell

Mel Doyle,* Assistant Secretary, WEA

It is often said — and validly so — that the 1973 Report of the Russell Committee of Inquiry into Adult Education defined for the WEA those areas of priority work which the WEA had first defined for itself, and later presented in evidence to the Russell Committee. The Committee Report confirmed that:

> . . . in its evidence to us the WEA has pointed to *four areas in which its recent experience shows possibilities of expansion that it would wish to pursue.* In general terms these are all concerned with sectors of the population who might not otherwise be touched by adult education and they are therefore a logical development of the Association's traditional concern for the under-privileged.

The four areas referred to were:
a)   Education for the socially and culturally deprived living in urban areas.
b)   Educational work in an industrial context.
c)   Political and social education.
d)   Courses of liberal and academic study below the level of university work.

Russell was convinced that these priority objectives would 'once again cast the WEA in the role of educational pioneer, bringing to those in great need services that they may have hitherto rejected.' The Committee gave its warm support to this development role but was conscious that in practice progress would be dependent on additional state funding. Recommendations were made, therefore, on changes to grant-aiding arrangements. In essence the Committee suggested that the DES should continue to pay to the WEA 75 per cent towards

* This chapter has been written by Mel Doyle in a personal capacity and does not reflect the policy or the views of the WEA.

the costs of an approved programme with a further 12½ per cent of total grant added as a contribution towards administrative expenses.

The Committee's minds must have been exercised wonderfully on devising a mechanism whereby it could have some confidence that the additional funding would lead to a genuine commitment to advance the defined priority areas. Laudable declarations of intent by the WEA at national level were one thing; the practice of Districts and Branches on the ground might be very different. As the Committee noted:

a shift of emphasis from a wide range of general provision to more specific priorities and a more general role in the promotion of adult education will require a substantial effort or reorientation on the part of branch and district committees.

The device chosen to influence the future direction of the WEA was the abandonment of the responsible body category from FE Regulations and with it grant payment directly from the DES to individual Districts. In its place the Report recommended that grant should be paid centrally to the WEA, which in turn would allow 'priority in the allocation of resources (to be) given to those forms of work or those regions which are regarded nationally as of high priority'. To put it bluntly the WEA was to be invited to put its new money where its mouth was!

The gentler language of the Report stressed that any voluntary body had to make its own policy for itself, but warned that a Committee of Inquiry could only indicate what aspects of the WEA's work should be particularly deserving of support from public funds. Russell was effectively making additional grant aid conditional on a change of emphasis in the WEA's pattern of work.

Within the WEA the three-year period following the publication of the Russell Report was dominated by attempts to negotiate new grant-aiding arrangements. Undoubtedly the task was made urgent by the serious financial plight of many Districts, yet made difficult by the Association's rejection of the Russell formula for centralized funding. At local level the WEA had read the implications of the Russell equation. The 'democratic rights of the voluntary movement' were rediscovered, refurbished and re-introduced against the centralized imposition of three of the four Russell categories – *(a)* 'Education for the socially and culturally deprived', *(b)* 'Educational work in an industrial context', and *(c)* 'Political and social education'. The fourth category — 'Liberal and academic study' — the bedrock of most Branch provision, tended to become increasingly detached from the other three categories in ensuing internal and external discussions.

When new grant arrangements were finally announced in 1977 they inevitably reflected a compromise between the Russell proposals and the anti-centralist position adopted within the Districts. Grant continued to be paid to individual Districts directly, but by using a cash limits mechanism it could be applied to non-teaching as well as teaching costs. These new arrangements were made on the assumption that the WEA should continue to shift the emphasis of its work towards Russell categories *(a), (b)* and *(c)* with target increases suggested for each category over a three-year period. The accompanying DES memorandum suggested that the Department would 'be looking to the Association to devise appropriate national liaison and co-ordinating arrangements so that it will be possible for the Department to monitor the change in the National picture.'

There is little doubt that the new arrangements eased the financial situation in Districts and it was that consideration which consumed attention for the first year under the new arrangements (1977 to 1978). The implications of any meaningful shift of emphasis did not arouse the attentions of the movement although one would have expected Russell to have encouraged a radical reappraisal within the WEA of its future role. After all Russell had given its blessing to a route which the WEA itself had chosen as appropriate for its future development.

But what in concrete terms had the WEA committed itself to? Whereas there had been full discussion at national level of what should constitute the Association's evidence to Russell, there is little to suggest that that debate ever encompassed the serious attentions of the movement at District and especially Branch level. This was not a matter of a nationally orchestrated grand deceit, but a reflection of the very nature of the WEA. The Association prides itself in being a voluntary self-governing movement with determination of the class programme residing with the student body. Add to this a federalist constitutional structure with governmental authority residing effectively with the Districts, then one can begin to appreciate the difficulties of determining national policy objectives let alone enforcing national policy decisions.

It is probably a reasonable supposition that when Russell reported, incorporating much of what the WEA had sought, WEA activists at local level thought the determination of so-called priority areas an irrelevance to the future development of *their* class programmes. There was no opposition as such to priority work, because the assumption was that liberal academic studies provision would continue very much as before. Indeed Russell itself had identified 'courses of liberal and academic study below the level of university work' as an appropriate area of development. The radical chic fringe could have their radical chic fringe-activities so long as there was no danger to the 'real' work of the movement defined in a 'traditional' branch image. When it came to pursuing the Russell categories the further problem emerged of giving a precise form to their meaning. The outstanding problems concerned categories *(a)* and *(c)*. Russell had this to say of the two categories:

Education for the socially and culturally deprived living in urban areas. Many other bodies are engaged in such areas — local authorities through community development projects involving housing and social services departments as well as education, the Home Office, universities, and local organizations such as Councils of Social Service, community associations, neighbourhood committees and local action groups. The involvement of the WEA would have to be in a strictly educational role and closely integrated with the work of the other bodies. It would also have to be of an experimental and informal character, requiring new forms of activity and unfamiliar techniques.

Political and social education. Traditionally the WEA has believed that much of its work in general education was directed to greater social and political awareness as well as intellectual enlightenment. This conception we feel to have special value today. New avenues for activity have begun to appear in courses run in cooperation with OXFAM, SHELTER and similar socially orientated organisations, and in certain kinds of 'role education' for those engaged in local government and in social and political activity.

These comments were never intended to be final statements of definition, nevertheless they did signpost a clear direction to be pursued. In 1977 an attempt was made at national level to give a more coherent form to the areas of development. Although the initial objective was to categorize more effectively existing provision it did identify also the main elements of *(a)* and *(c)* which were likely to form the substance of future work:

Work in areas of development (excluding Trade Union and Industrial Studies)

1   Political/social/community role education (i.e. the education of

people to occupy more effectively positions in the community including local councillors, play-group leaders, activists in community bodies).

2 Social, political and economic education for the citizen (open recruitment). This includes *all provision* whose primary aim is the better equipment of the student to understand the society in which he lives and therefore to be in a better position to exercise citizenship and influence decisions *other than* that classified elsewhere.

3 Rights education (including legal, welfare, and consumer rights, the rights of women and ethnic minorities. Here the emphasis is directly on equipping people to take full advantage of specific rights and to understand specific social responsibilities).

4 Education for retirement.

5 Basic education for adults (literacy, post-literacy courses to develop communication, comprehension, and other basic educational skills as necessary preparation for other study).

6 Training of tutors and other workers, professional, part-time or voluntary in adult education.

Additionally areas of development were defined by the special kind of student for whom the provision was made:

1 'Difficult' urban and suburban areas — urban areas in which a high proportion of the population left school at the minimum leaving age and have a low record of attendance at adult education classes, thus suggesting special efforts.

2 Rural areas which lack educational and cultural facilities.

3 The unemployed.

4 Shiftworkers.

5 The mentally ill and handicapped.

6 The physically handicapped. (This includes special provision in institutions or for other 'closed groups', provision in places where the handicapped are to be found that is open to all and provision for the general community with special arrangements or facilities to enable physically handicapped people to take part alongside the able-bodied.)

7 Immigrants and ethnic minorities.

8 Special provision for the elderly (see note to category 6 in this list).

9 Inmates of penal institutions.

This attempt at more effective definition would have allowed the WEA to report more accurately on the shift of emphasis of its work. One would have expected the DES to have encouraged the Association to pursue the exercise as an integral part of the monitoring process which the WEA had agreed to when the new grant arrangements were introduced. But incredibly the Department was unenthusiastic. Although since early 1977 the DES had required regular reporting of changes in class provision it tended to be incurious at the more fundamental questions involved. If one was forced to speculate on this, one might suggest that support for the traditionalist conception of the WEA within the Department suggested that it was best not to ask too many questions which might reveal no more than a marginal shift of emphasis and commitment to development work.

The inevitable consequence of inadequate definition of *(a)* and *(c)* was strongly revealed in the 1977–8 session. The absence of effective guide-lines allowed a number of Districts such flexibility in the categorization of their class provision as to question seriously the validity of much of the statistical data. Take for example category *(a)* If rural communities were to be generally viewed as suffering 'social and cultural deprivation', then if a District thought it appropriate within its own terms of reference, it could classify work in this area as Russell category *(a)*, irrespective of the subject matter of the class or the kind of student who attended. In other words it was perfectly possible to redefine traditional liberal studies provision in terms of development work. Thus 'real' progress made in categories *(a)* and *(c)* was most probably overstated.

What evidence then is there of a shift of emphasis? With the above qualification in mind class meetings for the 17 English and Welsh Districts have shown the following pattern over the years 1975 to 1978:

Category A: Education for the 'disadvantaged'

Year	Class meetings*	Percentage of total provision
1975–76	11,758	16
1976–77	12,954	17
1977–78	16,836	21

* A 'class meeting' is defined as a teaching period of 1½ hours.

Category C: Social and political education

Year	Class meetings*	Percentage of total provision
1975–76	10,037	14
1976–77	11,315	15
1977–78	11,590	15

At best, as far as *(a)* and *(c)* are concerned, there has been no more than a marginal shift in emphasis. In sharp contrast statistical evidence appears to suggest a marked decline in Liberal and Academic Studies provision (category *d*):

Category D: Liberal and academic studies

Year	Class meetings	Percentage of total provision
1975–76	39,955	55
1976–77	37,462	48
1977–78	30,753	39

The fall was considered dramatic enough for the WEA in its national submission to the DES in October 1978 to argue that:

Although the Districts have successfully changed the pattern of their class provision an increasing concern is developing about the reduction in the liberal and academic studies. The need for a more balanced programme has been accepted but the Association does not accept that much of what is now referred to as liberal and academic falls outside of the social purpose which makes necessary the development of the three other 'special' categories. The feeling is that the liberal and academic studies constitute the basis upon which the more varied programme can be developed, and that in some Districts this basis is being seriously eroded.

Most certainly there has been a decline in this area even allowing for redefinition of some Liberal and Academic Studies provision referred to earlier. But to suggest that a concerted attempt to shift the balance of work was the major contributory cause is incorrect. Three other major factors undoubtedly help explain the situation. Firstly, there has been a substantial rise in student class fees which may well have acted as a disincentive to student recruitment here in particular. Secondly, alternative provision by the Open University and by Colleges of FE extending their AE activities has weakened the WEA's competitive position. Thirdly, working relationships between WEA Districts and university extra-mural departments are now no longer as close as they once were with consequent effects especially on a District's administrative base.

But these factors, and possibly others, have been largely ignored. Instead attention has been focused on the growth and threat of the final Russell category to consider, 'educational work in an industrial context', or category *(b)*.

In the last three years the WEA has experienced an enormous quantitative increase in its Trade Union and Industrial Studies class provision:

Year	Total number of class meetings	Total number of class meetings in Trade Union and Industrial Studies	Trade Union and Industrial Studies class meetings as % of total
1975–76	72,800	11,122	15
1976–77	77,440	15,709	20
1977–78	79,044	19,865	25

In Trade Union and Industrial Studies these figures represent consecutive year-on-year increases of 41 per cent and 26 per cent and a total increase over the period of 79 per cent.

For most WEA Districts, provision under the TUC Regional Education Scheme is of central importance. In 1977–78, 19 of the Association's 21 Districts were direct providers of the TUC scheme, with 12 Districts promoting 20 or more 10 day-release courses during the year. All told some 90 per cent of total provision by WEA Districts in Trade Union and Industrial Studies is for the TUC scheme.

Given that no new tutor organizer posts had been created since 1975–6 this massive increase was made possible by three factors:

1 The re-direction of existing full-time tutorial resources towards Trade Union and Industrial Studies.
2 The introduction of greater 'flexibility' into the working arrangements (for example, class contact time) of full-time staff.
3 The employment of additional part-time tutor support for the Trade Union and Industrial Studies programme.

Of course such an expansion was not directly attributable to Russell. Throughout its history the WEA had made educational provision for trade unionists both directly and through its appendage, the Workers' Educational Trade Union Committee

(WETUC). With the winding up of WETUC and the National Council of Labour Colleges (NCLC) and their incorporation into the TUC Regional Education Scheme inaugurated in 1964, WEA provision very much reflected the conceived objectives and lines of development of the TUC scheme. It was inevitable therefore, that with the 'take-off' of the TUC scheme in the mid 1970s there would be a corresponding expansion in WEA provision. Thus by 1977 to 1978, of the 2008 day-release courses provided by the TUC Regional Education scheme, 533 or 27 per cent were provided by WEA Districts in England, Wales and Scotland.

The introduction of regulations implementing sections 57–60 of the 1975 Employment Protection Act and the safety representatives' regulations issued under the 1974 Health and Safety at Work Act ensured legislative support for the training needs of workplace representatives. From 1976 to 1977 the DES has made available to the TUC an annual grant towards the costs of its educational programme. Thus both legislative and financial support have underpinned the TUC's target of 180,000 training places annually by the early 1980s (for 1977–8 the TUC scheme provided 27,479 places).

Side by side with this quantitative expansion has come a major involvement in development programmes. On the initiative of the WEA and at the invitation of the TUC, WEA Tutor Organizers have contributed to the development of teaching materials and methods for courses organized under the TUC scheme. Largely this has reflected the view that the WEA's experience, expertise and credibility in Trade Union education is an invaluable resource for the Trade Union movement. WEA tutors have been involved in the design, piloting and evaluation of course materials at both basic and advanced level, and in both general and industrial sector courses. Furthermore, WEA expertise has been called on to assist in the TUC's tutor training programme. Also a number of individual Trade Unions have requested and received WEA assistance in curriculum development. In very general terms there has been common agreement that the WEA, and particularly its Tutor Organizers, should be continuously involved in programmes of development work which seek to *qualitatively* improve and broaden the nature of Trade Union education.

Since 1975 therefore, the WEA has linked into an area of provision which is now an identifiable mass provision. The implications of this for the WEA, as we shall see, have been and are, both structural and ideological.

The rapid expansion of WEA/TUC provision has tended to constrain attempts to focus on wider perspectives of Trade Union-based workers' education. Questions which have arisen have reflected organizational problems which were the inevitable consequence of the new volume of provision. The one exception to this narrow mechanistic approach has been the discussion on ways of building a *voluntary* basis to Trade Union and Industrial Studies. In concrete terms this has meant discussion on the role of WEA Industrial branches.

While the WEA has made a major contribution to the development of day-release provision for workplace representatives, its role in Trade Union education has been seen by some within the Association in a much wider, though often ill-defined context. There is the belief that the WEA can make a unique contribution to extending the definition of Trade Union education, to creating bridges between Trade Union education and other forms of adult education, and most importantly of all, to involving Trade Unionists in the definition of their own educational needs and in the structuring of participative provision to meet those needs. It is within this context of democratic workers' self-education that sections within the WEA have attempted to define its unique role in Trade Union education.

As we have seen, on the basis of the WEA's central role in the TUC scheme a vast body of students has been created through the transformation of Trade Union Studies into a mass provision. This has become a necessary prerequisite for allowing the WEA to build the connections between workplace representative training and the broader objectives of a workers' education movement. As yet in quantitative terms there are relatively few examples of these 'connections', nonetheless experience does suggest that major advances can be made to give organizational support to this objective. At present the WEA's programme of Trade Union education is carried on largely outside the traditional branch structure with heavy reliance on full-time tutor support. Trade Union students in day-release classes seldom come into contact with traditional branch provision. They face the immediate problems of identifying with an essentially bourgeois ethos and consequently of seeing relevance to their industrial and political experiences in a branch's class programme.

Industrial branches are a means of resolving these problems. Their central recruiting objective is to involve students from a variety of day-release provision in a programme directed at the longer-term and broader industrial, social and political education needs of Trade Unionists. Currently there are 15 Industrial branches, the earliest dating from 1971 to 1972, but with the majority formed after 1975 when work for the TUC scheme entered the period of sustained growth.

Although successive WEA Biennial Conferences (1977 and 1979) have called for support for Industrial branches, there has been little attempt to construct a coherent organizational strategy for their development. In essence while it is recognized that the majority of traditional branches are identified with so-called Liberal Studies provision and resistant to change, an alternative structure has not attracted sufficient support within the WEA to be pursued with any vigour.

This is not through the failure of argument — indeed it is generally accepted that the strength of the Industrial branches has been their ability to attract those whom one might think the WEA was most concerned to recruit; highlighting in turn the general failure to do so in traditional branches. No, the explanation lies in an appreciation of the implications of a strategy which would make the WEA something which at present it obviously isn't, an integral part of the broad Labour movement.

In earlier paragraphs it was suggested that where voices were raised in opposition to the new grant aiding arrangements they tended to be timorous and largely confined to fears of increasing centralization within the WEA. The major cause for concern was not the proposed shift of emphasis in class provision, but the fear that new administrative arrangements would weaken both local autonomy and the voluntary base of the movement. It could have been argued that this implicitly challenged the dominant position of liberal and academic studies, but that line of argument was not pursued. Therefore, because there was no generalized feeling that liberal and academic studies was under threat from the new arrangements, so no serious critique was offered in its defence.

But this is no longer the situation. A dramatic change in attitudes is now becoming evident. There is a growing view that the decline in liberal and academic studies is but a manifestation of a challenge to the very nature of the WEA. In its extreme form this perspective argues that the growth in trade union and industrial studies, crudely conceived as mere 'training', is anathema to 'traditional' liberal adult educational values.

While open hostility to further expansion in Trade Union Studies provision remains uncommon, opposition nonetheless is very real. Most usual are expressions of concern for District programmes showing signs of 'imbalance'. This argument involves criticism that new resources have been unevenly distributed in favour of 'new' work, that 'new' work is outpacing 'traditional' work, and that Branch provision (liberal and academic studies) is in some way subsidizing District provision (mainly Trade Union Studies). At the core of the argument is a deep suspicion of the academic legitimacy of Trade Union Studies, and more importantly of the implications for the WEA of growing institutionalized links with the Trade Union movement. It overspills into other areas of activity, for example the Women's Studies programme, and has manifested itself at times in the 'voluntary movement's' concern at the role of the professional field staff. As well there are signs that such fears are shared at the DES.

As we have seen currently 90 per cent of Trade Union Studies is provided under the TUC Regional Education Scheme. Thus the dominant institutional relationship in Trade Union education is with the TUC which encourages the charge that the WEA is in danger of becoming a mere adjunct to the TUC. Furthermore, at local level the institutional relationship increasingly extends to the Shop Steward, Branch, District and Regional bodies of the Trade Unions whose members attend WEA/TUC classes.

It is evident that two underlying themes of critical importance are associated with the expansion. Firstly, the very size of demand for Trade Union educational provision, especially at workplace level, has meant that expansion has fuelled further expansion and will continue to do so. The only restraints will be limitations on resources and a political decision within the WEA to go no further in this direction. Secondly, as more and more Trade Unionists participate in WEA Trade Union Studies provision so an increasing number will participate in the governmental structure of the WEA at Branch and District level. This in turn will lead to a more critical appraisal of the relevance of much of existing provision to the needs of those whose initial contact with the WEA has come through Trade Union day-release provision. In essence the question which will be asked is whether the Workers' Educational Association is a workers' movement or not.

7 Writers' workshops and working-class culture

David Evans, Lecturer in Creative Arts, Institute of Extension Studies, University of Liverpool

How can you tell what class I'm from?
I can talk posh like some
With an 'Olly in me mouth
Down me nose, wear an 'at not a scarf
With me second-hand clothes.
So why do you always wince when you hear
Me say 'Tara' to me 'Ma' instead of 'Bye Mummy dear?'
How can you tell what class I'm from?
'Cos we live in a corpy, not like some
In a pretty little semi, out Wirral way
And commute into Liverpool by train each day?
Or did I drop my unemployment card
Sitting on your patio (We have a yard)?
How can you tell what class I'm from?
Have I a label on me head, and another on me bum?
Or is it because my hands are stained with toil
Instead of soft lily-white with perfume and oil?
Don't I crook me little finger when I drink me tea
Say toilet instead of bog when I want to pee?
Why do you care what class I'm from?
Does it stick in your gullet like a sour plum?
Well, mate! A cleaner is me mother
    A docker is me brother
    Bread pudding is wet nelly
    And me stomach is me belly
And I'm proud of the class that I come from.

Mary Casey, 'The class game', in *Voices* (19)

A small event which illuminates an aspect of our contemporary culture took place in the Stephenson Room of Euston Station in September 1978. It was the launching of a book with the simple title

Writing [1] at the modest price of £1. The book was backed by no publishing house and predictably it was ignored by every national newspaper but one. [2]

Books, even modestly priced ones, are launched regularly. This book was different because it was a collection of short stories, tales, verse and recollections by people who are rarely allowed to break into print, though they often, and sometimes unconsentingly, provide the raw material profitably exploited by middle-class authors, including academic writers. The contributors to *Writing* included a dustman, an ex-docker, inner-city housewives, a welder, a taxi driver, unemployed building-site workers, alienated young blacks, school refusers; people living in the main in the poor, ravaged working-class areas of urban Britain. Most of them are people educationists are fond of referring to as the 'non-participators', a term only marginally less insulting than 'the deprived' or 'the disadvantaged'. Yet it is precisely these 'non-participators' who began and form the core of a vivid new cultural development: the importance of *Writing* is not simply that it offers evidence of creative energy and talent in people largely dismissed as failures by bourgeois educational standards, but also that it is the visible first fruit of a growing and vigorous national movement — the joint product of a congeries of predominantly working-class writers' workshops and community publishers.

The experiences leading to the emergence of the Federation of Worker Writers and Community Publishers (FWWCP) and the appearance not only of *Writing* but of numerous 'little magazines', area histories, individual and group biographies, collections of verse, literacy readers compiled from the work of the students themselves and, lately, sketches and short plays, can fairly be described as educational, creative or cultural. But they are far more, as this extract from a poem 'Culture for the Workers' by Chris Harris of the Scotland Road Writers' Workshop, suggests:

The worker puts pen to paper
He writes of life today
Expresses worker power
Solidarity his words say.

The worker becomes an artist
He paints our life today
Paints working class people
Models our strength in clay.

The workers develop their class
They live the life of today
They develop their own culture
They now practise all they say. [3]

For many people active in the writers' movement the workshops are as much an expression of working-class consciousness as an educational experience: they are an aspect of working-class politics, both in what they have achieved and the direction in which they point — towards an ever wider and increasingly conscious struggle to express (and, it is hoped, develop and refine) working-class preoccupations and values. Because of their aims and essentially democratic and collectivist style the workshops and publication groups challenge conventional bourgeois educational provision and raise the hope (or is it the spectre?) of a partisan approach in which the dangerous myth of a neutral yet somehow liberal pedagogy is displaced by an honest and explicit concept: the paramountcy of working-class interests and needs. And of course they raise the question: where in all this, if anywhere, does the adult educationalist fit?

The direction and style of the writers' movement has much to do with the conditions immediately preceding its genesis. Ken Worpole, one of the founders of the FWWCP has put it fairly accurately:

None of the groups represented . . . has grown out of an exclusive concern for 'Literature', 'Creative Writing' or 'History'. As often as not they have been born out of social action. [4]

He also confronts the question I posed earlier:

In each group there has been some contribution from people with 'higher education': teacher, journalist or college lecturer. . . . But this interaction has only been possible because of a common direction, a shared commitment to the working-class — in a word 'socialism'. [5]

The Scotland Road Writers' Workshop experience can be said to illustrate broadly the two points made by Worpole. It attempts to show how active residents of an area and extra-mural lecturers can together define a need and work out the means of meeting it — and in doing so create a ripple effect in other areas. [6]

The Scotland Road Writers' Workshop, started in September 1973, was the first of the six existing Liverpool workshops and by a month the first to emerge in the country. It is based in the Vauxhall district, locally known as Scotland Road, an area of about 13,500 people on 426 acres adjacent to the city's north docks.

The workshop was the result of a suggestion by an out-of-work electrician, the then chairman of the Heriot Tenants' Association. Most of the original members came from the Heriot and Over-the-Bridge areas and were to be its main supporters for the first two years of its life. [7]

Analysis suggests that the workshop has succeeded where other 'humane' courses have failed for a variety of reasons. Perhaps most important was that real need for it was felt. Then, the backing given by the residents associations which helped by informally publicizing the workshop and directing would-be writers its way was influential. We, for our part, in keeping with our belief in the seriousness of social action took great care that when a workshop session clashed with an important tenants' meeting or other political event it was the session which was postponed or stopped early so that members could go on to the meeting. Further it was made clear to new members that the writer had as strong a duty to be on the picket line as anyone else. And I tried to follow the example of my Liverpool colleagues by making myself as useful to the residents' groups as I could. [8] In addition I contributed a regular column to the community newspaper, the *Scottie Press*, about the activities of the workshop.

The workshop was also able to survive because we ignored most of the rules governing orthodox evening class provision, beginning with the 'numbers game', [9] fee-charging, rigid timetabling, inflexible course structures, regular attendance and political neutrality. Had we been playing the numbers game there would not today be one workshop in Liverpool, let alone six: the first months in the workshop brought nine people onto the roll with an average attendance of four each Monday evening, regularity of attendance being affected by a number of factors, among them the demands of shift-work. Output was modest too: one complete play, two part-plays, one poem, a few brief character sketches and an essay on economics. Yet by the middle of 1974 the group's enrolment had risen to twenty and the average attendance to six: now in mid 1979 about ninety people have passed through the workshop and average attendance is about eleven. By the middle of 1974, too, writing was coming into the workshop (some of it from non-members) in such profusion that there seemed point in publishing some of it in magazine form. Behind these advances was a feeling, enthusiastic and at times even passionate that the group individually and collectively was discovering and freeing creative energies denied and suppressed by the official culture.

This sense of denial and suppression is hardly surprising. Many would agree that working-class people are recipients of an education and a culture over which they have negligible control and in which they have little significant say. They have transmitted to them conditioning images and interpretations of their lives which have been largely refracted through middle-class perceptions. Furthermore, they are seldom allowed to use the media for a free and uncluttered debate among themselves: at best there is invariably a middle-class referee in the form of editor or interviewer or discussion chair-person. It is easy to see why the bourgeoisie wishes to maintain this state of affairs: it enhances their control of society. What is less easy to understand is why the situation is so tolerated by the working-class 'leadership'. The Labour Party, for instance, presses for more education for more people and the expansion of the state education sector as against the private. But it leaves largely uncriticized syllabuses and methods of teaching which uphold the bourgeois social and economic dominance and offer the student a pyramid whose point can only be reached, supposedly by the bright, the industrious and the aspiring few, while the rest work for lesser rewards below. [10] Similarly the trade union movement produces documents calling for more generous underwriting and a wider spread of the arts, but says very little about how people in working-class areas might be encouraged to generate and develop their own creative expression. In this, both are unconsciously abetting the bourgeois liberals who, argues Freire, see their interests as lying 'in changing the consciousness of the oppressed, not the situation which oppresses them, for the more the oppressed can be led to adapt to that situation the more easily can they be dominated.' [11] It is also regrettably true that the working-class 'leadership' too often acts as though the struggle is exclusively confined to the picket-line, the factory floor and the hustings; reinforcing the dangerous myth that social action and cultural activity are distinct and separable and having the effect of divorcing the 'artist' from the 'activist' in a disabling way for both art and politics.

All the same a recognition of the importance of cultural politcs has been slowly and painfully reviving. [12] The matter is complex but it seems true to say that since the war there appears to have been an increased class awareness in Britain, sharpening with the industrial and non-industrial campaigns of the late sixties and early seventies and the present capitalist-managed 'austerity'. One valuable consequence of the later campaigns has been that they have put a value on writing skills because of the need for leaflets, pamphlets, residents' newsletters and the growth of community newspapers; inner city residents have also been brought into contact with the theory and some of the hardware of 'alternative' communication (for instance, offset litho printing, tape-slide techniques, portable video and the ubiquitous and crucial duplicator). In the public culture the shift in consciousness seems to have been reflected in the increased interest in the work of Brecht and other left-wing European writers, the revulsion since the late fifties against the tyranny in British theatre of fashionable drawing room dramas and the growing tendency among writers to want to explore, not always too scrupulously, the rich heartlands of working-class existence. The weakness of this 'proletarian' trend in the arts was that its practitioners were concerned with, rather than emanating from the 'working class'. Sometimes the impulse was missionary rather than revolutionary: Arnold Wesker's Centre 42 experiment, which aimed to 'bring good art to the masses', failed I suspect, partly because it didn't see 'the masses' themselves as producers of art. [13]

From the outset the founders of the Scotland Road Writers' Workshop did see working people as producers of art. An early article in the *Scottie Press* made clear their attitude:

The writers' workshop is for those people in Scotland Road interested in writing down their stories, ideas, poems, plays, pieces of journalism, essays or whatever takes their fancy. . . . It's about everyday people who want to write. . . .

Similarly, the first magazine produced by the group, *Voices of Scotland Road and Nearby* insisted that ideas and creative talent were not the monopoly of a small class but 'exist everywhere and lack only discovery and encouragement.' It was also made clear to all comers that the audience workshop writers were seeking was a working-class one. *Voices* and its successors were sold by hand in alehouses and clubs in the Vauxhall area.

The ripples spread. The attitudes of the workshop members and the appearance of the magazine in 1975 found a response in another working-class area on the other side of the city, the Liverpool 8 area with its significant proportion of black people. Dorothy Kuya, a black militant, working as a community relations officer, had been wanting for some time to start a workshop. She approached the Scotland Road group and by 1976 she and I were convening the predominantly, but not exclusively, black Liverpool 8 Writers'

Workshop: it too went on to produce a collection of members' writing, *19 from 8*. Scotland Road was next to play a part in establishing the Red Star Writers' Workshop in neighbouring Everton, inspire a short-lived group in the outer city area of Skelmersdale, another on the Cantril Farm housing estate and yet another, still thriving, group in Netherley. [14] A group is about to form in the Garston area.

What was happening in Liverpool was happening in much the same way elsewhere. By 1975 there were groups in London, Brighton, Bristol, Manchester, Newcastle and other cities, most of them a mix of working-class writers and middle-class conveners or enablers [15], most of them stimulated by grassroots action. When in early 1976 nine of these groups met for the first time — each backed by a record of at least one publication — a national movement was born. Today the National Federation of Worker Writers and Community Publishers has 26 member groups.

The Federation is important for a number of reasons. Firstly, it reinforces the concept of solidarity among worker writers by bringing together groups from various parts of the country to share problems and preoccupations and to pool skills and experience: Centerprise in Hackney, London, for instance, has a successful record of publishing; the Brighton group has produced a street newspaper; the Scotland Road group demonstrated early the value of the workshop style, of writers reading their work in private and public, and of experimenting with plays written and produced by members of the group; Basement Writers in Stepney have links with young people and their off-shoot 'Controlled Attack' has proved the merit of setting out to entertain by means of a show which is half theatre, half revue. Secondly the Federation has created a sketchy, but crucial and expanding, series of outlets for worker writers: groups not only produce their own 'little magazines' but have been able to contribute to a quarterly national publication *Voices*, published from Manchester, and to various radical and feminist journals. Thirdly, it has emerged as a pressure group capable of negotiating at a national level: *Writing*, the anthology of working-class prose and verse referred to at the beginning of this chapter was made possible by money obtained from the Arts Council of Great Britain and the Federation has also been able to persuade the Gulbenkian Foundation to pay for a national co-ordinator. It has established links, too, though these are fragile, with the trade union movement and some community organizations.

I am sometimes asked about the methods and value of the workshops. How are people encouraged to write, what do they write about and what is the quality of the writing?

I find it difficult to answer any except the second of these questions with anything like precision: the first because the approach depends on the group, relations with its members, the nature and concerns of the area and the circumstances of the time; the third because I am too close to the material to be completely objective.

Broadly speaking, the methods used in the Liverpool workshops were evolved in the Scotland Road group in the early months. They were based on convincing members that *their* experiences, their thoughts, their feelings, hopes and even anger, were interesting and valuable and that they were writing not for the supercilious and possibly hostile eyes of school-teachers, editors or other middle-class readers but for potential sympathizers, their own class, their immediate fellows — not only as people exploited but as future inheritors. This is controversial and I have been accused of encouraging class and race consciousness, but the emphasis on working-class people as the first, though not only, audience for working-class writers and on black people as the primary target for black writers has created a sense of confidence and focus.

Members would be invited to bring in what they had written and the piece would be read out (and sometimes cyclostyled for distribution) for the group to discuss and comment on. There was particular insistence that what mattered was the criticism and approval of the group, as individuals and as a whole. As an English graduate, a lecturer and a published writer and as convener/secretary of the group I played the part of introducing stimulus material, producing comparisons between workshop writing and examples culled from the 'high culture' and leading — but not dominating — discussions on the mechanics of writing. I might take away pieces and advise a new writer. I might edit and correct work. But in the end members' writing was expected to be passed through the workshop for members' comments. In a sense members of the group became tutors. They shared in the rewards and agonies of creativity, midwifing each other's pieces by debate, argument and sympathetic criticism: in a sense, too, (as I have said elsewhere) [16] the play was everybody's play, the poem everybody's poem: people felt they were shaping their own literary consciousness. [17] In all this I was a fellow-writer rather than an academic tutor: my technical knowledge might be respected but my ability to move by my writing was no greater than anyone else's and my grasp of working-class realities considerably less; the hierarchical relationship which would have vexed a conventional literature class was dissolved — we were learner-craftsmen together. [18]

Because the honest writer must try to look unflinchingly at all of life, even the most sensitive aspects, because to be effective he or she must at times penetrate, if not permanently occupy, all viewpoints, crossing age, sex, racial, religious and political lines, workshop members have from the beginning found themselves debating every kind of controversial question. [19] Meetings often become consciousness-raising sessions at which people are perhaps the more likely to alter rigid views because the atmosphere is not narrowly sectarian, though arguably the shared, partisan class-attitude provides a sustaining base for members. It has been noticeable too that the reading-and-comment sessions bring out oral skills and confidence and most members have developed a willingness to read their work or speak in public.

A feature of most of the Liverpool workshops and the Scotland Road group in particular has been their capacity to evolve and change: the publication of the magazines has led to public readings in Scotland Road and other parts of Liverpool, in Manchester, Oxford, London and Sheffield; the readings have suggested dramatizations so that some members have written short plays for production by the group and, more recently, by amateur theatre organizations in up-town Liverpool. [20] At the same time some of the workshop verse has been turned into songs by a young area musician, though the plans for a rock musical based on the 1972 rent strike are still unrealized. There has also been a tendency to try to apply ideas and techniques learnt in the workshops to other projects, one example being a working-class history workshop begun in Scotland Road this year by a member, another a discussion group for former mental patients which borrowed the informality, the drop-in-style, the stress on class solidarity which the initiator of the group had valued in writers' workshop sessions.

The themes of the workshops are the themes of working-class life. Cindy Daley of the Scotland Road group writes about an isolated pensioner in her poem, 'High Rise':

If only I'd someone to talk to
I'm lonely up here by meself
It's no joke when you're old and forgotten
Like something just dumped on a shelf. . . . [21]

Her poem is one of many, some sad, some angry, some light-hearted.
Under the skilful pen of Jimmy McGovern the high-rise blocks are
shown to represent a grotesque denial of human dignity. In his story,
Tommy Taylor, a big tough, ex-building worker goes to pieces in the
notorious Crosby Heights [22] and jumps from a balcony:

I don't know who saw him first but in a few seconds everyone on the ground
was looking up, but I think there was a woman shoutin' something like, 'Oh
son, oh son.' Tommy only seemed to wait till everyone was lookin' then he
bent his knees and jumped. At first he started to call out somethin' — I think
he meant to shout 'Timber' but he stopped at the 'Ti. . .' and the rest was just a
kind of sob. . . . [23]

His brother, Albie, tries to protest by painting the silhouette of the
body on the concrete and next to it 'Killed by the Council'. But
mischievous kids add oversize genitals in purple paint, turning his
protest into pathetic and ludicrous obscenity. Corporation men come
to remove the eyesore and Albie submits. He is defeated and with him
the flat-dwellers who had hoped to see him resist. The collective
principle surfaces again in a more optimistic McGovern story in
which a drunken resident becomes a sort of representative of an entire
street's resentment against an arrogant, pushy priest. The priest is
flung into a gutter after trying to force his way into the man's house:
there his superiority becomes a disadvantage:

. . . people watched through rubber plants and lace curtains. How could they
cross the social chasm and have a superior being dependent on them? Perhaps
that teacher up the road might come past soon: he could help him. As long as
he takes him home like; we don't want him coming here tonight. . . . [24]

Predictably work, particularly the difficulty of finding it and its
unsatisfactory nature once found, features in inner city writing. There
are workshop poems and songs about the boredom of joblessness, a
story about the humiliations of a futile job interview, tales about the
uncongeniality of soul-destroying labour. But sometimes work is
perceptively seen to have a positive value apart from the monetary. A
former shop steward at KME in Kirkby writes movingly about an
odd, lonely and socially maladroit man who finds companionship at

work. Then it is announced that the factory is closing down. Most workers are philosophical: they have their families and the outside world and they believe they will survive, but

Jack was losing his job *and* his world. The only place he acted normally was in work. The only place he drank and chatted with men and women was in work.

Jack said nothing to anyone at the end of the meeting; he just went home and hung himself. [25]

Racism, unpleasant living conditions, individual and collective struggles against authority, the hurly-burly of pub, street and home get due treatment. Understandably there is much that is grim in the writing from the workshops, but there is always the humour for which Liverpool is justly famed. Norma Igbesoko of Liverpool 8 writes of a complacent racist that 'if she had had a third hand she would have patted herself on the back with it'. In one of John Bannister's stories of the impoverished 1930s, a young wife chops up the cellar steps for firewood with the result that her husband falls into the cellar and hurts his back. He rails at her in fury while her father hovers anxiously

'Jus' wait till I get out of here me lady!
I'll swing for you, yeh cracked mare!' Then weakly, 'Ooh! Me back's broke. God forgive me, I think I'm goin'.'

The father's voice comes through the darkness. 'Where yer goin'? I thought yer back's broke. Yer can't go anywhere with yer back broke.' [26]

Then there are the working-class feminists. If the men are oppressed so are the women — and sometimes by their men. Sometimes the response is direct and sarcastic as in Ann Blunt's sharp 'Scotland Road: a woman's view' ('The men love the ale — and their mates', [27] or sardonic as in Kim Rogers's poem for the Liverpool 8 group:

Why do men demand so much?
'Get me this, do such and such'
Why do men demand so much?

Why can't men be just like me?
Wash their own socks, make their own tea
Why can't men be just like me?

or bitter as in Val Newall's 'Sugar Daddy':

He'll wine you and dine you
and treat you like a queen
but when he cannot have you
he'll get positively obscene.

And all the time his little wife
is sitting on her own
with worry and with strife—
Does he put *her* on a throne? [28]

Though the disagreements between men and women are aired
frankly, workshop writers, whatever their sex, inevitably return — as
in the Mary Casey poem quoted at the head of this chapter — to the
need for class pride and solidarity — and for action against 'them', as
in this poem by a young Asian woman:

The dictionary of experience
Teaches:
Do the Deed
But remember the word.
Then our hands will be forged of iron
Our mouths will taste the strength of purpose
And our eyes will measure the future. [29]

Is there good writing here or not? How should the question be
decided and by whom — the working-class readers and listeners at
whom it is aimed or middle-class academics and Sunday newspaper
reviewers? Workshop writing is a relatively new phenomenon and
understandably suffers from neglect by the commercial publishing
houses and the mass media: if noticed at all it is likely to be disparaged
or patronized by critics who apply inappropriate criteria and there is
a great danger that it will be typified as sociologically interesting but
no more. I believe that at its best workshop writing is very good, and
most of it interesting, with even better work to come as output and
outlets increase: quantity does, in the end, bear on quality. [30] It
seems somewhat premature to be talking too pedantically about
criteria. These will follow more output. Meanwhile I would offer as a
guide to discussion the formulation in the 'Afterword' of *Writing*:

But while we do not see good bourgeois writing and good working-class
writing as utterly distinct (such matters as a feeling for words and a sensitivity
to the nuances of life are common, for instance), we are agreed that they are
recognizably different. Working-class writing is the literature of the
controlled and exploited. It is shot through with a different kind of
consciousness from bourgeois writing. Whatever its subject matter, working-

class writing, when it is any good at all, must contain in its tissues and exude through its pores, working-class experience. Politically the class struggle would be felt and communicated, even if indirectly, even if the writer has no such design on the reader.

I would add that at its very best, working-class writing is shaped by — though this may not be obvious — the longing for a very different society from the present. This is not necessarily the same thing as believing that the different society must come.

All things considered the writers' movement seems to be in a healthy state with regular readings and a stream of publications in the various centres, with steady and consolidating activity at workshop level and with constant requests from areas and organizations to advise them how to start groups of their own. The appearance of such venturesome groups as Controlled Attack in London and the small burst of plays in Liverpool promises the beginnings of a grassroots theatre movement.

But there are huge problems of funding and recognition. Because of its 'alternative' nature and lack so far of strong trade union support workshop writing depends heavily on aid from a variety of sources, including charitable trusts and is vulnerable to shifts of fashion and mood. The Arts Council of Great Britain, having financed *Writing*, in response to arguments that working-class creativity is neglected, has since drawn back from further commitment, retreating behind the weary old formula of 'literary standards', presumably under pressure from its more elitist protégés and their allies and despite abundant evidence that *Writing* and other federation publications have provable appeal to working-class readers — and others.

All this brings the challenge back to adult educationists sympathetic to working-class cultural expression, including those in university extra-mural departments who have in the nature of things greater freedom than local authority and WEA tutors to 'test the limits'. There is no doubt in my mind that radical tutors and other middle-class professionals can play a role in the development of working-class culture. That is to say, a more representative culture.

But confronted with requests to help establish writers' workshops, history workshops, political and economic theory workshops, black studies' courses and women's studies' groups, how will our conservative-liberal bourgeois institutions react? How, come to that, will those professed carers, the academic liberals, react? Will they risk even as much as did some of the women of the Netherley workshop who went on rent strike to finance their first magazine?

I doubt it.

8 Adult education and community action

Tom Lovett, Director, the Community Action Research and Education Project, The New University of Ulster

The role of adult education in community action has aroused a great deal of debate and discussion amongst socially committed adult educators over the last decade. [1] On the one hand are those adult educators who see in it an exciting possibility to extend the concept of adult learning, to make it more relevant to the interests, needs and problems of the working class and to open up educational resources to the latter so that they can make the maximum use of the opportunities it offers them. [2] On the other hand are those who feel that 'adult educationists should be wary when they are offered the resplendent new garments of community development, intended to transform their perception of themselves and their possibilities as they sally forth as community adult educators'. [3] The latter argue that the concept of 'community' should not be taken too seriously and that the role of adult education in the community development/community action process is more limited than the enthusiasts might have us believe. [4] Theirs is a more sceptical, cautious analysis; highly critical of the political naivety of the former and more explicitly Marxist, locating the origins of local community problems in the larger economic and social inequalities of a class society.

In the first model the role of adult education in community action is seen as one of providing the working class with an effective educational service so that they can take full advantage of the educational system *and* make the best use of their individual talents and abilities. Adult education is viewed as a general, comprehensive, community adult education 'service' meeting a variety of needs and interests amongst the working class, encouraging personal growth and development, and supporting greater community awareness and involvement. It provides for the general educational interests and needs of individuals (for example, informal group work, 'O' Levels, languages, keepfit, etc.) in working-class communities and offers educational assistance to groups engaged in local community action. This was the approach of the adult education work in the Educational Priority Area Project in Liverpool. [5]

The second model has been closely associated with the work of Keith Jackson and his colleagues from the Liverpool Institute of Extension Studies in Vauxhall in the early 1970s. Throughout the literature on this work there is a consistent emphasis on the need to engage the residents in relevant education of a high standard which makes no concessions to informal community discussion methods or the 'learning through doing' approach. Working-class activists are to 'be given the chance to come to terms with a subject skill or field of knowledge so that they can understand its internal rules, become an expert as far as possible'. [6] This is regarded as an essential educational contribution to social action.

The distinction between these two positions presents a number of problems for those involved in adult education with working-class men and women. On the one hand there is an increasing emphasis in many adult education institutions and organizations on community education, or social and political education. It is now part of the conventional adult education wisdom. However, the practical implications are rarely understood or appreciated. If they were then there might not be so much enthusiasm for the concepts! On the other hand the radical critique characteristic of the Vauxhall approach, and the educational emphasis arising from it — whilst important — is, I believe, unnecessarily limited in scope and in many respects does less than justice to the complexity of the situation on the ground and the opportunities available for linking adult education constructively to social/community action whilst avoiding the danger of both educational elitism and 'informal' education.

In my own view the relationship between adult education and community development is neither the grand opportunity seen by the optimists nor the more restricted role outlined in the sceptics' approach. I believe adult education *has* an important role to play in community action, that it is not necessarily a restricted one and that the concept of community should be taken seriously. However, before elaborating on this I want to look, not at recent experience in Britain and Northern Ireland, since this is dealt with elsewhere in the volume, but at two historically important initiatives outside our tradition of socially committed adult education. Both were attempts to link adult education more closely to movements for social and political change. Both were committed to, and intensely involved in, the process itself drawing no fine distinctions between action and education. One was the Antigonish Movement at the University of St Francis Xavier in Nova Scotia, Canada. The other was the Highlander Folk School in Tennessee, USA.

The Antigonish Movement

As with the Liverpool Institute experience, the Antigonish Movement was university based and initiated. It was also situated in a very economically depressed area. In this case a mainly rural, depopulated region on the eastern seaboard of Canada. It also emphasized the importance of the economic aspect of local community problems. However, the work took place in the 1920s and 30s and it was initiated and directed by two Catholic priests, initially by Father Jimmy Tompkins and later by Father Moses Coady.

It was a programme of adult education, self help and co-operative development which became world famous. It was far from being non-directive and, in fact, the leading figure in it, Coady, was a charismatic personality who passionately believed in the role of adult education as an agent for social change in society. To him adult education was an aggressive agent of change, a mass movement of reform. [7]

He condemned the excesses of capitalism and placed his faith in the common people and the need to release their energies so that they could take over their own affairs. This he saw as the 'scientific' way to peaceful radical change. Adult education was the method he believed would bring this about by:

... finding a technique that is practical, inexpensive, widely applicable and capable of fanning out into the higher levels of culture. It would be a great mistake to think that such a programme can be solely academic. Such a procedure would be to ignore completely the nature of man. Common people — in fact all people — must parallel their learning with action. The action can best be found in the social and particularly in the economic field. Action in the economic field is two-fold. It can be individual economic action or group economic action. Individual efficiency in the economic field is highly desirable and goes a long way to produce a good society but individual action alone will not solve the economic problems facing the people. Economic group action, or what is called economic co-operation, is also required and offers the greater possibility. [8]

Generally speaking there were two phases to the movement. One in the 1920s when Tompkins put a great deal of pioneering effort into persuading local people to tackle the social and economic problems in the community. And the second in the 1930s when, as a result of Tompkins's efforts, the University opened an extension department with Coady as Director. During this period there was more emphasis on training and education but both men regarded the whole process as essentially educational and drew no fine distinctions between action and education. The methods used ranged widely, for example, mass meetings, study clubs, radio listening groups, short courses, kitchen meetings, conferences, leadership schools and training courses.

The mass meeting was the place where the educators preached their message. They took the initiative because, although Coady believed that education should be concerned with the everyday problems facing people in the region, he did not believe in just responding to 'felt needs'. He put more emphasis on the creation of awareness explaining that 'a fish doesn't know he lives in water until he is taken out of it.' [9] He did not believe that the educator should avoid unfamiliar words and language:

... don't be afraid to use hard and unfamilar words, even though people don't understand in the beginning they'll soon know the meaning ... when I started in adult education work twenty years ago, not five per cent of the people I talked to understood what was meant by production, economic, natural resources, proletariat, exploitation, or any such words, but now they all know — people catch on fast. [10]

After the mass meeting people were organized into study clubs or discussion groups. This was regarded as the key educational technique in the Antigonish Movement: 'the foundation of the people's programme for adult learning'. [11] Everyday problems were discussed and success depended on intelligent local leaders and proper study materials. The study clubs quickly advanced to direct action. A variation of the study club was the radio listening group which enabled the movement to reach a larger number of people with relevant learning material. This basic work was complemented by the more intensive work at conferences, short courses and training schemes on the university campus. It was in fact a comprehensive and extensive programme of adult education and social action which owed a great deal, not only to the charismatic quality of Coady's leadership and Tompkins's pioneering field work, but the basic philosophy behind the movement. This was simple and straightforward, understood and accepted by the network of voluntary workers (many of them clerics!) which formed the backbone of the movement. The basic principles were:

i) The needs of the individual must have primacy.
ii) Social reform must come through education.
iii) Education must begin with the economic situation.
iv) Education must be through group action.
v) Effective social reform involves fundamental changes in social and economic institutions.
vi) The ultimate objective of the movement is a full and abundant life for everyone in the community. [12]

It was a populist movement with a vision of a new society. Although it was strongly anti-communist it was nevertheless influenced by, and imbued with, certain co-operative and Christian socialist principles based on a critical analysis of the existing social order. It stressed the need not only for working people to build their own, alternative, co-operative society but for full participation in all the major institutions in society.

Although most of the literature on the movement is uncritical, and not particularly analytical, there are suggestions that this very public and active commitment to social change produced tensions between the movement and the local political and educational establishment. For instance in 1938, at the height of the movement, a university report stated that, 'It will be difficult for the University to continue to carry the burden of the Extension Department' [13] — apparently the latter was considered expendable!

When Coady died in 1959 the movement appears effectively to have died with him and it became institutionalized and enshrined in the establishment of a Coady International Institute. Little of the work remains and a recent analysis of the movement states: 'In Canso and Little Dover 50 years after Father Jimmy started his work there the people are still struggling with poverty and deprivation. Women working in the fish plant in the early 70s made $14 a night before taxes. In their efforts to organize the people here got help from Father Gerry Rodgers of the Extension Department of St Francis Xavier University, the living embodiment of the Antigonish Way. But he's a very lonely man.' [14]

Antigonish believed that radical change would come about through education, public participation and the establishment of alternative institutions, that is co-ops and credit unions, not explicit political action. It was not a revolutionary movement and it has been argued that it damped down radical political agitation, directed the attention of the workers from striving for a new social and political order and, 'removed the need for the political system to perform efficiently and to meet the needs of the people instead of the elite. It may have prevented its collapse.' [15] This view is supported by comments made in a 1933 report from the Extension Department, discussing its activities amongst urban industrial workers, which states: 'The educational activities of these industrial workers resulted in quietening down the radical agitation of the area.' [16] Obviously Antigonish was a reform movement!

Nevertheless, although the Antigonish Movement lacked any explicit class analysis or radical political philosophy it did succeed in engaging large numbers of workers in relevant education linked to social action with methods and techniques which even today would be regarded as too radical for many educational institutions. It drew no barriers between social action and adult education and was engaged on a number of fronts linking one to the other. Despite its limitations it is still a good example of how such work can be developed from a committed adult education base.

Highlander

The Highlander Folk School in the USA was established in the 1930s by Myles Horton. Like Antigonish, it was situated in one of the most socially and economically depressed regions in North America, a mixture of mining and agricultural communities in Tennessee. Like Antigonish its founder and leading figure throughout its early history was strongly imbued with Christian/socialist principles and deeply influenced by the Danish Folk High School Movement. [17] The latter was regarded by both as a prime example of how an educational movement could be linked effectively to movements for social change and the development of a sense of national pride and identity. Highlander also had a simple philosophy which was, however, based on a more explicit class analysis.

Highlander's basic philosophy is summed up well in the following extract from a letter written by Horton in 1933 shortly after the school was established:

As I understand our purpose correctly, we will all be working at the same job but will be using different approaches. Our task is to make class-conscious workers who envision their roles in society and to furnish motivation as well as technicians for the achievement of this goal. In their words, we must try to give students an understanding of the world in which we live (a class-divided society) and an idea of the kind of world we would like to have. We have found that a very effective way to help students to understand the present social order is to throw them into conflict situations where the real nature of our society is projected in all its ugliness. To be effective, such exposure must be preceded, accompanied by and followed by efforts to help the observer appreciate and digest what he has seen. This keeps education from getting unrealistic. While this process is going on, students need to be given an inkling of the new society. Perhaps this can be done best by having our communal living at the school come into this picture as an important education factor. The tie-in with the conflict situations and participation in community life keeps our school from being a detached colony or utopian venture. But our efforts to live out our ideals makes possible the development of a bit of proletarian culture as an essential part of our programme of workers' education. [18]

However, although committed to a revolution to alter basic political and economic relationships, Highlander was not ideologically rigid.

It was deliberately vague about its governing concept, letting the people it serves and the times in which they live define precisely what brotherhood, democracy, mutuality and united social action mean. . . . Highlander had to learn that ideology, no matter how firmly grounded in objective reality, is of no value if it is separated from a social movement of struggling people. [19]

Like Antigonish this meant placing the emphasis on working with people on real issues and problems and emphasizing the importance of co-operation and acting in unison.

Once Horton and Highlander realized that society would not be changed by individuals acting alone or by radical political analysis alone, Highlander sought to educate people away from the dead end of individualism and into the freedom that grows from co-operation and collective solutions. [20]

Unlike Antigonish however, Highlander was an independent educational establishment with a more explicitly socialist philosophy and its approach was radically different. It did not *initiate* programmes of social action, like Antigonish. Instead it concentrated on identifying and working closely with emerging social movements thrown up by the times and people, providing them with practical advice and assistance on the ground as well as educational support in the form of workshops at Highlander. The latter generally fell into two distinct categories. As the particular movement gathered force the workshops were broad and loose in range, usually without a specific topic. As the movements gained momentum more concrete information was requested and greater use was made of experts.

In the 1930s Highlander played an active role in the bitter struggle to organize trade unions in Tennessee, not by providing classes and courses, but by being actively involved on the picket line and in the mass demonstrations and providing information and opportunities for discussions on strategies and tactics. Horton was arrested during one of the most bitter campaigns in a mining town called Wilder and charged with: 'coming here and getting information and going back and teaching it.' [21] It was the first of many such arrests. The strike had a powerful effect on the Highlander staff who were involved in it. They were themselves ideologically committed but realized that to accomplish their goals workers themselves would have to state their own beliefs and that Highlander had not only to serve the people but be of the people.

During the 1930s work with the unions meant this sort of active commitment and involvement, complemented by conferences and residential workshops at Highlander and study groups out in the local community. As the unions became more organized these increasingly developed into union training schools and Highlander became somewhat disillusioned by union conservatism.

Highlander's early hope that the union movement, especially the CIO, would become a powerful force for social and economic change had dimmed with experience. Any struggle on behalf of the working-class had been submerged beneath a bureaucratic struggle for power. By 1949, an organization which had thrived on militancy was fearful of militancy, afraid the bottom would upset the top. [22]

That statement has a certain contemporary ring about it!

However, as indicated earlier, Highlander had always seen its work as a long-term process adapting to new movements and circumstances and, during the 1950s and 1960s, it turned its attention, increasingly, to the problems of black workers. It played an important supportive role in the growth of the Citizenship Schools (designed to assist illiterate negroes to read and write so that they could pass the voting test) and in the civil rights movement. As a result of this, and its earlier work with the trade unions, Highlander was labelled a communist training school by the racialist and reactionary forces in the south. Eventually in 1961 the State of Tennessee seized the school's property and revoked its charter. The idea and the institution were, however, quickly reorganized and rechartered under its present name, Highlander Research and Education Centre Inc.

Since 1964 Highlander has concentrated on the problems of poverty and inequality in Tennessee — still one of the most depressed regions in the USA. However, it has also attempted to unite the various depressed minorities throughout the United States. For example, in 1970 it held a workshop attended by militant blacks, Puerto Ricans, Indians from six nations. Mexican Americans and people from the Appalachians which, although it highlighted the antagonisms between the various groups, illustrated the fact that none of them were free to determine their own destiny and all were poor. This was one of numerous attempts by Horton and others to assist the growth of a bottom-up radical coalition in the USA.

Highlander's original purpose, educating for a revolution that would basically change economic and political power relationships to the advantage of the poor and powerless, has clearly not been achieved. That was obviously an impossible task for one Folk School! However, Highlander's educational methods and techniques are now used in various grassroots initiatives throughout the USA and there is evidence that a radical coalition is emerging. [23] Highlander has played a pioneering role in encouraging that process.

Northern Ireland

Much of the recent British debate about the theory and practice of adult education in the field of community development and community action finds an echo in the two North American examples discussed above. Many of the 'new' concepts and methods in community development and community education (and the related theories of radical educators like Freire), were understood and practised at Highlander and Antigonish over forty years ago. As is so often the case in adult education it is not a matter of new theories and concepts but new arrangements responding to different circumstances and influenced by prevailing social/political and economic theories.

In some respects the situation facing Highlander and Antigonish was less complicated, more clear cut, than the situation facing radical committed adult educators today. The inequalities and the injustices were starker, more obvious, and the choices facing the educators concerned clearer than those facing their counterparts today. Maybe this accounts for their faith in the power of adult education; their simple message; their vision of the new society; their open, public sense of social commitment, dedication and active involvement in building that new society. They both paid a price for their radical commitment, however. Antigonish is now a lost dream. Highlander survived better probably because of its cranky independence, its non-institutional base, its ability to adapt to new movements and most important, its radical critique.

In terms of their *educational* contribution both took a broad view and did not seek to define too precisely what shape that contribution should take. They utilized a variety of methods and techniques ranging from the informal to the formal depending on the time, place and circumstances. Highlander placed more emphasis on educating leaders for emerging social movements whilst Antigonish sought to create and shape a 'movement' providing educational support at a variety of levels. Both, however, used real issues and problems as material for an educational process which — although it did not ignore the need for hard information and training — placed more emphasis on the development of the will, the imagination and creative human relationships than analytical skills. Highlander in particular stressed the important educational role of music and songs and other aspects of local culture in its work.

In their respective ideologies and strategies they reflect the two aspects of the contemporary debate about community development, community action and adult education mentioned earlier. On the one hand, Antigonish placed its faith in the creation of alternative social and economic institutions and structures at local, community level. On the other hand, Highlander placed its faith in providing educational support for emerging social movements which would fundamentally alter existing political and economic structures.

In Tennessee the open oppression of the people — black and white — was a spur to such social movements, thus creating conditions which have made it possible for Highlander to adopt its role as an involved, but supportive, educational 'arm'. In Nova Scotia the problems of rural poverty and depopulation did not present obvious 'oppressors' and Coady and Tompkins were faced with the need to take initiatives to create a movement. Generally speaking the latter adopted a community development strategy with an emphasis on the creation of alternatives, whilst the former adopted a community action strategy with an emphasis on conflict and radical political change.

Similar choices face adult educators today (depending on the community they work in and the degree of grassroots organization to be found there) i.e., helping to create local community organizations (or alternative institutions) or assisting existing organizations. In practice the situation is usually a combination of both but the *educational* emphasis will depend on the political ideology of those involved. Thus in the Liverpool Institute the emphasis has been like Highlander, on an educationally supportive role based on a socialist critique but stressing the need for the development of analytical skills. The EPA work was, like Antigonish, less openly political and took a broader view of its educational role. It was involved both in the practical work of setting up community groups and organizations and supporting existing ones, seeking to find an educational role in a range of activities.

Here in Northern Ireland, at the Institute of Continuing Education, Highlander and Antigonish have been important influences, along with the recent English initiatives in deciding the educational strategies and methods we in the Community Action Research and Education Project should adopt in this divided, conflict-ridden society. There are many similarities between our situation here and the examples discussed above. Religion plays a large part in people's lives here as it did in Nova Scotia and Tennessee. Many of the settlers in Tennessee were Ulster Irish and the music of that area has roots in Irish culture. Northern Ireland is a mixture of rural and urban communities and farming is still one of the most important industries in the province. There is still a traffic in evangelical ministers between Tennessee and Ulster, Ian Paisley received his degree from the Bob Jones University there. No wonder Northern Ireland has been described as Britain's Tennessee!

However, I do not want to push these comparisons too far. Northern Ireland is part of the economic and political structure of the United Kingdom — one of the most economically depressed regions in that economy with a long history of unemployment and poverty. It is a region which has not only gone through the pangs and torments of civil and military conflict but one which, within the last ten years, has witnessed great changes in its economic and social structure as a result of industrial decline, urbanization and redevelopment. [24] New bureaucratic structures have been established to assist in planning and developing the infra-structure to attract new industries. These structures, created in the 1960s, have survived intact throughout the present conflict, despite various political changes.

The political vacuum means that we have a civil service and bureaucratic machine, like any government, but no political watchdogs except the Secretaries of State appointed by Westminster who act like colonial administrators and governors. Of course this is not to suggest that in the rest of Great Britain political parties are effective in regulating the bureaucracy. Evidence suggests that often they become part of that machine. [25] Our situation is just more extreme. Northern Ireland is, in fact, the clearest manifestation of a process at work generally in British society.

A recent analysis suggests that it has a higher level of poverty than any other part of the United Kingdom. [26] It is a divided community. Its tragedy is that the conflict has often assumed the proportions of a civil war between Catholic and Protestant working class. It is also a colonial society, one of the last remnants of the British Empire and one in which the concept of 'cultural invasion' has real meaning.

However, despite the conflict and the divisions between the working class, the social and economic changes referred to above have resulted in the growth of numerous community organizations throughout Northern Ireland in both Catholic and Protestant areas. [27] They have found common ground in the midst of communal conflict. This is the constituency we have decided to work and identify with, viewing it as the only hope for a united working-class movement which, through this common struggle, might find a solution to its larger political problems and divisions. In doing so we have had no option but to take the concept of 'community' seriously since it was one which is used by the people themselves to describe their work and to articulate their hopes and ideals. Thus 'community' is not a concept imposed from above but one which springs from the grass roots and is held sincerely and passionately by very articulate community leaders.

Our base is an institutional one. However, it is only recently established (1972) and initially had a public commitment to community education. In numerous public documents reference was made to the 'large-scale development of community oriented education'. This means putting 'educational resources at the disposal of the community' [28] to help in resolving the social and economic problems of the area. Such public statements of intent and purpose are always suspect until they are matched with practice. It's doubtful if the implications were understood or appreciated at the time. However, since it was a new institution with new staff, able to develop their own roles without any prior commitments to fulfil, it was possible to take these statements of intent seriously and to develop work in the community in the knowledge that it was official policy and a priority for the institution. Of course it soon became obvious that people had different views about what community should be served. Our emphasis on working-class communities and organizations has always been something of a minority interest and priority, but at least we have been able to pursue it, unencumbered initially by other responsibilities, free to develop and define our role. However, this proved to be a difficult situation and, until money was provided from outside sources, it was an uphill struggle.

Like Antigonish and Highlander we have over the years since then sought to support, and identify with, the two sections of the working class in their common struggles and to provide what resources and assistance we can, making a point of stressing the extent of university resources and our commitment to making them available.

This has not proved easy. On the one hand our practical interpretation of 'putting education resources at the disposal of the community' — which often meant simply using Institute premises for meetings and discussions about all sorts of social, economic and political problems facing working-class communities (they were one of the few neutral premises available) — was viewed with some suspicion by the Institute and meant that they had to be 'dressed up' as classes or seminars. On the other hand community activists were, and still are, suspicious of academics and their intentions. This is something which can only be resolved at a personal level, over time, by active involvement and it remains a 'personal' rather than an institutional solution to the problem.

Our work like Highlander has, generally speaking, fallen into two phases. During the first phase, when the community movement was gathering strength, we were involved in various local initiatives, such as setting up resource centres, organizing conferences on broad topics and issues and assisting in the creation of a province-wide federation. In the second phase we became more actively involved in running workshops and seminars on more specific topics and issues, providing opportunities to learn certain skills and obtain items of information. [29] At present we are engaged in producing radio discussion programmes; [30] organizing local study groups throughout Northern Ireland; [31] assisting in a programme of linked weekends for community activists; running a research workshop for local activists interested in the Derry economy; organizing a two-year extra-mural certificate in community studies in which we hope to link theory and practice, using materials arising out of the work here, as well as experiences and analysis from abroad.

In all this work we have taken a sympathetic but critical approach to the prevailing community ideology and the strategies arising from it. We have encouraged active discussion and debate about the latter and the role of socialists within it. This has taken the form of seminars and workshops at which a variety of activists presented their written views and opinions for discussion and debate. We have found, like Antigonish and Highlander, that the people we are involved with are suspicious of what they regard as the cold clinical 'academic' approach. They tend to emphasize the practical, the affective, the imaginative, the need to create new structures out of new relationships.

A range of views, opinions and philosophies are held by those involved in community action, i.e., a welfare service approach, a human growth approach and a socialist political approach. Many initially denied that they had a 'philosophy' which influenced their work and approach to community problems. Our seminars illustrated that this was not the case and that those involved were often indirectly influenced by prevailing theories and practices in group work and community development and thinkers like Illich and Freire.

Some were also influenced by the sort of approach expressed for instance in *Zen and the Art of Motor Cycle Maintenance* [32] that rejects the traditional 'academic' logical/analytical approach in favour of a search for 'quality' because the former is seen as contributing to the technological/scientific culture we live in, whether socialist or capitalist.

We feel that these views and opinions must be treated with respect and that socialists should engage in a democratic dialogue with those concerned about ends and means. Our seminars were a useful initial step in that direction. We are now encouraging the production of written material by activists and others so that this debate can be widened and used as 'learning' material in educational programmes in which we are involved. This is part of our general effort to provide a range of learning materials for community action, some based on people's views and experiences, others more critical and analytical.

In some respects our task is both easier and harder than it is elsewhere in the UK. We do not have a strong Socialist/Labour/Trade Union tradition, although that can on occasions be a hindrance rather than a help! The changes of the last decade in

Northern Ireland have, comparatively speaking, radicalized some sections of the working class here — including some sections of the Protestant working class. [33] This, as indicated above, provides opportunities to engage in a dialogue about what shape a new society should take and the role of socialism in it. Our task is more difficult not only because of the divisions within community groups about their role but the divisions between them about the future of the state. [34] Many on both sides associate socialism with planning, bureaucracy and lack of freedom. That is what they know of the socialist dream. The struggle of the working class to achieve that dream is not, with some exceptions, seen as part of their heritage. We have thus placed some emphasis on finding ways of illustrating the common culture and problems of the Northern Irish working class for example, through the radio discussion programmes which are a sort of oral social history and material which helps to illustrate the similarities with working-class problems elsewhere in the U K and relates this to earlier working-class struggles — to develop in fact a sense of working-class history and culture. In all this work we have sought to combine the affective and the analytical, using aspects of the local culture as well as art, music, literature to help people articulate their dreams and aspirations, to investigate the major themes in their lives and to provide opportunities for serious analytical study and the acquisition of skills and information.

Freire sees this process in stages, that is, an initial stage of 'investigation' by the educator; a second stage in which learning material is produced which uses cultural artefacts familiar to the people, to explore major themes in their lives as reflected in the issues and problems they face. In the third stage, this material is discussed in cultural circles and it is interesting to note that Freire quotes the Brazilian novelist Rosa as the 'investigator par excellence of the "meaningful thematics" of the inhabitants of the Brazilian hinterland'. [35] Novels, drama, radio, music are very effective mediums for such an investigation because they personalize and dramatize issues and problems. This is a common experience for adult educators and explains the emphasis at Antigonish and Highlander and elsewhere, on the role of such methods in social and political education. However, in the fourth stage Freire stresses the need to use specialists, like economists and sociologists, to assist in the more detailed analysis of the themes discovered in the third stage.

We have found Freire's analysis and classification of this process helpful. However, his emphasis on *stages* does an injustice to the complexity of the evolving situation on the ground where different people, and different groups, are at various stages at the same time. We for example are involved on a number of fronts simultaneously, providing 'courses' for leading activists, whilst also involved in more informal work in workshops, seminars, study groups as well as practical action on the ground.

We are also aware that a simple 'economic' analysis and explanation of community problems does an injustice to the complexity of the 'themes' shaping and changing people's lives here. We have sought, therefore, not only to insert an economic perspective into the community debate, but also to include the political, the social and the cultural. Thus one of our radio discussion series was on religious stereotypes and another on changes in family and community life.

We feel, like Ralph Miliband, [36] that the search for a modern interpretation of the socialist dream, especially in the situation we find ourselves in here, entails a long search — a continuing dialogue which of necessity encompasses a wide variety of groups and individuals who are experiencing tremendous changes in their everyday lives and relationships. Miliband regards this as an aspect of 'democratism' which has been neglected by the left and which needs to be conceived in much larger terms; especially he argues, 'the demand for more democratic relations in daily life, between men and women in the home, between parents and children, in schools, in all spheres where people come together by necessity or choice. This is a formidable task which undermines strongly-held attitudes and deeply ingrained customs and modes of behaviour and which presents a manifold and diffuse and still unfocused challenge to a class-ridden and class-encrusted society such as this. The 'cultural revolution' which this currently signifies is now well under way. It has still a long way to go but it is obviously strong and almost certainly irreversible, and it will form an intrinsic part of the socialism to be'. [37]

We agree with that analysis. Because of the absence of a strong socialist tradition here we accept it as an opportunity to open the socialist debate, by engaging in action and dialogue on a number of fronts — the cultural, the social, the economic, the political — providing educational resources, support and assistance, in an attempt to bring together the affective and the analytical, to marry the best of our 'academic' approach to that of Antigonish and Highlander.

We hope in this way to assist in the creation of a radical social movement which will, of necessity, bring together people belonging to different groups and parties as well as individuals who belong to none. Like Miliband we visualize that some form of loose federation or alliance will be necessary and that it will attempt to articulate the 'themes' and visions implied in various aspects of the community struggle as well as to offer a radical critique of the existing order. Thus we have not concentrated specifically on community organizations but, through workshops and conferences, brought together activists from community groups, women's organizations, trade unions and those concerned with creating alternative institutions at local level. We have also assisted in organizing conferences on political options in Northern Ireland and the problem of human rights. All of this work has brought together not only Catholics and Protestants, but also supporters of various para-military groups in a debate which offers some hope for the future.

However, we realize there are dangers in over emphasizing the need to establish links with organizations like the trade union movement. It can result in a form of educational elitism which, while providing classes in political economy and work on research, only reaches a tiny proportion of the working-class population. The need is to marry this form of social action with community action on the ground. Attempts by those involved in the latter to establish community control or work towards community 'development' should not be dismissed, as they often are by those on the left. They have historical parallels in the history of the working class, that is the building up of local working-class organizations and informal social structures whilst engaged in wider social and political action.

They are two sides of the same coin and it is just not true to argue that all problems and issues facing the working class can *only* be resolved by mass movements for social and political change. The search for 'quality' in human relationships and convivial local institutions, a feature of the work of many local people involved in community development, tends to be ignored by political activists or dismissed as irrelevant. The mass movements' struggle is, however, long-term and new relationships and new structures at local level can be created which at least will illustrate what the new society might look like. It was done in the past in the most adverse conditions. It can be done today.

We have no illusions about that process but we believe radical educators must play a role in it whilst providing support for a social movement. However, it is doubtful if such a role will, or could be, undertaken by the formal adult educational system. Universities and other institutions have a great many resources to offer for such work. Radical adult educators often find a haven in the former and a freedom to develop their work which is the envy of colleagues in other adult education organizations and institutions. However, this is often a lonely vigil, a constant struggle which saps the will.

There is no sense of common purpose and commitment which could create the dynamism necessary for radical and effective involvement in the community struggle. What is required here — and elsewhere — is a new educational 'movement' based on existing independent initiatives — like the local resource centres.

It is indicative of the situation here that *no* formal educational institution is prepared to take up that challenge despite the conflict of the last ten years. The emphasis is very much on carrying on as if things were normal, providing credits and certification and the sort of community education which means hairdressing and keepfit, turning a blind eye to the essentially abnormal situation here and the need to assist actively in the search for political solutions to our problems. In that sense it is, as I argued earlier, only an extreme manifestation of the general attitude of modern social, economic and political institutions to social and political change. They are part of the whole machinery which effectively de-politicizes issues. This de-politicization is carried to an extreme here affecting the community movement by the familiar process of co-option and the search for political solutions by ignoring the essentially political nature of the present conflict and treating those involved as 'ordinary' criminals. Adult education is, unfortunately, increasingly part of that process, particularly as it becomes more established and accepted as an important part of the total educational system.

Our one hope lies in the possibility of establishing a residential centre which would link in to the network of local resource centres to provide research and educational facilities, concentrating on weekend, and week-long workshops, with staff employed in the centre and in the field. It would be clear about its purpose and methods as the creation of the radical working-class movement, in which adult education would assist in encouraging a dialogue and analysis, not only about community action, but about wider social and political problems. Such a dialogue would seek to go beyond narrow Republican and Unionist stereotypes to a realization of the heritage and culture shared by both communities, an appreciation of the strengths in their different traditions, and the opportunities available to create a new future based on their common efforts and aspirations. That is the challenge for adult educators here in Northern Ireland. A similar challenge and opportunity faces all committed adult educators involved in community action.

9   Second Chance to Learn, Liverpool: class and adult education

Martin Yarnit, WEA Tutor Organizer and Co-ordinator of Second Chance to Learn

We are living somewhat dangerously through the most promising revival of independent working-class adult education since the heyday of the National Council of Labour Colleges in the 1920s or even Chartism. The contours of the resurgence are still blurred and its momentum not yet consistent, but we can identify the features that locate it in the British tradition of class education, the oldest in the world.

The new movement has sprouted out of the crevices of the working-class movement, at the points where new pressures have arisen in conflict with the traditional ideas of labourism. Black people, women, socialist trade unionists, inner city tenants: these are some of the forces, disillusioned with Labour government and parliament, which have begun to organize on the edge of mainstream politics. Often there is more hostility than harmony between these dissident forces; on the whole, they have developed in isolation from each other. What they have in common is a belief in their own ability to organize for change and a firm commitment to the value of education. They learn because they want to understand how the world works and how they fit into it and how they change it.

A key question for these new forces is how to interpret the relationship between the notion of working class and their own specific condition or oppression. This kind of inquiry has given rise to the almost obsessive concern with self-history which has resulted in new accounts of the origins of racism and of women's political history, for example. Alongside the history workshops have grown the writers' workshops. In both cases, a concern to understand one's present situation goes along with an attempt to rediscover lost realities and experiences. At the same time, urban and industrial decline coupled with the loss of Labour's radicalism, has prompted some sections of the working class to re-examine their world view, to try to understand why earlier dreams have not been realized.

This renewed popular interest in learning, history and creative expression is in many ways reminiscent of previous movements. Political movements like syndicalism and suffragettism gave rise similarly to forms of education and reflection. The initial impetus was political but the activities were often much broader than this. Working-class art flourishes in a period when the working class is feeling its way towards defining a new society to replace the old. In his discussion of hegemony, a word which means far more than domination, Gramsci recognized the significance of the wider cultural developments to which proletarian political advance gives rise.

Turning to specifically educational activity, we can see today a concern with collective rather than simply individual advance, with the informal but structured and with the appropriation of the written word by those deprived of its use: these are the features which link the developments of the 1970s to a long-standing tradition of class education in this country. There are also important differences with that tradition. Most crucially, the present revival of interest in education has coincided with a period of setback which probably began during the first Wilson government but which made itself felt after the return of Labour in 1974. As the old dominating presence of the industrial working class has ebbed, new social and political forces have arisen which are for the moment incapable of turning the political tide away from the right. Education has a different function in a long drawn-out period of class stalemate than in a period of working-class advance. It is more reflective and less idealistic. It is less immediately related to today's activity and more conscious of the need to make long-term advances.

The second distinctive feature of the new movement is linked to this. Outrageously political activities are unlikely to attract official funding, particularly in a moment of class polarization. The 1919 Report on Adult Education, in which the socialist educationalist Tawney played a guiding role, refers to an unnamed director of education who was reluctant to permit the use of his schools for 'anarchist' adult education classes. In the 1970s the state has felt sufficiently secure to enter into a partnership with diverse species of radicals to promote educational and social action experiments. The Community Development Projects can lay claim to a shelf-ful of studies charting the social impact of the decline of Britain's manufacturing base, especially on the inner areas of the great cities. But CDP overstepped the mark and was closed down by the Home Office. Nonetheless there still remain many examples of state-supported projects staffed by the critical intelligentsia.

In education, this reality demands a reassessment of our inherited notion of independent adult education. Truly independent working-class education remains, on a restricted basis. The development of the modern state has opened up opportunities in education which the pioneers of the NCLC would have found hard to comprehend. As long as some of the most exciting developments are taking place with the aid of public finance, we must keep an open mind about how widely we define 'independent'. For me, the key consideration is less the source of the money than the degree of autonomy. How freely can we respond to the needs expressed by 'students'? How readily can students shape educational initiatives to support their own aims? These are the questions which count.

What I have tried to do is to write an account of the development of Second Chance to Learn, in Liverpool, in the light of these considerations. If there is an argument, it is that this course has attained its present shape and outlook as a consequence of a prolonged *political* relationship between professional adult educators and local working-class organizations and networks.

Origins

In 1970, Keith Jackson, a lecturer in community development in Liverpool University's Institute of Extension Studies, began to put together an action-research team to work under the Community Development Project recently set up in the Liverpool dockside Vauxhall area. The aim was to make adult education an integral part of the Project's programme. With funding from the Home Office, which was responsible for the national CDP scheme, and the Gulbenkian Foundation, Bob Ashcroft was appointed in 1971 to a full-time action-research post attached to Vauxhall CDP. Early in the following year, I began work as a lecturer in community development with a large slice of my time devoted to our joint activity in Vauxhall. The team was completed in May 1973 by David Evans, whose responsibility was to be the development of local creative writing and journalism.

Apart from Keith Jackson, none of us was appointed permanently or paid by the University. Financial independence gave us a degree of political independence, but if in the end we were largely accountable to ourselves, we were also very vulnerable economically. When the money ran out, we had to go.

The manifesto of the team was first presented publicly at a conference on social deprivation and change in education held in York in April 1972. A paper, written by Ashcroft and Jackson, argued that the starting point for working-class adult educators should be the recognition that exploitation was the central feature of class society and that the purpose of education was to confront the student with his/her class position, helping them towards a critical understanding of their position. [1] Much of the paper was taken up with a highly critical appraisal of the notion of social relevance put forward by Eric Midwinter, then director of the Educational Priority Area programme in Liverpool. Midwinter, like many exponents of community education was prepared to countenance a link between education and action, subject to severe self-imposed limitations. For him, the social possibilities of a critical education are casually abandoned with this credo: 'For valid reasons, society insists on a differential system of status, income and circumstances which critically affects educational performance.' [2] Thus, relevance is for him a useful way of overcoming the middle-class cultural domination of the schools to make a direct approach to the minds of working-class children. For us the key word was, instead, consciousness.

Without an understanding of the position of the working class, the individual would be hard-pressed to locate the levers of effective, collective political action.

These statements were generally treated with scepticism by our colleagues and collaborators. The dominant trend in our field was represented by Eric Midwinter who fitted in well with the fashionable concern with community development. In these early days of the national CDP experiment, Vauxhall could probably be located a little to the right of the orthodoxy emanating from the Home Office and its academic advisers. The conventional view of the problem in areas like Vauxhall put the emphasis on improving the institutional arrangements of the welfare state to improve 'service delivery'.

The CDP is a modest attempt at action research into the better understanding and more comprehensive tackling of social needs, especially in local communities and within the older urban areas, through closer co-ordination of central and local official and unofficial effort, informed and stimulated by citizens' initiative and involvement. [3]

Accepting this as a starting point many of the CDPs decided to devote their resources to developing residents' organizational capability as a pressure group to reform local services. [4] Vauxhall, whilst sharing this view and helping to set up advice centres and community legal advice schemes, placed at least an equal emphasis on the internal reform of the local authority's procedures. The project's crowning achievement was to persuade the City Council to create a local multi-service centre which brought together on the same premises almost all local and national state institutions operating in Vauxhall. Local area management, it was thought, would shorten the supply lines between the officials and the people, reduce the risk of conflict caused by mutual misunderstanding and ignorance, and finally, help to bring about a budgetary re-distribution in favour of the inner city.

The emphasis on building local residents' organizations helped to draw the majority of the CDPs closer to a conflict-orientated notion of community development. Many CDP workers found, through their commitments to tenants' organizations, that problems could not be resolved within the official schemes. Although the staff of the Vauxhall never denied the wider economic causes of the social problems they were employed to deal with, [5] they remained steadfastly loyal to their original conception that area management could help to focus the public services on the points of greatest need in the community. The conflict which was latent in our relationship with the CDP staff continued until the autumn of 1972 when we all found ourselves caught up in the mounting concern in the local community about the Housing Finance Act, a measure shortly to come into operation. This issue was intensely embarrassing for the CDP which strove to remain neutral in what eventually became a battle between tenants and councillors, once the Labour-controlled City Council had bowed to Whitehall pressure and abandoned its opposition to the Act. The tenants' associations voted for a rent strike and called on the CDP to support them. They were refused; tenants' leaflets could no longer be printed on the machines in the CDP offices.

The rent strike brought us our first major experience in the area as a team and also an opportunity to put into practice what was until then largely untried theory. [6] Invited by the tenants' organizations to explain the implications of the Act, Ashcroft wrote a short pamphlet summarizing its workings and gave a series of public seminars, in front of 200 people on one occasion, at which the impact of the Conservatives' housing measures was assessed. Invited to join the tenants' co-ordinating committees as a technical adviser,

Ashcroft accepted and the rest of us began to work closely with the organizers of the rent strike, helping in the production of leaflets and bulletins. This identification with the tenants continued into the following year when they opposed the sitting Labour councillors with tenants' candidates, one of whom came perilously close to displacing a senior member of the Labout Party. [7]

The more we distanced ourselves from the CDP, the closer we found ourselves working with the activists in the area. The experience of the rent strike and then the local election campaign had brought together a hard core of militants, 10 to 15 strong, with whom our team was involved in a continuing discussion about the politics of education. From this group emerged the plan for a People's Centre, an independent community centre with a strong emphasis on learning activities. Ashcroft ran a series of seminars on political theory and Evans led a season's discussions of 'favourite books' which gave way to the Scotland Road Writers' Workshop (see Chapter 7 in this book). For a new breed of working-class community workers emerging at this time in central Liverpool, some of whom had cut their teeth in the rent strikes, Jackson and I mounted a course leading to a Certificate in Neighbourhood Work whose core component was a study of the rise and fall of the Port of Liverpool and its social consequences. Jackson also obtained official funding for a residents' inquiry into law and order in central Liverpool. The researchers, who were paid a sessional fee for their work, were mostly young men, several of them with a criminal record. Under the guidance of a sociologist, they prepared their own report on the causes of crime and vandalism, *We Live Here*, a direct and lively alternative to the official report of the Lord Mayor's Committee on Vandalism.

Out of these involvements, we later drew a series of educational conclusions which were to guide our work henceforth:

Education for the working class

Most of our work has grown out of a collaborative relationship with people in the working-class communities of central Liverpool. Our starting point has been that education has a usefulness in the development of political confidence and strength, provided it relates to the issues which the people define as important and relates to their experience of life. In practice, this means that we frequently work with the activists, a comparatively small group in any area.

There is another reason why we direct out attention towards the activists. Since the time of the Chartists, it is the potentially committed amongst the working class who have formed the backbone of the movements for independent education and (as Chapter 7 suggests) that is still the case today. We have little confidence in the ability of professional adult educationalists to create a permanent demand for education in the working class where so little exists today. Adult education will remain a lost cause until the working class takes it up on its own terms — with the support of sympathetic professionals. After almost a decade of committed adult education in Liverpool, there are now clear indications that a generation of local militants is emerging for whom education is a priority.

Content before form

In its desperation to appeal to all the deprived categories red-lined by the Russell Report, adult education has frequently fallen foul of the vacuous gimmickry of much that passes for 'community education'. While the political approach of this brand of education is easily revealed as social democratic, its superficial radicalism can be seen as an obsession with form at the expense of content. Typically, there is much talk of access and student-centred pedagogy and at best this is combined with a recognition that working-class students are disadvantaged in education. But the solution to this problem, since it must avoid a political commitment to working-class demands, is to present bright and lively techniques as the breakthrough. Sometimes they are, but rarely lastingly.

To put content before form is not to deny the importance of pedagogy or to equate content with a perpetual diet of politics. It is merely to affirm that in the end if education is to grow deep roots in the working class then they will be nourished more by what people learn than by how they learn. Too often adult educationalists have searched for exotic and exciting remedies to cure the working-class alienation from education rather than admit the obvious: the initial motivation to learn is often linked to the desire for change, personal and social. It is worth recalling Robert Owen's claim that the working man (or woman) has a right to 'learn what he is in relation to past ages, to the period in which he lives, to circumstances in which he is placed, to the individuals around him, and to future events'.

This is not an argument for a standardized approach to working-class adult education. On the contrary, I feel strongly that a thousand schools should contend.

Second Chance has moved a long way from the early informal, action-orientated approach we adopted in Vauxhall because students have demanded an increasingly tight internal regime from us. But that should not mean that highly structured classroom courses are the only valid ones for us.

Paid release and positive discrimination

Successful middle-class students are paid to study, for life. Grant-aided through university, they are released by their employers for periodical in-service training courses, and on their successful completion they are habitually rewarded with promotion and enrolled for more advanced courses. The system works in reverse for those discarded by education at 16. If they want more education they must pay for it. Grants are usually discretionary and small, opportunities narrower. *Public spending is structured to widen the gap between those who leave education at 16 and those who make it to higher education at 17+.*

Working within but on the fringes of the state education system, we set ourselves three aims:

a) To win paid release for workers to attend day-time courses. To have to study at night after a day's work is a double penalty.

b) No fees. People should not have to choose between learning and feeding themselves and their children.

c) Favourable conditions of study. People returning to education need at least as much support as university students: to be discriminated in favour, not against. On Second Chance we have identified the crucial role of the personal tutor in providing personal and intellectual support.

Second Chance to Learn

When we decided to launch Second Chance, it was with the aim of extending what we had learnt in Scotland Road/Vauxhall to Liverpool as a whole. We are now in the fourth year. Our intake includes housewives, factory workers, hospital workers, clerical workers, young black community workers and the unemployed; none of them with much more than a basic secondary schooling, drawn from all over Liverpool.

As they talk about their reasons for applying for Second Chance, two things become clear. Everyone is conscious of what a conventional education has left him without. They want to express themselves fluently and clearly. And they want to understand their own position in life and the workings of the society they live in.

From these needs emerge the structure of the course, the stress on attainment in the written language and for a logical and analytical approach to problems, as well as the centrality of history as a key to understanding society. We aim to stimulate a critical consciousness of the way society works, to counter the view which presents the inner areas of Liverpool and other cities as victims of circumstances, as regrettable accidents. We attempt instead to chart Liverpool's decline historically, to show that the slums are just as much the products of a market economy as the lush suburbs of south Liverpool.

Whilst denying the notion of a value-neutral education, I have more enthusiasm for providing students with a framework for understanding than in trying to instil a given set of values. Systematic study does cause a shift in political values for many. Often, as well, it leads to a personal reassessment. The return to learning sometimes coincides with, sometimes provokes a personal crisis. Students may leave Second Chance further to the left than when they started, but this is likely to be part of a more profound change in outlook. In my experience political consciousness is closely related to personal confidence and awareness. And that is probably the most important gain to be made. It is certainly the effect of attending Second Chance most regularly referred to by students who have completed the course.

Organization of Second Chance

Second Chance to Learn is a day-a-week social studies course stretching over 20 weeks. It is aimed at people active in the community or in trade unions who have gained few or no formal qualifications since leaving school at the minimum leaving age. The course offers no certificates but several students have used Second Chance as a launching pad for mature entrance to university, polytechnic or the new Northern College.

On paper, it is a joint university—WEA course but the real position is anomalous. Urban Programme funding under the Inner Cities Partnership scheme has been used to create a structure unlike the norm in adult education. A full-time team of eight people — two secretaries, and six tutors — are employed mainly by the WEA, while the University's Institute of Extension Studies contributes the part-time efforts of three of its staff, plus one full-time Partnership-funded lecturer. The local authority, which is represented on the management committee for the course, contributes 25 per cent towards total costs, under normal Urban Programme arrangements. [8] Since no fees are paid by students, a sum total of about £50,000 p.a. must be found by the state (locally and nationally) and the responsible bodies.

What is the return on investment? We begin each course with two intakes of about 20 each, which attend on separate days. The day consists of a history seminar, history workshop and writers' workshop, each 90 minutes long. In addition, each student is allocated a tutor for regular weekly meetings. Perhaps twice a course, students are expected to attend a weekend residential school held at the Northern College, with which we are linked through tradition–Keith Jackson, a founder of Second Chance, is now senior tutor there — and through joint participation in a Partnership project which provides funding for courses at the Northern College for students from central Liverpool. A local charitable trust makes grants for childcare, fares and other essential costs for those of our students who are involved in community activity.

The students

We recruit mainly through contacts and media coverage. There is a growing demand for the course, particularly from those areas or workplaces from where we have already drawn students. Applications outnumber places available by about three to one. Applicants are overwhelmingly women in their middle 20s to middle 40s. Students are usually in the same age range but we consciously select more or less half men, half women. There are housewives, employed and unemployed, and one or two retired. In giving priority to activists, we normally end up with about a third of our students in this category. The very young and the very old are in a minority, as are black people (particularly since the opening of the nearby black community's Charles Wootton Centre).

The intake of Second Chance is remarkable for the number of people drawn from the untouchable castes of adult education, the partly skilled and unskilled categories of the Registrar-General's Classification. The contrast is heightened if we compare the student profile of Second Chance for the 1979 course with the results of a survey of students of Liverpool Extra-mural Department and WEA, West Lancashire and Cheshire district, carried out just over a decade ago. These figures are from John Lowe's *Adult Education in England and Wales.*

Social class (Registrar General's classification)	Census (%)	Survey (%)	Second Chance (%) 1979 Men	Women*
Professional	3 ⎫15	11	–	
Intermediate	12 ⎭	40	–	–
Skilled	51 ⎫	37	20	25
Partly Skilled	12 ⎬85	7	20	55
Unskilled	22 ⎭	–	60	

Note: Unemployed have rather arbitrarily been grouped with unskilled (on Merseyside there is a strong link).
*The three women who refer to themselves as housewives have not been classified. 20 men and 17 women provide the sample for the Second Chance figures.

An overwhelming majority of Second Chance students is drawn from precisely those sections of the working class which remain largely uncatered for by formal institutions. A review of the applicants we reject suggests, moreover, that there is a lively interest in education, especially amongst women in the middle ranges of the social spectrum, which isn't being met at present.

Three main reasons are given by applicants in interview for joining the course. An almost universal priority is a desire to improve facility in the written language. We now know of the shame felt by the illiterate when it comes to revealing their ignorance, but many working-class men and women who are quite literate are deeply conscious of their own shortcomings in writing. Next comes a desire to learn more about politics and economics. Equal second is an interest in qualifying for further and higher education. Housewives cite as a further reason for applying for the course that they are at a loose end, particularly if their children are all at school or have left home. Women of this kind often display an exceptional commitment to study.

A growing number of Second Chance students are drawn from the ranks of the industrial workers. The present intake includes dockers, typographers, local authority workers, a carpenter, an engineering worker and a postman. Our selection procedure gives priority to full-time workers because we want to establish the right to paid educational leave (PEL) for workers on non-TUC courses.

Two senior shop stewards at the nearby Ford plant who believe that Second Chance is a useful course for trade unionists typify the problems all our worker students face. They have been trying with little success for over six months to win their union's backing for their claim for PEL. Unfortunately, our experience is that trade unions have as little enthusiasm for paid release as the employers, although we have found some isolated exceptions. Most full-time workers on Second Chance attend at the cost of their holidays or their rest days since most employers will concede unpaid leave only so long as they are not inconvenienced. The difficulties of coping with work when no proper release arrangements are possible accounts for the major part of absenteeism and drop-out on Second Chance. We expect to lose 30 to 40 per cent of our students in this way, although some each year maintain their relationship with the course by continuing to attend tutorials or even by completing their written assignments as if they were on a correspondence course.

Course content

Why so much history: this is the most frequent query from visitors. Not only is two-thirds of the day taken up with history, but history forms the major topic at weekend schools and in tutorials. Most written work is set on historical themes. History is our chosen vehicle for examining some related questions in British social and economic development since the Industrial Revolution.

Our starting point for inquiry is the rise and fall of Liverpool as a port and a city, a fruitful avenue of exploration. Liverpool's past is closely tied up with Britain's imperial era, with the exploitation of the Third World, with slavery and racism; with Ireland, and with the changing fortunes of the staple industries of the industrial north. The course tries to answer three basic questions:

a) How did Britain's early start in industrialization turn to economic decline?

b) What were the economic and social consequences of this trajectory for Merseyside?

c) What were the origins of the working class and how have its conditions of life changed since the Industrial Revolution?

Within this framework we try to lay the basis for some key concepts: class, nation, race and sex; and to try to understand how they have combined to produce the society we know today. Women students and tutors have helped us to see the importance of sex as a social and economic dimension, and in the same way black students have argued for a greater emphasis on the economic contribution of slavery and colonialism to western development. And the tutors as a group have learned to compensate for their own and the students' ingrained parochialism by constantly restating the importance of *global* events to British history.

Each week students receive a set of history notes — 12 to 15 pages long, duplicated with illustrations and diagrams — which provide the factual and conceptual basis for the forthcoming seminar. The notes contain suggestions for further reading and a series of review questions as a prompt to self-assessment. The tutor's aim in the seminar is to make sure that everyone has grasped the main points in the notes and then to develop by discussion some of the more stimulating questions raised by that week's theme.

The history workshop tends to run parallel to the seminar thematically. The topic for the 1979 course was Liverpool around the time of the Great War with Pat O'Mara's contemporary autobiographical account, *Memoirs of a Liverpool Irish Slummy*, as our starting point. For the first term, students examined the Liverpool of the early decades of the century through O'Mara's often unreliable account, through archives and newspapers and through film. We dealt in detail with selected events and themes: religious riots; the Tories and the working class; housing and social conditions; childbirth. Having laid a basis for understanding the period and the techniques of historical investigation, we went on to organize interviews with people who could recall the period and talk about significant aspects of life at the time.

In the tutorial and to a degree in the writers' workshop, students learn the basic techniques of study and written composition. Students are taught how to use a library, how to take notes, how to plan an essay, not as skills in themselves but as necessary adjuncts to the reading and writing required by the course. What is a sentence and how do you use the apostrophe: these are our main concerns in grammar, and for them alone we have developed special drills. We use writing to clarify ideas, to gain intellectual confidence and to improve use of language. Written assignments are graduated from the first month's straightforward 'What were the main changes brought about by the Industrial Revolution?' to 'Why was the General Strike defeated?', a far more complex question, two-thirds of the way through the course.

The most unusual aspect of Second Chance is the tutorial, a conventional teaching method in the university but almost entirely absent from adult education, apart from literacy classes. Every student is allocated a tutor at the start of the course and can expect a weekly meeting, usually alone but sometimes with three or four others, until the end. A lot of tutorial time is occupied by the monthly essay and in discussing that week's history seminar. But tutorials serve many other functions. They provide the students, especially less confident ones, with a constant personal link to the course, with an opportunity for talking through problems raised by Second Chance or which affect attendance. Tutorials also act as an early warning system in the case of students who are finding the going too hard, or, as is more usual, can't solve the problems which make attendance difficult. A one-to-one relationship with a tutor can act as a safety net for students who find the seminars or workshops impossible to participate in, and, at the other extreme, provide additional stimulus for more able students. A wide ability range can be taught without a high fall-out if there is the individual tutor available to provide support. It is the tutorial system above all which boosts the cost of Second Chance to about £500 per student, a comparatively large sum in adult education, a sector where penury has come to be borne with pride. And, yet, is there any good reason why working-class students should not expect the same investment as an undergraduate? When you consider that many of our students are losing a day's wage to attend a course which provides no obvious final reward, it seems just that we should underwrite their commitment with an effective system of student support. In any case, a measure which effectively cuts the rate of drop-out as well as the tutorial system must remain a vital element of the course.

Second Chance in its natural habitat

The political and educational events of the 1970s in Liverpool and Britain have generally provided the basis for Second Chance's development. Alongside us, several other educational experiments have taken similar directions. A network of projects is emerging, parallel to the conventional provision and dedicated to the notion that adult education is for change.

The ponderously named Liverpool Inner Areas Adult Education Consortium came together in 1978 to make a joint application for funds to the Inner Areas Partnership programme. The application argued, immodestly, that the Consortium represented a tried and tested, integrated adult education system for central Liverpool. [9]

The underlying logic of the Consortium's composition is that it aims to serve three functions for those sections of the population who are worst served by present educational provision. Schemes such as Home Link and Vauxhall provide initial access to adult education, through strong local roots, sensitivity to local needs and concerns and a programme of basic education, although not exclusively that (Vauxhall and Charles Wootton, for example, both have schemes for students interested in GCEs and higher education). Second Chance, particularly but not exclusively, provides access to more advanced study and prepares students for mature entrance to higher education. Finally, the Northern College, with Partnership finance, undertakes to provide places for a number of students from Liverpool as well as to provide shorter courses, created jointly with one or more of the Consortium members.

Within the framework of a series of diverse but educationally and organizationally complementary courses, the consortium is moving towards a more rigorous definition of its own objectives, partly in response to growing local authority interest in working-class adult education. We have started to set ourselves priorities, which are reflected in a new application to Partnership, for over £200,000 a year. Black people, women and paid educational leave for workers are three of our main concerns simply because these are the ones we judge to be worst served by existing arrangements.

A significant development in the short life of the Consortium is the move towards student participation. A small but growing number of working-class people are beginning to gain appointments in schemes such as the Charles Wootton Centre and the Scotland Road Writers' Workshops. None of the schemes has adopted the falsely populist policy of jobs for the locals, but there is an assumption that when candidates of equal merit present themselves for interview, the scales should be weighted in favour of the working class.

Adult education and the movement

The development of the Consortium reflects the rise in interest in education in Liverpool's working-class communities and it points to the possibility of creating a new system of adult education, more accessible and more daring than the local authority provision. As I have tried to show here, the vital factor underpinning this development is the growing link between working-class activists and committed professionals.

The most impressive aspect of the Liverpool developments has been the break through to the communities and organizations. This will seem commonplace to people who have taught in the traditional bastions of workers' education, in South Yorkshire and South Wales, where the trade unions have for decades provided a constant demand for education. Second Chance represents an attempt to apply the lessons of that practice to a population which has never known that kind of tradition. In some mining areas, for instance, education is as much a part of the culture as sport or the pub. The labour movement and the trade unions have a different history in Liverpool, a city which has always depended on casual labour and uncertain commercial links. Even today, over one-third of the population lives in run-down inner city areas where unemployment and low pay is the norm. In some areas, over half of the potential workforce is unemployed. A sample survey of the Vauxhall area in 1972 confirmed an infinitesimal take-up of local authority adult education provision. [10] Nevertheless, seven years later, this area now supports two growing education projects and attracts students from other parts of Liverpool. A tradition of adult education is beginning to take root in Vauxhall, and elsewhere in Liverpool. (WEA/TUC provision for shop stewards now amounts to one of the largest provincial developments in this field.)

Once education puts down permanent roots, new possibilities are opened up. In the first place, a popular tradition in education subverts the normal dependence on professionals and the local authority and may lead to a working-class definition of priorities and contents. The schemes described in this article could expect to be dwarfed by a flowering of a truly popular educational movement. And that must be our aim, if we see education playing a significant role in the development of a working-class challenge to bourgeois hegemony.

In a limited way, the projects involved in the Consortium have demonstrated that a deeply rooted educational tradition can point to real alternatives to the present system. We are a long way from being able to offer a satisfactory alternative to the serious intellectual challenge presented by some degree courses, nor can we pretend to comprehensive provision, but an alternative model is emerging. Teaching materials and techniques are being developed *with* students in a way that is rare in mainstream adult education. More important, perhaps, the debate is opening up about the purpose of education.

Education for individual or for collective advancement, this is the vexed question in working-class education and it underlies much of the work that Keith Jackson and others of us have been doing since the early 1970s. It is far from a theoretical issue too. It is raised whenever students decide to seek admission to university or to a residential college. It has to be faced when selection policy for Second Chance is under discussion. Are we favouring some kinds of applicants at the expense of the activists, the people who are most likely to use education for social ends? This is an impossible debate unless it can involve class-conscious students, people who are deeply aware of the personal and political ambiguities involved. The growth of a committed system of education offers hope of some solution to the dilemma. First, in time it may provide students with jobs in the communities or close to the areas in which they were raised. The experience of Ruskin students shows that this is a far from completely satisfactory solution. Second, it may be possible to avoid the creaming-off of activists if the priority is given to the development of forms of education closely tied to the needs of the community. This is not to deny the right of students to expect support in their efforts to reach the university. On the other hand, the vast majority who don't make the break with work or community have at least an equal right to forms of education which advance their struggles and interests.

Recent discussions on Second Chance involving students and tutors point to a revision of course content towards a more direct link to current concerns: unemployment, investment, the decline of council housing, the future of public transport. We are keen to avoid creating a model of academicism which would deepen the isolation of the course from its roots among the activists.

Yet, education which exists exclusively for the struggle is necessarily limited in its scope. Second Chance has always had to come to terms with the tension between the interests of the politically committed, who form a coherent and vocal minority of the students, and the needs of often minimally class-conscious students. We have recognized the advantages, for both types of student and for tutors from this mix, but we also hold that adult education for the working class has to offer stimulus to both the committed and the uncommitted. Many students will never identify with our outlook, but it is crucial that they should feel at ease in arguing with it. Educationalists have always laid claim to truth and freedom. We can and must do the same with a serene conscience, knowing that if we fail it won't be long before we are being vilified by some students as indoctrinators. And that's a risk which the bourgeois educationalist should run, but rarely does.

10 150 Hours — Italy's experiment in mass working-class adult education

Martin Yarnit, WEA Tutor Organizer and Co-ordinator of Second Chance to Learn

We're workers because one day society threw us out of school and made us factory fodder. With our labour we've paid for a school system that chucks us out and pushes our kids to one side. Culture is used only to make people unequal, but with 150 hours the aim is to unite ourselves and make ourselves equal. We began the 150 hours with tremendous problems and real experiences and, after a lot of difficulties, I think we've all really developed, teachers as well. This will help us to deal more effectively with the problems we have to face every day.

Last year, nearly 100,000 Italians went back to school to take their middle school diploma. The curriculum is apparently the same as for the diploma their children sit for at 14 or 15. In fact, the approach, contents and underlying aims of the adult course are quite different.

Since 1973, when the 150 Hours courses got under way, the number of workers, housewives and the unemployed enrolled for the one-year part-time diploma has quintupled. Well over 200,000 have been through the course in the first four years. Paid educational leave (PEL) arrangements to attend the 150 courses now extend throughout industry to about 8 million workers. Most workers are now entitled to 250 hours' PEL. Suddenly Italy has moved from totally inadequate provision for working-class adult education towards a dramatic attempt to create a universal system, paid for by the state and the employers but with a distinctly working-class outlook.

Why the government and the bosses should tolerate and finance education often highly subversive of their interests only makes sense in terms of recent Italian political history.

The origins of the 150 Hours (the name refers to the number of hours paid by the employer towards the total course in the early years) have to be looked for in the massive upsurge of workers' and students' struggles in the late 1960s and early 1970s. The influences which combined to produce the courses are diverse, but everyone recognizes the 150 Hours as a political advance for the Italian working class, as well as a purely educational gain. And, in Italy of all places, that was badly needed. A Workers' Educational Association tour of inquiry of Italian adult education in 1956 concluded that the system was 'patchy and chaotic'. Outside the training courses for union officials, they could hardly find any trace of *workers'* education.

How the education system doesn't work

Apparently more open than the British system, the Italian schools are among the world's most selective and class biased. A rigid hierarchy of educational opportunity consigns the children of poor, peasant, dialect-speaking parents to almost instant failure. A small proportion of manual workers' children manage to leave school at 14 or 15 with their diploma, the equivalent of a few CSEs; a tiny proportion go on to prepare for entrance to a degree course or equivalent. 73 per cent of Italians of 15 and over were without a diploma in 1971, equivalent to 30 million people, and 50 per cent of those in the age range 15 to 44 had no diploma. These figures tend to be worse in the south and for women. Even in the big cities of the north, the level of illiteracy is high. Library lendings in Italy are 1/200th the UK level. Not only are school hours short — students are back home by about 2.00 p.m. in most cases — but overcrowding is so acute that many schools work a shift system.

Manuele, a ten-year-old who enlisted my help with his English homework, explained how the teaching was organized at his school, in a working-class area in central Milan. The Italian school day has always been short, but now the children are taught in shifts since the Director of Education decided to lower pass standards to keep kids off the dole and enrolments shot up. So Manuele attends on Friday afternoon and comes back for a Saturday morning class.

Not surprisingly, many parents conclude that school is a farce, preferring anyway to have their children at work and earning, especially in the south where child labour is still prevalent. Many state teachers double their earnings by giving private classes in the afternoon. Before the 150 Hours, hundreds of thousands of Italians went back to night school, as adults, to gain their diploma as an aid to advancement at work. Apart from that, there was almost no provision for workers' education. There were liberal education courses, dominated by the middle classes and their cultural outlook, and cadre courses organized by the trade unions.

What is unique about the 150 Hours is that although it seeks to provide students with a basic level of education and a diploma which can be significant in job-hunting, the whole outlook of the courses, the teachers and the unions, leads to a stress on collective rather than individual solutions to social and educational problems. This echoes a tradition in British workers' education which is as weak today as it is long — it stretches back to the Chartists, continuing into this century with Tawney's Tutorial Classes and the work of the NCLC. At a time when that tradition is being re-examined in Britain, it could well be that the Italian experience has a lot to teach us.

Political origins of the 150 Hours: the 'hot autumn' of 1969

In 1946, the communist partisans in the cities and factories laid down their arms. For the next twenty years, the trade unions and the workers' parties guaranteed industrial peace for the sake of national reconstruction. The economy, fed by an endless supply of immigrant labour from the south, boomed and productivity soared. And as the big industrial cities flourished, the gap between north and south widened. Tens of thousands left the parched, silent villages of Sicily and Sardinia in search of work in Milan and Turin. Between 1950 and 1967, one-third of the entire population emigrated, many of them abroad.

The competition and patronage on which Christian Democratic rule depends and which is deeply hostile to planning, helped to ensure a growing abyss between industrial development and the social needs it generated. The employers provided jobs, but the public authorities declined to meet the consequent demand for housing, education and health facilities. Workers slept on park benches. Schools arranged shift systems.

The whole social situation in Turin blew up, what with the shortage of housing, lightning price increases, the building speculation and everything. [1]

Between 1951 and 1969, Turin's population doubled to 1.5 million. Over 60,000 alone worked in the various Fiat plants which sprawl all over the centre of the city.

In 1969, the unions opened negotiations for a new 3-year contract. According to the traditional formula, workers were invited to participate in a series of staggered strikes, designed for minimum inconvenience and as a warning against procrastination by the employers. But in April 1969, when two rioters were shot by the police in the southern town of Battipaglia, the growing unrest with unemployment overflowed into the northern industrial belt. Young immigrants leading the protests against the shooting, turned their anger against the union—employer orchestrated wage manoeuvres.

A general strike called by the unions on 3 July led to a 'day of almost insurrectional demonstrations in Turin [which] has brusquely reminded Italy that it has not yet had its May' (*Le Monde*, 5 July 1969). A key element in the day's events was underlined by the *Economist*:

The notion that students and workers cannot find common ground was disproved when the hard core of student revolutionaries was joined on the barricades by large groups of young workers. Even workers loyal to the trade unions notice that pay increases won through the unofficial strikes are much greater than those gained after regular management–union bargaining. [2]

To the workers' hostility to the factory and the wretchedness of immigrant life, the rising student movement added an overall political consciousness. The combination of young worker and student radicalism, which burst on Italian society with more force than anywhere else, brought to an end two decades of social peace and constant growth.

After the riots on 3 July, the government collapsed and the trade unions abruptly changed their tune. The unofficial workers' movement's demands — for the abolition of differentials and grades, for the abolition of the differences between staff and workers, for a shorter working week with no loss of pay, for slower line speeds — were all taken up by the union negotiators. Adjusting to the new mood of the shop floor, a proof of whose power is the abolition of the night shift in the big factories, the trade unions advanced a new bargaining strategy based on the need for workers' unity and changes in the organization of production.

The unions also posed a series of 'policy' demands related to social questions outside the factory. They began to campaign, for example, for an increasing share of public and private investment to go to the south. They argued for long overdue reforms to the school system which they identified as the indispensable accomplice of the divisive tactics used by factory management. Characteristic of the unions' attempt to ride the tiger of the unofficial movement led by revolutionaries, the workers' demand for a shorter working week with no loss of pay and their radical challenge to the class-bias of the education system was neatly side-stepped and replaced by the proposal from the engineering workers' union, the FLM, for paid educational leave. [3] To see how this led to the 150 Hours, it is first necessary to look specifically at developments within Italian education in the 1960s.

The struggle over education

In Italy's schools the impact of selection on children from the poorest sections of society is horrendous. But several years before adult students began researching the facts of discrimination in the schools, a group of school children had assembled their own devastating critique of selection. They were the pupils at a small school founded by a concerned priest, don Milani, in the isolated Tuscan village of Barbiana. Their book, *Letter to a Teacher*, has made a deep impression on millions of people involved with education, inside and outside Italy. Published in 1968, this simply written but powerful condemnation of the traditional teacher figure, coincided with the beginning of the student movement, first in the colleges and later in the high and middle schools. 'I've learnt that others have the same problems as I do. To tackle them together is politics. To tackle them alone is selfishness', they write. They cite the comfortable sentiments of article 34 of the Constitution: 'Competent and deserving students have the right to pursue their studies to the highest levels', adding, 'To be a happy student in your schools you have to be a social climber at the age of 12.' [4] They confirm their claims through a painstaking analysis of the fate of successive national intakes of pupils. Out of every 100 children entering first grade elementary school, only one student will become a graduate. An OECD report substantially confirmed their results in 1969 that during the period 1955–63, out of 1000 primary school children in Italy as a whole, only 117 got as far as the middle school certificate (148 out of 1000 in the centre-north, 86 out of 1000 in the south). [5] Only 8.1 per cent of graduates, in 1963, were from working-class families. [6]

Two factors in particular are crucial to this educational under-development:

a) the demands of the labour market

b) the nature of Italian education.

Despite the enormous reduction in the size of the agricultural workforce — from 7.2 million in 1951 to 3.8 million in 1970 — agriculture still represents an enormous demand for unskilled, badly paid labour. Ironically, the new industries which have been such a magnet for immigrants, all call for a largely unskilled or semi-skilled workforce: in cars, rubber or consumer durables. Add to this a traditional dependence on child labour — by employers and parents — in the country and in the south, and it's easy to grasp the connection between the needs of the labour market and the output of the schools.

What makes the schools so well-suited to their role is their fundamental lack of seriousness as a system. Only since 1962 has the law required educational provision beyond the age of 11. But this reform has to be set against the scandal of the morning school. Assuming that they are lucky enough not to be taught in a big city where the schools can cope only by running a shift system, Italian children only attend school in the morning for four or five hours a day. For teachers and the children of the well-off this is an admirable arrangement since it provides the time for private afternoon schooling (*doposcuola*), which advances the interests of everyone except the majority of children whose parents cannot afford to pay tuition fees. To add insult to injury, the state schools manage to lose 180 days of the year in holidays and a further 30 days with examinations. 'School, with today's timetable,' said the pupils of Barbiana, 'is a war against the poor.'

This picture varies. In Naples, local industry is long used to the services of child labour and many teachers have resigned themselves to the expectation that a large proportion of their pupils will fall at or just beyond the primary-middle school hurdle. [7] In Bologna, which has avoided many of the problems of the northern industrial belt cities with its fairly slow rate of growth, the school system has expanded to meet the needs of the unusually stable population. Illiteracy is low and standards are higher. Milan presents a grimmer picture. To offset growing unemployment among youngsters, children are being encouraged to stay longer at school, which is being used openly for its traditional function as a parking lot — *parcheggio.* [8]

The consequences of the class bias of the education system are in turn related to wage levels. The school of Barbiana showed how in concrete terms:

An MD has cost the poor L4,586,000. The father has invested L244,000. Later, with that MD degree which was a gift from the poor, the doctor will charge them L1,500 for a fifteen-minute visit, will go on strike against the Mutua and will oppose socialized medicine of the English type. [9]

Taking as an indicator the fact that fewer than 20 per cent of engineering workers left school with the middle school certificate — the figures are worse, of course, for the south and for women — it is easy to see why there should have been about 1 million workers in 1970 studying, mainly in private night schools, for qualifications. Explains one in Turin:

I attend a private institute; L210,000 just for fees, and the books cost L25–30,000 a year; then there's the bus fares. . . . Altogether, for a year it amounts to L260–300,000. Now, I take home L120,000 a month, although it was much less at first. [10]

The hunt for qualifications sustained the ethos of individual advancement, a dubious notion particularly in an era of rapid technological change. Workers found, to their chagrin, that changes in the organization of work had emptied the jobs they strove for, of skills. Promotion, at best, meant little more than a pay rise.

Qualifications are an instrument of the boss who picks out and divides the workers among themselves. [11]

The bitterness and financial costs generated by this situation led in two directions. In one way, shopfloor workers were developing a critique of the causes of their own disunity in the workplace. In another, they could identify clearly the responsibility of the education system in all this. The resulting demands for an integrated pay system for white- and blue-collar workers — *inquadramento unico* — and for time off for study, paid by the employer, emerged together logically.

The very scale of the problem of the worker students compelled some recognition by the government. The law of May 1970 on the right to study should be seen as preparing the ground for the 1972 agreement between the unions, and the state and the employers for 150 Hours' paid educational leave. [12] It seems clear that the intention behind the Right to Study Act was to show willingness rather than to take concrete steps towards PEL. Spending on Italian adult education was in constant decline from 1967 to 1974. [13] Not only did adult education command a minuscule proportion of all educational spending, but it was more thinly spread as well. Per capita, the state was spending about L184,000 a year on adults compared with L458,000 for high school students and L700,000 for university and college students. [14]

The struggle against the divisiveness of the school system — in society generally and at work — drew on the emerging strength of the popular education initiatives which arose out of the convergence of revolutionary students and workers' movements. As early as 1969, student activists, fresh from the contestatory battles in the universities over syllabuses and control, had begun to campaign in working-class neighbourhoods to create 'People's Schools'. Almost always the demand for alternatives to the official education system was firmly linked to and arose from some local issue.

In Primavalle, a working-class district in north-west Rome, a people's school was set up by a Housing Action Committee. The Committee had received its initial impetus from an independent group of leftist activists who now helped to create a school to provide middle school courses for adults who had missed out on their education.

By 1972, together with about ten other people's schools, the Primavalle committee was fighting the LEA for the right to hold its own exams for the middle school certificate. Finally, in May 1973, about the same time as the FLM was signing the 150 Hours contract with the employers, the Rome people's schools secured the right to conduct independent exams. Enrolments immediately rose and, the great obstacle to a mass involvement in middle school courses now overcome, the idea of the workers' school began its rapid spread to other cities. In Primavalle, as in most other cases, they decided to merge their efforts with the FLM. There were two important consequences. First, from the start the right of non-workers to enrol for 150 Hours courses was established. As the first entry got under way, only one-third of the students in Rome were engineering workers. In Primavalle, an area dominated by four large hospitals, the main group tended to be service and health workers, with a largish contingent of building workers. Housewives were also present on the courses from the very beginning. The second contribution of the people's schools was to a revolution in techniques in adult education. In contrast to the competition and authoritarianism of the state schools, the people's schools stressed a collaborative effort in learning, based on methods of collective work and drawing whenever possible on the students' own experiences and intellectual resources. In Primavalle, they learnt their Italian by learning about the housing struggle in the locality. They studied the school system by examining their own educational experience. These are approaches which are by now traditional to the 150 Hours.

A militant battle over control of the schools and universities and the uses of education is a key background factor in understanding the emergence of the 150 Hours not merely as a form of education but as a movement for change in education. The 150 Hours' programme launched in 1973 may not have followed the people's school tradition in all respects, but there can be no mistaking its popular roots. In this crucial respect, it is distinguished from most current trends in adult education in Europe and north America. But then there are few countries where the working class has grasped the importance to their struggle of education and culture generally. Perhaps it is not totally surprising that this should occur in the country of Gramsci, a founder of Italian communism (the largest, most influential communist party in the west) and the man who grasped the significance of hegemony for the working-class.

In the autumn of 1974, 4000 students and teachers from over 40 Turin schools and colleges struck against the cuts in education. They marched to the gates of the city's main Fiat plant, Mirafiore, to show their support for the car workers' fight against sackings. The Fiat workers' banners expressed that link between school and work which is the main motif of the 150 Hours:

Cutbacks, Teachers on the Dole, Overcrowding . . . The people they fail at school they lay off from the factory.

The unions and the 150 Hours

In spring 1973, a delegate conference of the engineering workers' joint union, the FLM, met to consider proposals for the 150 Hours scheme. They concluded that it should be

free.
on a scale sufficient to eliminate the demand for private courses.
established in state schools, taught by state teachers.
one school year in length: 12 hours a week for seven months.
based on programmes chosen by the students.
examined locally by a commission drawn mainly from the course teachers and the unions involved.

With minor caveats, that conception has largely been realized. Since 1973, the number of courses and students has roughly doubled and in many areas, especially the south, demand continues to outstrip supply. The key to the scheme's success has been the energetic pioneering spirit of the FLM and the national official responsible, Paola Piva, which have held up through the successive annual negotiating rounds with the Minister of Education (Franco Malfatti during the first formative five years).

The greatest problems for the 150 Hours have arisen from the side of the Ministry which has always been at pains to limit the growth of the scheme or, at least, to cripple its internal freedom of action. From the first, Malfatti was reluctant to see the 150 Hours as an integral part of the school system, even though it fell within the competence of the local authorities, was accommodated in middle schools in the afternoon and evening, after normal hours, and drew on a basic middle school syllabus of Italian, maths and natural science, a foreign language, and geography, history and civics. Thus, Malfatti knew that the unions saw the 150 Hours as a dagger aimed at the heart of a grossly unequal school system. 'He knows that our school has put his in crisis,' says Paola Piva, 'and he wants to gag us.' The proposal for an integrated teaching service was opposed, Malfatti instead offering a discriminatory non-tenured contract to 150 Hours staff. Conscious of the union's conception of the scheme as a kind of Trojan Horse for exerting public control over the schools, the minister was determined to maintain the distance between the new programmes and the schools. He was also reluctant to accept the principle of union control of courses involving non-unionists. The long-established, obscure and money-starved CRACIS programme — which had provided a lengthy route to the middle school certificate for a few, out of working hours and without any form of paid release — was rediscovered by the authorities and revamped. Brought within the paid release provisions and drastically shortened, from three years to one year, CRACIS grew from 15,000 in 1969–70 to 40,000 in 1975–76. It has been used as an alternative pole of attraction to the more radical 150 Hours, and with some success, especially in the south, which takes some 40 per cent of the places. Run by groups linked to the Christian Democrats, CRACIS is termed a 'ghetto' by the unionists. Malfatti would clearly like to have established from the beginning that CRACIS would deal with housewives and the unemployed, whilst the more advanced content and methods of the 150 Hours were confined to the workers. The essential weakness of the CRACIS courses remains their reliance on traditional approaches.

Within all these limits, the agreement to create the 150 Hours represented a considerable triumph, especially for the FLM. It had been handed, in effect, sufficient resources by the state and the employers (who, by the way, have always been excluded from any say in the contents of the courses) to mount the most extensive adult education programme ever conceived in Italy. Apart from housewives, the unemployed (about 2 million), and the precariously employed (another 2 million), a total of eight million workers are now covered by the 150 Hours scheme.

The 150 Hours for the middle school

The core of the programme is represented by courses for the middle school certificate. But the 150 Hours scheme also involves university (so-called 'monographic') courses and a grossly inadequate number of literacy courses. What unites them is the 150 Hours PEL agreement and a common form of organization, based on the trade unions, and increasingly the teachers' unions.

The origins of the 150 Hours are political; the dynamic of its development reflects the changing political situation in the years since the scheme started. Educational factors tend to have a smaller impact overall. The main changes, in summary, are:

a) a slowdown in the momentum of the workers' struggle in Italy since the energy crisis of 1974. The struggle over education and control of schools has lost priority in the eyes of the workers' movement which is fighting hard to retain the gains it made after 1969 on wages, jobs and working conditions.

b) the engineering workers have been displaced as the dominant force in the 150 Hours, especially in the centre and the south. Away from the traditional industrial centres of the north, the composition of the student body becomes increasingly diverse as you move south. Without such a nucleus the course is in danger of losing its political edge and simply furthering personal advancement.

c) the pressures to consolidate are a force for a more traditional approach to education.

Organization

Arrangements for the 150 Hours vary between industries and areas, but the norm is a course 350 hours long, spread over the months of the school year. This amounts to, roughly, 4 hours per week on each of the four components of the course: Italian, science, history and a foreign language. Two hundred and fifty hours — in some industries and throughout most of the public sector — of this total are paid for by the employer. The remainder is contributed by the worker, usually by unpaid release from work. In practice, the 350 hours often extends to 420 to 450, once time is added for research projects or further tuition in any of the main subject areas. Courses, which usually take place in middle schools at the end of the normal day, are organized on a modular basis: 4 teachers, one for each of the main subject areas, take responsibility for 4 classes, each containing 20 to 25 students, arranging the week's timetable between them. A variation on this arrangement which I saw in Milan is a kind of team teaching, with two teachers always serving a group together.

The national programme provides meagre funding for overheads: administration, materials, porters, nurseries, teacher training. This makes a sympathetic LEA and head-teacher a crucial element. In some areas — Bologna and Val d'Aosta, on the Swiss border — local authorities have topped up the Ministry's permitted funding with some of their own money to raise the number of courses and to provide more generous back-up services.

At none of the schools I visited was there a nursery for students' children. The FLM is campaigning for either a room and other facilities to be set aside as a crèche in every school used for 150 Hours classes or for facilities to be made available in the nearest state nursery. The union would also like to see women given priority in the recruitment campaigns and in the planning of course material. Courses are co-ordinated within each school by a committee representing students, teachers and the unions involved. In an area, schools are linked through a co-ordinating committee, sometimes served by a full-time worker appointed by a union (often the FLM), which will probably include representatives of factory councils or community organizations. Cities have their own central co-ordinating committee which negotiates with the local authority and the employers over arrangements for the course.

In choosing who should go on the course, the factory councils give priority to women, illiterates and then to those who didn't complete their basic education.

After a slow start in 1973, whilst teething troubles were dealt with, demand in many areas has outstripped supply. Demand is increasing, particularly, in the south, amongst women and the unemployed, and in those sectors where the certificate counts towards promotion: health and public services.

150 Hours – courses and students

Middle school courses	Students	North	Centre	South
74 – 776	14,237	9,327	2,819	2,091
75 – 2036	38,790	19,665	10,177	8,948
76 – 3696	77,436	33,237	14,889	29,310
77 – 4079	89,977	36,302	16,622	37,053

(Source: Nadio Delai) [15]

The table above shows clearly the dramatic rise in the proportion of courses located in the south, from 14.7 per cent to 41 per cent in 1977. Failure rates are hard to come by. Just over 20 per cent of the 1974 intake dropped out. Presumably, as the course has found its feet, that level has fallen. Problems with shifts, childcare and transport — as in remote Sassari province, Sardinia, where only 26 out of an intake of 100 completed — all take their toll. The number of examination failures is very small. Students who are likely to fail are not entered for the end-of-year exams.

Bologna

I looked at the 150 Hours in detail in two cities, Bologna and Milan, mid-way through the 1977 course, attending classes and speaking to students, teachers and trade union organizers. It is clear from the evidence and my own experience that the 150 Hours shows marked variations from city to city. Although there was no time to visit the south or centre of the country, it is easy to see how different the situation must be in Naples, where 50 per cent of students are housewives and the unemployed, from say, Turin, still the stronghold of the car workers, despite the recession.

In 1977, Bologna provided just under 100 courses, about half of them financed by the city council. The composition of the 2000 student body was mixed: hospital workers, shopworkers, housewives, young unemployed. Engineering workers accounted for only 40 per cent of the students. 'The 150 Hours' — and this was a story I continually heard wherever I went — 'has lost the initial momentum which the engineering worker militants gave it.' The result, argued Elda Guerra, the FLM's 150 Hours organizer in Bologna, was that the courses had lost their earlier links to the workers' struggles.

Daniella, a 150 Hours teacher involved in far-left politics, was disillusioned with the FLM's role (which effectively means the PCI in Bologna). 'It's completely failed here and becoming more and more like the traditional school.' Daniella blamed the rigidity of the FLM, which lays down the syllabus from its local offices, and failure to recognize the changing nature of the student body. At the same time, she observed that the new type of student, who was concerned above all to get the certificate, wasn't too keen on unconventional methods of learning.

'In Bologna, we made the mistake of beginning with an explanation of the balance of payments,' I was told by another teacher, Sonia. Whether this was an example of left-wing political enthusiasm or PCI dogmatism wasn't clear.

Elda Guerra, who admitted that the course was 'in crisis' and that there was a need for a change in the content, identified three key problems for the 150 Hours. First, there was the inexperience of the teachers in a country where adult education has traditionally been neglected and where teacher education is in the doldrums (see p 210).[16] Second, there was the need for 150 Hours to devote more time to basic education, to language and concepts. This is significant: Bologna, with its relatively stable population and high spending on education, could expect fewer problems with illiteracy and semi-literacy than, say, Turin or Naples. The final problem, according to Elda Guerra, was that 150 Hours alone couldn't be expected to cope with all the deficiencies of the school system. Certainly, the spread of attainment, if only in basic study skills, in the average 150 Hours class, presents an immediate challenge to the usually under-trained teachers. (One month of training before the courses begin with in-service seminars interspersed throughout the year is usually the best a teacher fresh to the unfamiliar techniques of adult education can expect from the 150 Hours.) This problem is generally recognized and ways of coping with it are being developed. Extra hours can be devoted to literacy tutorial work or used for 150 Hours preparatory courses.

Since the early heady days of the course, there is a growing realization that the balance between hard graft and advanced contents must change to take account of the difficulties most students encounter on the return to study. In discussion with students after classes at Dante Alighieri School one afternoon, the major criticisms were reserved for the foreign language and the teaching: 'I want to be taken more seriously. There should be a tougher approach by the teachers,' I was told by one of the housewives in the group. Another disagreed: 'It would become like a normal school then.'

There were sixteen in this group, eight of them women:

2 hospital workers
4 housewives
3 engineering workers (2 from the Weber vehicle components factory just down the road which has sent altogether about 50 workers to the 150 Hours)
2 local authority workers
1 shop worker
4 busmen

They arrived just before the end of the day shift and sat down to a two-hour session on English. The foreign language is the least successful component of the course everywhere and nearly everyone would like to see it become an optional subject with the time used for more pressing priorities. In practice, the attempt to teach the language has been all but abandoned. In some areas, there is a token encounter with the basic elements of grammar and vocabulary, but in this class the teacher, Sonia, devoted most of her session to a study of history and culture. She began by reading an article about Northern Ireland. Italians in my experience are rather better informed about world affairs than the British and certainly have a superior grasp of the realities of the Irish situation. The ensuing discussion, in Italian of course, assumed the root cause of the problem to be imperialism, and touched on Zaire and Lebanon and the differences in the handling of these situations by the super-powers.

After a short break, the group went on to a maths class. They were learning how to construct graphs from tables of figures about unemployment in the textile industry. A few, who finished early, assisted the slower ones. Iolanda, one of the housewives, 23 and married, explained how she heard about 150 Hours:

I live in a village near Bologna. Before this I never read the papers or did anything really. I was at home all day long and I suppose I just got depressed. I went to see a neurologist to see if there was anything he could do to help me. He works at a hospital where a lot of people have gone on to the 150 Hours and he said to me, 'Why don't you try it?' I think that I'm more open, more confident since I've been on the course. I talk to my husband more. I'm thinking about starting a course as a typist when this one finishes. I think it's a good idea for women to go out to work.

From her classmates I heard the full range of reasons for enrolling on the 150 Hours:

'I come for the education. Certificates are useless for engineering workers.'
'I've found out some interesting things although I only came for the certificate.'
'I wouldn't come if there wasn't a certificate at the end of it. I couldn't afford to take the time off without being paid for it.'
'I come because I want to be able to help my kid with school.'
'I'm here to get away from the family.' (housewife)
'Before, I used to hear terms on television like "balance of payments" without understanding a word. But I do now.'

Milan

The 150 Hours has a different feel to it in Milan where the original imprimateur of the engineering workers is still perceptible. There is also a strong sense that the scheme has grown real, popular roots in a way that perhaps the efficiency and centralization under FLM control militates against in Bologna. The very strength and autonomy of the shopfloor workers' organizations in Milan is reflected in the firm local roots put down by the 150 Hours in each of the 15 zones for which the unions provide a full-time co-ordinator.

Lilliana Bellinvia is the co-ordinator for the industrial zone of Sempione, north-west of the city centre. Every Friday morning during term, the local commission of teachers, factory delegates and delegates elected from the classes meets to review the course. The job of the local commission is to ensure an adequate take-up of the places available and to iron out difficulties with the schools. Lilliana recognizes all the inherent problems of a scheme like the 150 Hours. New techniques require a very high level of preparation by teachers who find it hard to adapt to the collaborative approach that the course demands. Then, there's the gap between students' needs and a syllabus that evolved from the early years when students were more highly politicized and more united as a body. And, as elsewhere, there is the tension between the use of the 150 Hours for individual as opposed to collective advancement. Which are the problems that we have to learn to live with, and which could be resolved by improvements and changes? Lilliana I found relatively optimistic about progress, especially in the genuinely popular way the 150 Hours was being taken up by the working class. Of course, people are keen to get the certificate, and that's what we want,' she told me, 'and that's fine as long as the course is serving more general ends as well.' Some ex-150 Hours students from local factories had recently launched a kind of mass seminar series on political economy. Some weeks up to 100 people attended the course in a local library. This was an important sign that 150 Hours students were feeling their way towards independent, self-sustaining forms of workers' education. Also useful was their success in persuading the librarians to provide space for this kind of activity. At Seveso, outside Milan, the scene of the notorious chemical plant disaster, 150 Hours students had set up their own seminar — inquiry into chemical hazards to life. Material of direct use in social and industrial activity and researched by 150 Hours students and teachers is widely available.

To see how the scheme worked in Milan I visited a middle school, Via Frigia, on the north-eastern borders of the city, in Sesto San Giovanni. The local commission for this zone is responsible for 12 classes held in 5 schools. In addition there are several literacy classes, aimed at people who aren't yet ready to deal with the middle school course, and an involvement in the various 150 Hours university seminar courses. Here the commission meets fortnightly, spending most of its time on three areas of discussion:

a)   Relations between students and the unions
b)   School–student relations
c)   Syllabus

There are continual problems with awkward head-teachers and there seems to be a constant battle to persuade factory councils to make recruitment a priority. The teachers all remarked on the significant fall-off in support for the courses in the traditionally committed large factories. Magnete Marelli, the biggest employer, had sent only 50 per cent of last year's number of students. They still hadn't solved the drop-out problem which could be traced to two main causes:

uncertainty and confusion in the early stages of the course (in Primavalle, Rome, some preparatory courses have been organized with success); and the difficulties of coping with shift work. As far as course content is concerned, the twin demands in Sesto San Giovanni were for more maths and more rigorous study overall. 'They say that they don't study enough, they learn little and talk a lot, that there's no programme', says the 150 Hours Bulletin for Sesto San Giovanni reporting the most common criticisms of the courses.

The courses, which run from October to the end of May, usually begin with a questionnaire for each student to complete about their school experiences. Apart from providing an early indication of educational attainment, the material gleaned in this way formed the basis for the first part of the Italian classes, a discussion of the relationship between individual school experiences, the school as a system and the labour market. The value of this approach is that it begins from the student's own experience and understanding, working from the particular to the general and establishing that each student, apart from his or her personal history, shares in a class experience. This point cannot be made so easily in Britain where the stigma of failure often blinds students to the deficiencies of the schools. From there, students went on to a review of the period of fascism and the resistance. Incidentally, some classes had refused this fairly standard 150 Hours' approach in favour of a greater concentration on present-day political and economic questions.

The first class I visited was divided into small groups, carrying out a comparison of the way the press had treated an incident. Two teachers were working together, a normal arrangement in this school. After 6 drop-outs, the remaining 19 were heavily dominated by a group of ten engineering workers from Marelli. The other nine included two school porters, two food industry workers, four hospital workers and just one housewife. A firm in Treviso had been prosecuted for vetting the political backgrounds of job applicants, a bad old habit dating back to the fascist era. The students compared the reports in four newspapers — *l'Unita* (PCI), *Corriere della Sera* (centre), and the dailies of the Manifesto (left of the PCI) and Avanguardia Operaia (far left) groups — looking particularly at the selection of facts, the headlines, the attention to fact rather than opinion and the prominence it received.

Next door, a second smaller group, mainly male workers in their 20s and 30s, were reading together an article from *Corriere della Sera* about the government's negotiations with the IMF. In the space of a few hours it's hard to gain any very reliable impressions about how well a course works, although there was a seriousness about the work that the students confirmed in conversation afterwards.

Coming back to school after so many years was confusing and a bit frightening, but after learning about things here, you go back to the factory seeing things differently,

explained an engineering worker. He was emphatic about the need for a still more rigorous approach on the part of the teachers.

The teachers responsible for the first of the classes I visited were unusual in having transferred to the 150 Hours after two years' teaching in a middle school. The Minister of Education has dug in his heels against the notion of transfers in the reverse direction, partly because it would mean giving long-term contracts to 150 Hours teachers and partly, according to the FLM, because the authorities are terrified of a political contamination of the middle schools. The teachers found the work more interesting, the students both more committed and demanding than school children, but conditions were inferior on the 150 Hours, as I could see for myself. Books and materials are scarce and the teachers were denied the use of the staffroom.

Students and teachers: national profiles

150 Hours teachers are noticeably different from middle school teachers and from the adults they teach. There were 4100 in 1977, mainly employed on one-year contracts. Because of the attractions of a fixed contract and better conditions and despite the difficulties of making the transfer, there is a steady filtering off of the most experienced 150 Hours teachers into the middle schools. This is the 150 Hours' loss, as the Minister of Education must know. It also means that the teaching body is very young. Only 3.3 per cent of them are over 35, compared with a massive 67.7 per cent of middle school teachers.[17]

Only 15 per cent of students were women in 1974, but 62 per cent of the teachers were women, usually younger than their students too. Only 13.8 per cent of teachers were over 30 compared with 39 per cent of students. 11 per cent of the teachers had previous experience of working on evening adult courses, but the vast majority had to rely on crash conversion courses.

'A lot of teachers are completely unprepared for the discovery that normal methods are a complete failure with adults,'

observed Enso Mingione, better known in Britain as an urban studies writer but in Italy actively involved in the 150 Hours at two levels. He works for CRP, a body set up by a black sheep of the Pirelli family to carry out research into the Third World which since has developed an interest in the production of 150 Hours teachers' texts. In Messina, he has helped to set up a teachers' training course for the 150 Hours. All in all, the 150 Hours has been a remarkable stimulus to educational activities. The bookshops are full of *dispense*, texts written for students or teachers on standard themes: the Industrial Revolution, the state under fascism, inflation, women's health and work. Then there are the cartoon exegeses: the engineering workers' contract in pictures, an introduction to Lenin, the Communist Manifesto.

150 Hours teachers work an 18-hour week on average. In the Milan schools, they put in 12 hours on 'modular' teaching (three or four sessions in their own subject), plus four hours a week for literacy or experimental work. Then, there would be two hours' preparation time which everyone agreed was nowhere near adequate considering the enormous burden of curriculum development. Finally, 20 hours a month was paid for course development meetings and work, again not nearly enough.

Since 1974, when 78 per cent of students were engineering workers, nearly three-quarters of them in medium and large firms, there has been a steady widening of the recruitment zones in favour of smaller firms, public services, unemployed and housewives (who are three times more likely than males to have left school at the age of 11). By 1977 engineering workers formed only 22 per cent of the 150 Hours student body (13 per cent in the south, 33 per cent in the north), and manual and skilled workers had fallen from 90 per cent of the intake in 1974 to 45 per cent in 1977. Women students have risen over the same four years from 15 per cent of the total to nearly 33 per cent.

Differences between north and south are particularly marked. The unemployed from the largest single category of students in the south. In the north, students tend to come from much larger firms, as you might expect from the structure of Italian industry.

According to Piero Carizzoni, the co-ordinator for the 150 Hours in Vimercate, Milan, 'Students' expectations about personal advancement quickly vanish and what is left is their curiosity about this completely new school.' This may be so, but the CENSIS survey suggests a tendency on the part of teachers to give more emphasis to political and trade union motivations than the students themselves are prepared to attribute.

It is impossible to know to what extent students regard vocational/educational motivations as more respectable than political ones, but the reasoning makes sense if one considers the rise in the number of students who benefit from qualifications. Auxiliary nurses can only enrol for courses leading to the equivalent of SEN/SRN once they have surmounted the obstacle of the middle school certificate.

The university courses

In 1976, almost 5000 workers participated in the 150 Hours seminar courses in universities and high schools. Economics, social science, health and safety at work and the organization of work form the most popular categories of 'monographic' courses. And with the growing presence of women, more and more courses about women's health or women's conditions have been developed.

The university courses have a lot of advantages over the middle school courses. They are autonomous and not subject to the various stifling regulations of the middle school precisely because there is no certificate at the end of the course. Students can usually be expected to be highly committed and more than literate and specializing in a single topic means that the courses can aspire to a degree of seriousness which would be unusual in the middle school courses.[18] On the other hand, although monographic courses often arise out of problems experienced in struggle, there is a danger of academicism and social and political isolation which is rarely felt to the same degree on the more down to earth middle school programme.

Similar starting points have been adopted for the middle school and monographic course. They should pose a challenge to the normal purposes of the university and, at the same time, the workers should establish their right to use the facilities of the university. The university should be seen not as a separate entity but as directly linked to the process of the reproduction of knowledge, ideas and labour power.

Putting these principles into practice has proved more difficult in the case of the university courses. In the first place there is the continuing debate about whether there should be a mass assault on the university or whether, as the union centres have proved, the monographic courses should be viewed as a higher level more suitable for militants and officials with, as the end result, research documents which could be used in the day-to-day struggles. This is fundamentally a political issue with a subordinate educational issue. But the question has long since been settled by virtue of the nature of the 150 Hours itself. There is a limit to the number of workers who can be given paid release at any time and it's also clear that the priority has to be given to the basic education courses. So, ironically, whilst the unions declare themselves against the creation of workers' education ghettos on the edges of the educational institutions, there is a tendency for the monographic courses, because of the kind of students who attend them, to become isolated from the mainstream of the whole 150 Hours experiment.

Another problem arises from the practice of involving university students in as many of the seminars as possible. In principle this is sound. The contact and debate between workers and students can be valuable and mutually instructive, and the presence of workers in a seminar in the university is one way of establishing the workers' right to be there on a permanent basis, to open up the university to the service of the working class. The problem is that the workers tend to lose control over the process and the pace of learning, in a way that doesn't happen in the middle school courses. From here the road to abstraction and irrelevance is wide open, and then workers begin to abandon the courses to the students.

What they learn

'On the courses, we generally use two ways of working. One of them consists in reading books, magazines, extracts. In turn, every student reads a part, and then, after all the words have been understood, explains the passage's meaning, if necessary with the help of other students and the teachers. At the end, there's a discussion to clarify ideas, and finally everyone makes a note of what has been learnt.

Sometimes, instead, everyone individually writes a report. This is then corrected by the teacher with the student.

The other method used in the courses is the work group. The class is divided into groups of four or five persons. Every group has books and magazines available which are read collectively, discussed and then a summary is written of the conclusions. Each group then reports back to the class.'

That explanation comes from the information bulletin distributed in Sesto San Giovanni by the local 150 Hours Commission.

The educational aims of the 150 Hours approach are these:

1   Acquiring the indispensable instruments for knowledge and autonomous expression of one's thought; speaking, writing, reading, calculating, using logical procedures and scientific method.
2   Being able to understand in a critical spirit one's personal experience of life and work within an overall historical frame of reference. [19]

Regardless of other variations, 150 Hours courses seem to have adopted the standard procedures referred to above, which rely on collective clarification of individual experience within a clear historical and conceptual framework. This approach lends itself well to educational inquiry, and it can also work well for a study of industrial organization. My first contact with the 150 Hours came when I was asked by an Italian friend to transmit questionnaires about wages and working conditions to car workers on Merseyside. This was part of an international survey organized by a 150 Hours class in Bologna.

In the teaching of Italian, these techniques mean that the language is treated as a medium of communication, with the rules and patterns of the written and spoken language, isolated and discussed in a structured way, arising out of the needs of the students to improve their command of the language. This is more complex even than it sounds because illiteracy poses an initial problem to a greater extent than in Britain.

At every stage students are encouraged to write up their findings as an aid to clarifying their ideas as well as to gain fluency in expression. The end result of the year's work in history, for example, could be a joint report to which each student contributes one section. There are obvious similarities to projects in Britain and in other countries where workers' education schemes take a class-conscious starting point. Freire stresses the importance of relating literacy work to the social condition and causes of workers' illiteracy. The Second Chance course in Liverpool parallels the use of collective investigation. The importance of autobiography or biography as a valid contribution to a global social analysis can be seen in the growing network of workers–writers' workshops in Britain and the production of workers' autobiographies.

The mathematics and science component of the 150 Hours shows the potential for developing a relevant approach to these areas, in comparison with the mechanical and abstract approach normally followed in the schools. There is also a world of difference between the 150 Hours approach and the schema proposed by Eric Midwinter for Educational Priority Area education in Liverpool. The notion of social relevance is common but whereas Midwinter wants to teach addition and mechanical skills in the environment in which they are actually used — in a supermarket at the checkout — the 150 Hours method is *critical* in intent not merely explanatory. The historical importance of the development of scientific observation (in Bologna they have shown Lilliana Cavani's film of Galileo) or of the development of the steam engine takes its place alongside the discussion in other parts of the course about the causes of the industrial revolution or the necessary burden of value borne by the simple fact and its selection.

'The maths programme should help the worker to a deeper understanding of the reality of the factories and the society as well as leading to a more general discussion about the non-neutrality of science'.[20]

Mathematical method consequently can be seen as part of the panoply of technology utilized by the employer in the search for productivity and profit.

There are two conditions for preventing this approach itself taking a turn towards abstraction, as Lorenzo Dore explains *(Fabbrica e Scuola: le 150 Ore)*:

to involve the workers, the point of departure of the research should constitute an objective and subjective contradiction in the eyes of the students.

In other words, there has to be a problematic, understood personally and as a general political or social problem:

to develop independent analysis and judgement . . . the research should start from the terrain on which the workers can exercise effective control at every stage of development. . . .

I have already mentioned the publishing outgrowths of 150 Hours, but the publication of students' research work [21] has a wider significance that shouldn't be missed. In political and cultural terms, students are laying hold of the conceptual tools, hitherto wielded exclusively by the intellectuals, by which society can first be grasped in its entirety and then changed. They are also subverting the monopoly over the printed word enjoyed by the bourgeoisie and the critical intelligentsia. These are difficult ideas, even in the birthplace of Gramsci, and not every 150 Hours student or teacher will see their importance. Those who commend the 150 Hours for its immediate value, may not necessarily grasp the long-term significance of these changes in the *cultural* division of labour. But these changes seem to me crucial if the working class is one day to abolish wage labour.

The political impact of the 150 Hours

In April 1977 1500 people took to the streets in Milan to protest against the obstructionist tactics of the LEA towards the 150 Hours. When people demonstrate for the right to learn, then it is clear that education begins to mean something for them. How effective has the 150 Hours been in meeting the early aspirations for it? What is its educational and political value today in Italy? I think that the impact of the scheme can best be assessed under two headings:
a)   Italian education
b)   The working-class movement

Italian education

'The 150 Hours courses have overturned the methods and materials used by the schools and, not without a lot of hard slog, created a new way of seeing culture and knowledge.'

That is Paola Piva's assessment. She goes on:

'They've begun to break down the barriers between those who work and those who go to school, and between the teachers and the taught.'[22]

A start has been made in all these directions but it's doubtful how far the 150 Hours has gone beyond an initial impact on attitudes towards real change. This, of course, is a very tall order, yet it was a central aim of the workers' organization after the 'hot autumn'. After all, the unions launched the scheme in an attempt to take control of the schools rather than to revitalize adult education. Superficially, the gap between the working class and the schools has narrowed, in that parents and trade unionists are now represented on the schools councils created by Malfatti. Adults who have been through the 150 Hours courses, and the total number to date is over one-third of a million, are probably better informed about the purposes of the schools, the way they work and what's wrong with them.
    There is a case, made by the far left, that the most effective action taken to change the schools has occurred from outside them. Lotta

Continua, until recently the largest of the extra-parliamentary organizations, warned that the 150 Hours might be used to reduce the risks of confrontation, defusing the challenge to the schools by putting the workers in the classroom. [23] It seems more likely that the challenge to the schools failed to come about because the workers' movement lost overall momentum from 1975 onwards.

Nobody I spoke to in Italy felt that the innovations of the 150 Hours had had more than a glancing impact on the normal school, although the inadequacies of the present system had probably been more clearly highlighted by the public knowledge that so few people left school with a qualification or basic education. While dubious about the impact of the 150 Hours on the middle school, Enzo Mingione told me that there were signs that the 150 Hours had stimulated an appetite for educational reform in Italy.

It's at this level that I think that the major impact has been. The 150 Hours has awakened appetites for progressive methods and content in education. Ironically, many of the ideas for reform originate in the student challenge to the universities since 1967 but have made little headway there. Along with a tremendous outpouring of course books and student inquiries the 150 Hours has firmly established a democratic, participatory notion of education in a country where hitherto Montessori had shone like a beacon in the wilderness.

But that is a long way from the workers' school that the Italian left once talked about.

Within adult education, the 150 Hours has marked a complete break with the past, perhaps more so in Italy than it might have done in, say, Britain. Franco Malfatti, whilst Minister of Education, had gone out of his way to promote the CRACIS courses at the expense of the new scheme, but the result has been that CRACIS has had to reform in order to pose as a serious rival. Spending on the 150 Hours is still inadequate, especially on the support services, but the commitment to adult education this spending represents is on a quite different scale to what went before.

The working-class movement

Throughout Europe, the struggles of 1968 and after pinpointed the class basis of knowledge and culture. The 150 Hours has gone further in providing an organized framework within which the working class might develop its own ideas.

On the other hand, there is a great deal of debate about whether the

150 Hours is a ghetto, isolated from the real struggles of the working class. Much of the criticism has been directed against the university courses, which could veer towards academicism and elitism.

The truth of the matter is that the 150 Hours is at the mercy of the state of organization and morale of the working class. The declining centrality of the industrial working class, particularly the engineering workers, has struck a hard blow at the 150 Hours which certainly felt the weakening of its early supporters in the north. On the other hand, the growth of the movements of women, youth and the unemployed have given a new impetus to the 150 Hours in some areas. This is the answer to those who fear that the hunger for certified advancement has consumed the scheme's political commitment. Of course there are areas where the 150 Hours has settled down to a hum-drum existence, light years away from the original crusading spirit. At the same time, there are dozens of examples of the way that 150 Hours students have used the course to fight industrial pollution or discrimination against working women.

'Best results have occurred where the programmes have taken account of what's going on in the workers' movement and the world of work and have developed teaching which always relates to this'.[24]

In this respect, the 150 Hours differs from nearly every existing state adult education scheme. By definition it is aimed at the working class, and by practice it relates to the issues and experiences which its students define as of paramount importance. Consequently, it has clearly begun to establish genuinely popular roots for adult education. Obviously, it helps that workers are paid to study and that there is the incentive of a qualification at the end of it, but this isn't its central feature. The 150 Hours has demonstrated that the Italian working class is serious about an education which it controls and which reflects its interests as a class.

11   Adult education for a change

Jane L. Thompson, Lecturer in Community Education, University of Southampton

There will be many readers who feel by now that we have been unduly critical about the organization and practice of adult education as we have depicted it in this collection of articles. Certainly we would not wish to imply that all of the many individuals who, in either a voluntary, part-time or full-time capacity, give vast amounts of energy and enthusiasm to the development and expansion of adult educational opportunities, are all malevolent or mischievous in their intentions. The real situation is, of course, quite the reverse and we recognize that there are countless numbers of people who in a variety of ways are doing valuable work.

But in being critical about some of the conventional assumptions and familiar practices of adult education, we have been forced to recognize the contradictions between the intentions of many well-meaning adult educators and the functions their commitments serve in the essentially conservative contexts in which they work. It is not the teachers themselves in the main, but the institutions they subscribe to, the ideologies they inherit and the types of provision they are expected to make available which are the aspects of adult education we have set out to question in this book.

Theory and practice

A number of contributors have commented upon the absence of much critical theory in adult education, though as Nell Keddie hints in Chapter 2, an undue reliance on behaviourist and psychological prescriptions about teaching and learning have had a certain pragmatic appeal to those engaged in training and research. And despite the fact that writers like Lawson and Patterson [1] have begun discussions about the nature of knowledge from a philosophical perspective, the status of knowledge itself, the way in which it is selected and made available to students, the reasoning which underpins a differentiated curriculum and the assumptions which constitute the 'hidden curriculum of the great tradition' are all aspects of the 'content' of adult education which are rarely treated as a problem. In other words, at least one of the most important recent debates in the sociology of education, about the relationship between knowledge and social control, has been largely ignored by those involved in adult education.

There are a number of reasons to explain why adult educators seem to underestimate the value of theory. Most of them are to do with the ramifications of being 'practical people' who judge credibility in terms of action. The 'numbers game' is a significant discipline. And certainly there is a characteristic about adult education which E. P. Thompson has often referred to as one of the 'peculiarities of the English' — a noticeable resistance to theoretical discussion and an undue responsiveness to empiricism. In our discussions with adult educators, consequently, we have sensed a preference for descriptive rather than analytical accounts of practice. Much of the continuing acrimony generated by notions of community education, for example, is, as Colin Fletcher points out [2], only rarely grounded in theoretical analysis. A weakness which is particularly unfortunate at a time when 'community education is all too rapidly becoming a type of education appropriate to a type of people', as distinct from 'derived from a theory' and so a 'full educational perspective'. [3]

The perspectives outlined in Part One of this collection are, of course, by no means comprehensive, and in arguing for the examination of adult education within a sociological and political frame of reference, we are aware that we are merely initiating a debate which needs considerably more development. It would be more than arrogant to suggest that the introduction of critical theory into the analysis of adult education constitutes a 'new paradigm' in the sense that Thomas Kuhn uses the term, but in identifying the features which make for a 'new look' at 'old ideas' his recognition that they must be 'sufficiently unprecedented to attract an enduring group of adherents away from competing modes' and 'sufficiently open-ended to leave all sorts of problems for the redefined group of practitioners to resolve'[4] seems to reflect some of the spirit and intention of our collective enterprise.

But neither has it been our intention to be critical in a destructive sense. All of those who have contributed here are deeply involved in the practice of adult education and are committed to changing rather than destroying it. Tom Lovett, David Evans and Martin Yarnit, for example, all give illustrations of what is being done and what might be done more enthusiastically to promote adult educational opportunities for working-class men and women. [5] And clearly there are lessons to be learned from experiences in other countries. It is not merely a matter of changing the location of classes or improving the methods of publicity or tinkering around with a variety of cosmetic innovations designed to change the image of adult education. Perhaps the most important lesson from the contributions presented here by Lovett, Evans and Yarnit is the recognition that their practice is based upon a different kind of philosophy about adult education, and a different analysis of society than the kind which provides, almost without question, the remarkable uniformity of provision identified by Wiltshire and Mee. [6]

The important insight discussed by Nell Keddie [7] that, despite claims to the contrary, adult education is *very like* initial schooling, and that if bad experiences at school are held to be largely responsible for the non-participation of working-class adults in adult education, then it might well be the case that the correspondence between adult education and schooling also explains its appeal to middle-class students. If, as she says, this is the case, then we must consider whether adult education is pursuing practices which hinder rather than help its claim to be a resource for the whole community. If adult education is to 'radicalize the nature of its enterprise' it must be prepared to 'examine its practice critically'. To recognize, in fact, that 'the problems lie within the nature of the provision which adult education makes and not in those who do not avail themselves of the resources it offers'. [8]

Sallie Westwood and Geoff Brown make a similar plea — not in the spirit of negative criticism — but in full recognition of the fact that if adult education is to become genuinely democratic and regain some of its lost radicalism, adult educators must be prepared seriously to re-examine what they do in the context of the stratified society in which they operate. [9]

The way forward

And what of the next ten years? As so often in the past, the future of adult education is still one of uncertainty.

Despite the expansion of provision in the early and mid 1970s, the impact of expenditure cuts in more recent years has found adult education to be an easy target. The part-time teachers who staff so many of the local authority classes are rarely unionized and their students, spread about the city in other people's buildings, lack the tradition of association and allegiance which could be united to defend their interests. And the ideology which has presented local authority provision as a non-political and recreational activity is not well placed to think and act politically when the circumstances demand it. And yet simultaneously it seems, an expanded adult education service is rapidly becoming regarded — in words, if not in deeds — as the obvious corrective to the anticipated problems brought about by unemployment and the side effects of technological change. And all this at the same time as notions of continuing education, lifelong learning and paid educational leave are gaining momentum.

It should be clear, however, from the views expressed in this book that whatever the outcome, 'more of the same' is not, in our opinion, the way forward. Though as far as we can see, recent discussion documents about, for example, continuing education, [10] and basic education [11] give little hope that any major change in the institutional provision of post-school education is envisaged by their authors. Similarly the rapid expansion of training and professionalization in recent years seems to be more about entrenchment than development. The proliferation of courses reflects, in my view, more the concern of those responsible to strengthen and confirm their professional identity, and to ward off the challenge from other institutions, than any recognition of the need to re-examine their behaviour in any kind of radical way.

As Nell Keddie has observed, as institutional bureaucracies develop in adult education, in response to expansion and differentiation of expertise, the idea that the adult education organizer is an entrepreneurial jack-of-all-trades has given way to the more sober concept of management in adult education, and the idea that what the organizer needs is a multiplicity of managerial skills. Likewise the long-defended notion of the value of the amateur teacher who imparts or shares a skill is rapidly losing ground in the face of the conviction that the teaching of adults requires an expertise which cannot be left to chance.' [12] In practice, of course, this means providing new recruits with the skills, knowledge and professional ideology which those who are the decision makers and opinion leaders in the profession consider to be appropriate. If, as we have argued earlier, the prevailing orthodoxy is empiricist rather than analytical, liberal rather than radical, frequently responsible for practices which demonstrate a middle-class bias, and which constitute a hindrance to expansion, then the confirmation of these institutional and professional characteristics in the socialization and training of new recruits may improve institutional definitions of 'good practice' but will constitute little, if any, change in the definition of adult education or the redistribution of educational resources to the majority of adults who currently find little meaning in what we have to offer.

Clearly there are examples of instances in which some of those involved in adult education have been able to challenge the prevailing view of the world and involve, with real commitment, working men and women, who have in turn been able to use education as a cultural and political tool. But the much more general will to restructure the curriculum, to challenge the conventional definitions and distribution of knowledge and to regard education as an important part of the struggle for socialism are still the tasks which need to be taken up with intelligence and vigour by all those who genuinely want adult education to be a radical force in an unequal society. And to provide, for all those who have had least in the past, adult education for a change.

Notes and references

Foreword

1 N. Harris, *Beliefs in Society* (Pelican, 1971), p. 27.
2 P. Wilby, 'Education and Equality' (*New Statesman*, 16 September 1977).
3 Within the politics of educational practice this concept has been eloquently described by Paulo Freire in *Pedagogy of the Oppressed* (Penguin, 1972), and *Cultural Action for Freedom* (Penguin, 1972).
4 D. Harvey, *Social Justice and the City* (Edward Arnold, 1973), p. 10.
5 ibid., p. 15.
6 ibid., pp. 17–18.
7 ibid., p. 18.
8 This is part of a full report which, it is hoped, will be published in some form during 1980.
9 R. H. Tawney, 'Adult education in the history of the nation', paper read at the Fifth Annual Conference of the British Institute of Adult Education (1926), p. 20.
10 ibid., p. 22.
11 This quotation is taken from Brian Simon, *The Two Nations and the Educational Structure 1780–1870* (Lawrence and Wishart, 1974). Simon's account of adult education may be compared with Thomas Kelly's 'official' *History of Adult Education* to indicate the limited forms of analysis which result from scholarship within the field of adult education alone.
12 See Cynthia Cockburn, *The Local State* (Pluto, 1977), for a useful presentation of the community movement in this light.

Introduction

1   See, for example, the arguments expressed in E. Hutchinson and
    E. Hutchinson, *Learning Later* (Routledge & Kegan Paul, 1978);
    Michael Newman, *The Poor Cousin: A Study of Adult Education*
    (Allen & Unwin, 1979); and Jennifer Rogers and Brian Groom-
    bridge, *Right to Learn* (Arrow, 1976).
2   Department of Education and Science, *Basic Education
    Statistics for the UK, January 1978* (HMSO, 1978).
3   Hutchinson and Hutchinson, *Learning Later.*
4   Basil Bernstein, 'On the classification and framing of educa-
    tional knowledge', in M. F. D. Young (ed.), *Knowledge and
    Control* (Collier-Macmillan, 1971).
5   See, for example, S. Bowles and H. Gintis, *Schooling in
    Capitalist America* (Routledge & Kegan Paul, 1976); Dale,
    Esland and Macdonald (eds.), *Schooling and Capitalism: A
    Sociological Reader* (Routledge & Kegan Paul, 1976); and Geoff
    Whitty and M. F. D. Young (eds.), *Society, State and Schooling*
    (Falmer Press, 1977).
6   Bowles and Gintis, *Schooling and Capitalism.*
7   Hutchinson and Hutchinson, *Learning Later.*
8   See, for example, 'Adequacy of provision', *Adult Education*,
    vol. 42, no. 6 (1970); Tom Lovett, *Adult Education, Community
    Development and the Working Class* (Ward Lock, 1975); and P.
    Fordham, G. Poulton and L. Randle, *Learning Networks in
    Adult Education* (Routledge & Kegan Paul, 1979).
9   Raymond Williams, in *The Long Revolution* (Penguin, 1961),
    distinguishes four sets of educational philosophies or ideologies
    which rationalize different emphases in the selection of the
    content of curricula, and relates these to the social positions of
    those who hold them. The liberal position he associates with the
    nineteenth-century aristocracy and gentry.
10 K. H. Lawson, 'Community education: a critical assessment',
    Adult Education, vol. 50, no. 1.
11 *Adult Education: A Plan for Development* (Russell Report)
    (HMSO, 1973).
12 See Chapters 5 and 6 in this book.
13 Russell Report.
14 See Bernstein, 'On the classification and framing of educational
    knowledge', in Young, *Knowledge and Control.*
15 See the Russell Report and Graham Mee and Harold Wiltshire.

Structure and Performance in Adult Education (Longman, 1978).
16 Michael Newman claims in *The Poor Cousin* that the fear of beer and bingo was a popular myth among his staff which had to be overcome when innovating at the Addison Institute.
17 Russell Report, par. 284.
18 Rogers and Groombridge, *Right to Learn.*
19 Fordham, Poulton and Randle, *Learning Networks in Adult Education.*
20 ibid., p. 21.
21 Jane Thompson, Chapter 4 in this book.
22 Lawson, *Community Education.*
23 Colin Kirkwood, 'Adult education and the concept of community', *Adult Education*, vol. 51, no. 3.
24 Bernstein, 'On the classification and framing of educational knowledge', *Knowledge and Control.*
25 Paulo Freire, *Pedagogy of the Oppressed* (Penguin, 1972).
26 Q. Hoare and G. Nowell Smith (eds. and trans.), *The Prison Notebooks of Antonio Gramsci.*
27 Bernard Jennings, 'Revolting students: the Ruskin College dispute, 1908–9', *Studies in Adult Education*, vol. 9, no. 1 (1977).
28 In *Studies in Adult Education*, vol. 8, no. 1 (1976).
29 Jackson, Yarnit and Evans, 'Adult education and the partnership' (Unpublished resource proposal, 1978).

1 Adult education and the sociology of education

1 National Institute of Adult Education, *Adult Education: Adequacy of Provision* (NIAE, 1970)
2 P. Fordham, G. Poulton and L. Randle, *Learning Networks in Adult Education* (Routledge & Kegan Paul, 1979), p. 20.
3 V. Houghton, 'Recurrent education', in V. Houghton and K. Richardson (eds.), *Recurrent Education* (Ward Lock, 1974), p. 8.
4 cf. J. Lowe, *Adult Education in England and Wales: A Critical Survey* (Michael Joseph, 1970), pp. 32-41.
5 Scottish Education Department, *Adult Education: The Challenge of Change* (Alexander Report) (HMSO, 1975), p. 19.
6 Lowe, *Adult Education in England and Wales*, p. 286.
7 M. Newman, *The Poor Cousin: A Study of Adult Education*, (Allen & Unwin, 1979), p. 26.
8 A. H. Halsey, J. Floud, and A. C. Anderson, *Education, Economy and Society* (New York: The Free Press, 1961).

9 Alexander Report, and the ACACE discussion paper, *Towards Continuing Education* (1979). See, for example, p. 6.

10 Floud, Halsey and Anderson, *Education, Economy and Society*, p. 5.

11 J. Floud, A. H. Halsey and F. M. Martin, *Social Class and Educational Opportunity* (Heinemann, 1956). For a recent review of relevant literature, see W. Tyler, *The Sociology of Educational Inequality* (Methuen, 1977).

12 R. Collins, 'Functional and Conflict Theories of Educational Stratification' reprinted in B. R. Cousin (ed.), *Education: Structure and Society* (Penguin, 1972), pp. 175–99; I. Berg, *The Great Training Robbery* (Penguin, 1974).

13 Collins, 'Functional and conflict theories', p. 187.

14 L. Althusser, 'Ideology and Ideological State Apparatuses: Notes towards an investigation', in L. Althusser, *Lenin and Philosophy and Other Essays* (New Left Books, 1971), pp. 123–73.

15 Althusser, 'Ideology and Ideological State Apparatuses'; S. Bowles and H. Gintis, *Schooling in Capitalist America* (Routledge & Kegan Paul, 1970). P. Bourdieu and J. Passeron, *Reproduction in Education, Society and Culture* (Sage, 1977).

16 R. Deem, *Women and Schooling* (Routledge & Kegan Paul, 1978). A-M Wolpe, 'Education and the Sexual Division of Labour' in A. Kuhn and A-M. Wolpe (eds.), *Feminism and Materialism: Women and Modes of Production* (Routledge & Kegan Paul, 1978), pp. 290–328.

17 Althusser, 'Ideology and ISAs', p. 127.

18 Bowles and Gintis, *Schooling in Capitalist America*, p. 48.

19 ibid.

20 It is clear, however, that education can offer personal fulfilment and occupational mobility to *the individual*.

21 Althusser, 'Ideology and ISAs'; Bowles and Gintis, *Schooling in Capitalist America*.

22 Bowles and Gintis, *Schooling in Capitalist America*.

23 Althusser, 'Ideology and ISAs'.

24 cf. N. McIntosh *et al., A Degree of Difference* (SRHE, 1976). R. Woolfe, 'Education, inequality and the role of the Open University', *Adult Education*, vol. 50, no. 2. (1977), pp. 77–83. Woolfe notes in conclusion, 'the the Open University can be seen to reflect many of the inequalities which exist in society. In this way it functions in a way which is similar to many other educational institutions' (p. 82).

25 Bourdieu's work is most accessible to the English reader through a series of articles that are referenced below.

26 P. Bourdieu, 'Cultural reproduction and social reproduction' in R. Brown (ed)., *Knowledge, Education and Cultural Change* (Tavistock, 1974), pp. 71–112.

27 P. Bourdieu, 'Intellextual Field and Creative Project' in M. F. D. Young (ed.), *Knowledge and Control: New Directions for the Sociology of Education* (Collier-Macmillan, 1971), pp. 161–88.

28 P. Bourdieu (trans. J. C. Whitehouse), 'The School as a Conservative Force: Scholastic and Cultural Inequalities' in J. Eggleston (ed.), *Contemporary Research in the Sociology of Education* (Methuen, 1974), pp. 32–46, p. 37.

29 ibid., p. 38.

30 G. Murdock, 'Class Stratification and Cultural Consumption: Some Motifs in the Work of Pierre Bourdieu' in M. A. Smith (ed.), *Leisure and Urban Society* (University of Salford, The Leisure Studies Association: 1977), p. 3.

31 Bourdieu, 'Cultural Reproduction and Social Reproduction'.

32 P. Freire, *Pedagogy of the Oppressed* (Penguin, 1972).

33 G. Mee and H. Wiltshire, *Structure and Performance in Adult Education* (Longman, 1978), p. 110.

34 A review of Gramsci's work is presented in C. Boggs, *Gramsci's Marxism* (Pluto Press, 1978).

35 R. Williams, *Marxism and Literature* (Oxford University Press, 1978), p. 108.

36 Althusser, 'Ideology and ISAs'.

37 Q. Hoare and G. Nowell Smith (eds.), *Selection from the Prison Notebooks of Antonio Gramsci* (Lawrence & Wishart, 1971), pp. 3–43.

38 cf. Boggs, *Gramsci's Marxism*, pp. 85–100.

39 Newman, *The Poor Cousin*, p. 214.

40 T. Schuller and J. Bengtsson, 'A strategy for equality: recurrent education and industrial democracy', in J. Karabel and A. H. Halsey (eds.), *Power and Ideology in Education* (Oxford University Press, 1977), pp. 635–47.

41 R. Miliband, *The State in Capitalist Society* (Weidenfeld and Nicolson, 1969), p. 19.

2 Adult education: an ideology of individualism

1   References to adult education tend to raise definitional problems. This paper is primarily concerned with the provision of adult education by LEAs, extra-mural departments, the WEA and other voluntary agencies, where the ideology of individualism is least constrained by the ethos of an occupational training or the requirements of formal certification.

2   See David Ingleby, 'The psychology of child psychology', in *The Integration of a Child into a Social World*, ed. M. P. M. Richards (Cambridge University Press, 1974) and reprinted in *Schooling and Capitalism: A Sociological Reader* (ed.) Dale *et al.*, (Routledge & Kegan Paul in association with The Open University Press, 1976).

3   See Nigel Harris, *Beliefs in Society: the Problems of Ideology* (Watts, 1968). This formulation of ideology is quoted by Michael Apple in 'Commonsense categories and curriculum thought', in Dale *et al.*, ibid.

4   See Bucher and Strauss, 'Professions in process', *American Journal of Sociology*, vol. LXVI (January 1961). 'It is characteristic of the growth of specialities that early in their development they carve out for themselves and proclaim unique missions. They issue a statement of the contribution that the speciality, and it alone, can make in a total scheme of values and, frequently, with an argument to show why it is peculiarly fitted for this task.'

5   See Nell Keddie, 'Classroom knowledge' in Michael F. D. Young (ed.), *Knowledge and Control* (Collier-Macmillan, 1971), an empirical study of teachers' classroom practices which suggests the difficulties in interpreting teachers' ideologies as indicators of their practice.

6   Ettore Gelpi, *A Future for Lifelong Education*, vol. 1, translated, Ralph Ruddock, Michael Pilsworth *et al.* (Manchester Monographs 13, 1979).

7   Sally Westwood, Chapter 1 in this book and Colin Griffin, 'Curriculum analysis of lifelong education' (Unpublished article, 1979).

8   See 'Systems of education and systems of thought', *International Social Science Journal*, vol. XIX (3 November 1967). This paper is also published in Young (ed.), *Knowledge and Control*.

9 R. K. W. Paterson, *Values, Education and the Adult* (Routledge, 1979).

10 A significant difference between schooling and adult education is, of course, that adult educators are not expected to be responsible for the behaviour of their students or to exercise any overt control over it.

11 Graham Mee and Harold Wiltshire, *Structure and Performance in Adult Education* (Longman, 1978).

12 Colin Griffin, *Recurrent and Continuing Education – a Curriculum Model Approach* (Discussion Paper 3, Association for Recurrent Education, December 1978).

13 Ronald King, *All Things Bright and Beautiful: A Sociological Study of Infants' Classrooms* (John Wiley and Sons, 1978).

14 See, for example, Rosabeth Moss Kanter, 'The organization child: experience management in a nursery school', *Sociology of Education*, no. 45(2), (1972) which is reprinted in Dale *et al.*

15 Most adult educators have stories of difficult or troublesome students: these students tend to be the exception to the rule. Garfinkel suggests that the commonsense world of everyday life is taken for granted so that the problem is to make the norms that govern social interaction in any situation visible. One method for doing this is to observe violations of social intercourse — those actions which call forth surprise, disapproval, embarrassment, etc. Accounts of troublesome students would indicate what expectations govern 'normal' student behaviour. See Harold Garfinkel, *Studies in Ethnomethodology* (Prentice-Hall, 1967), esp. chapter 2.

16 The degree to which initial schooling is held responsible for unfavourable attitudes to adult education is more readily expressed verbally than in print and often extends to a distrust of the fitness of school teachers to teach adults. The Russell Report, however, speaks of a population 'whose attitudes are indifferent or hostile to education; . . .the main impetus must come from involving that public in active experience of learning, so that they discover, or re-discover, the nature of education. They must see it as something relevant to their chosen aspirations and the quality of their lives, and not as the mysteriously testing and rejecting process that their own schooldays seem to be.' (paragraph 46, 2). Willis, in his study *Learning to Labour* argues that to the 'counter-school culture' the testing and

rejecting process is well understood.

17   Mee and Wiltshire, *Structure and Performance in Adult Education.*

18   For an overview of the research see Olive Banks, *The Sociology of Education* (Batsford, 1968).

19   Mee and Wiltshire, *Structure and Performance in Adult Education,* p. 41, suggest that adult educators are dealing with several publics distinguishable by reference to their allegiance to certain subjects or subject groupings. In terms of the analysis I am suggesting it would be important to investigate whether or not these allegiances support differentiated lifestyles in wider social contexts.

20   For an analysis of this view of women's traditional role in psychological terms, see Jean Baker Miller, *Toward a New Psychology of Women* (Penguin, 1976).

21   Bridget Barber (personal communication), suggests that adult education supports women's diffuse domestic management role both because a class can be fitted into the way their time has to be managed in terms of a series of short-term tasks and because skills classes enhance their expertise as managers of the home. She also suggests that the greater number of women in their thirties and early forties in more academic classes may be related to an interest deriving from their children's secondary school work which both stimulates their interest in study and challenges them to do as well as their children. While this hypothesis has yet to be investigated it suggests that some women's use of adult education may be related to their changing role within the family life cycle in quite specific ways.

22   'Second chance' courses may, of course, open up new roles for women through enabling them to gain access to formal courses of study and training.

23   It is not clear that in many classes, students are invited to exercise even this amount of choice.

24   Jones and Charnley, 'Adult literacy: a study of its impact' (NIAE, no date).

25   Jane L. Thompson, Chapter 4 in this book.

26   See, for example, *Let Loose* (Write First Time, Acacia Road Centre, Acacia Road, Bedford, 1978) and Jane Mace, *Working With Words: Literacy Beyond School* (Chameleon Books, 1979).

27   *A Strategy for the Basic Education of Adults* (published and dis-

tributed by the Advisory Council for Adult and Continuing Education).

28 It is significant that academic pupils receive very little moral and social education of this kind and that there are few demands that their curriculum be made more relevant. They may be presumed not to need social education because their place in the academic stream is witness to their commitment to the values the school seeks to transmit.

29 Ingleby, 'The psychology of child psychology'.

30 Paul Willis, *Learning to Labour: How Working Class Kids Get Working Class Jobs* (Saxon House, 1978).

3   The theory of community education and its relation to adult education

1   A. Stock, Review article, *Adult Education*, vol. 50, no. 1 (1977), and this stance may represent a change in perspective; cf. A. Stock, *Adult Education*, vol. 49, no. 2 (1976). 'Community is essentially a dynamic concept; and recent evidence from follow-up studies suggests that some established communities, formerly rich in interactive networks (and therefore rich in options, stimulus and support) are becoming more limited, bland, stereotyped. Which suggests that *development* and *action* may be even more appropriate than provision when we think in community terms.'

2   D. Selby, 'Ideas for action', NWAE Annual Conference (8 June 1978), *Adult Education*, vol. 51, no. 4, 245–47.

3   A. N. Whitehead, *Science in the Modern World* (Mentor, 1925), pp. 142–55. A. L. Stinchcombe, *Constructing Social Theories*, (Harcourt, Brace and World, 1968) pp. 15–17. J. Galtung, *Theory and Methods of Social Research* (Allen and Unwin, 1967), 451–4, e.g.: 'A theory is an integrated set of relationships with a certain level of validity.' D. Willer, *Scientific Sociology*, (Prentice-Hall, 1967) p. 9 or 'Properly Speaking, theoretical laws (or formulae) cannot be considered true or false . . . they are simply more or less useful in generating empirical laws.' M. Lessnov, *The Structure of Social Science* (Allen and Unwin, 1974).

4   'Since one of Adult Education's goals has always been to help

students to develop their creative capacities and to participate more effectively in a democratic society many adult educators should find themselves sympathetic towards work with such groups.' K. Jackson, 'Adult education and community development', *Studies in Adult Education*, vol. 2, no. 2 (1970), p. 162.

5 T. R. Young, *Red Feather Dictionary of Socialist Sociology* (Colorado: Red Feather Institute, 1978), p. 27.

6 D. Holly, 'Education and the social relations of a capitalist society' in M. E. D. Young and G. Whitty, *Society, State and Schooling* (Falmer Press, 1977), p. 172.

7 Manifest and latent functions are said by R. K. Merton in *Social Theory and Social Structure* (Free Press, 1952), to be part of a theoretical analysis. The practical aspect of this approach is adeptly used in 'Relations between agent and employer are always two-edged. Contradictions start to emerge when the agent begins to regard himself as his own employer, and when he is in a position to do so. At that moment he becomes a competitor.' H. M. Enzenberger, *Raids and Reconstructions: Essays in Politics, Crime and Culture* (Pluto Press, 1976), pp. 128–29. The contradiction of functions is cogently expressed as a dilemma by Head: 'It is a dilemma of community education that, while individuals can go away and put words into practice, group action leading to change (as distinct from speech and thought leading to change) is too involved, too ambiguous, too controversial to be part of a statutory educational programme. This is unfortunate, since so much learning is by doing and learning about society by social doing.' D. Head, 'Education at the bottom', *Studies in Adult Education*, vol. 9, no. 2 (1977), p. 138.

8 'To say that someone is an adult is to say that he is entitled, for example, to a wide ranging freedom of life style and to a full participation in the taking of social decisions; and it is also to say that he is obliged, among other things, to be mindful of his own deepest interests and to carry a full share of the burdens involved in conducting society and transmitting its benefits. His adulthood consists in his full enjoyment of such rights and his full subjection to such responsibilities.' R. W. K. Paterson, *Values, Education and the Adult* (Routledge & Kegan Paul, 1979), p. 13.

9 ibid., p. 42.

10 G. H, Mead, *Mind, Self and Society* (University of Chicago

Press, 1934), pp. 186–91.

11 ibid., p. 171.

12 'One of the defining characteristics of critical social theory is precisely its attempt to overcome the empirical/normative split and the separation of theory from practice that follows from it. At the level of philosophical foundations, this requires a reconceptualisation of the notion of theoretical truth and the establishment of an intimate relation between truth and freedom.' T. McCarthy, Introduction, (X) to J. Habermas, *Legitimation Crisis* (Heinemann, 1976).

13 K. Jackson, 'Some fallacies in community education and their consequences in working class areas', in C. Fletcher (ed.), *Community Education '77* (Department of Adult Education, University of Nottingham); reprinted in C. Fletcher and N. Thompson, *Issues in Community Education* (Falmer Press, 1979).

14 J. P. Satre has expressed the decision upon authentic engagement as lying between 'gauchist intellectuel' (left intellectual) and 'intellectuel gauchist' (intellectual leftist).

15 'When capital and revenue resources for the development of adult education and youth work are scarce (and this is the rule rather than the exception), the Community College concept offers a practical and economic way in which Local Education Authorities can make progress. But a "college" is more than a building: a nucleus of full-time professional staff is absolutely necessary if the quality of work done is to be raised beyond what is possible where this vital cultural, recreational and leisure service is dependent wholly on part-time service.' 'A Community Tutor — Those members of staff in community colleges who spend between 60 per cent and 80 per cent of their time organizing adult education, youthwork and community education and 40 per cent to 20 per cent of their time teaching in the secondary school — generally the school leavers.' A. N. Fairbairn, *The Leicestershire Community Colleges and Centres*, Nottingham Working Papers in the Education of Adults, no. 1, Department of Adult Education, p. 104.

16 'The adoption of a community education approach involves all-round changes in emphasis: institutions through which learning takes place should change in accordance with people's wishes, and needs and aspirations; and there has to be a broadening of the range of subjects taught, and of teaching methods; much more flexibility in timing and a proliferation of the sites where

educational activities are arranged. . . . The larger aim should be to encourage people to understand and participate in the necessary decision-making about the use of adult education and other community resources. . . .' Anders *et al., Community Education Seminar Report*, University of London, Goldsmith's College, 1978.

In association with British Association of Settlements and Social Action Centres, pp. 22–23.

17 cf. '. . .for the unemployed, which includes most of the married women in all social classes, Community Centres for Education would be . . . effective. A possible model for this might be the Community Law Centres which have lately developed in many urban areas.' E. Hopper and M. Osborn, *Adult Students: Education, Selection and Social Control* (Francis Pinter, n.d.), p. 155.

18 H. Calloway, Review, *Adult Education*, vol. 51, no. 4 (1978), p. 257.

19 ibid., p. 161.

20 These terms and their use in this way form a cornerstone in management thinking, T. Burns and T. Stalker, *The Management of Innovation*, (Tavistock, 1962).

21 T. Lovett, 'Community adult education', *Studies in Adult Education*, vol. 3, no. 1, (1971), p. 13. In a characteristic burst of fine phrases Tawney wrote: 'Education is not put on like varnish. It springs like a plant from the soil, and the fragrance of the earth is upon it.' R. H. Tawney, *The Radical Tradition* (Penguin, 1966), p. 81.

22 K. H. Lawson, 'Community education, a critical assessment', *Adult Education*, vol. 50, no. 1, (1977), pp. 6–13.

23 'Mr. Lawson seems to be harking back to a familiar stance — that he is both the arbiter of the values of others and at the same time somehow above the field of contending values.'
C. Kirkwood, 'Adult education and the concept of community', *Adult Education*, vol. 51, no. 3, (1978), p. 147.

24 ibid., p. 410.

25 ibid., p. 13.

26 C. Bell and H. Newby, *Community Studies*, (Allen and Unwin, 1972). R. Frankenberg, *Communities in Britain* (Penguin, 1966).

27 J. R. Seeley, R. A. Sim, E. W. Loosley, *Crestwood Heights: a Study of the Culture of Suburban Life* (Wiley, 1956). A. J. Vidich

and J. Bensman, *Small Town in Mass Society: Class Power and Religion in a Rural Community* (Princeton, 1968).

M. Stacey, *Tradition and Change: a Study of Banbury* (Oxford University Press, 1960).

28 C. Fletcher, 'Issues in community education', in Fletcher and Thompson (1979). The sets of conditions are said to be necessary, sufficient and emergent.

29 'In many ways it is convenient that the systematic practice of community development is new in Britain, so that the situation is fluid enough to work out new relationships before demarcation becomes too rigid. The opportunity is there for adult educators to take the initiative.' Jackson, (1970), p. 160.

30 *Vide* Colin Kirkwood's evaluation of the myths of community, 'Adult education and the concept of community', pp. 149-50.

31 'A survey conducted for the Royal Commission on Local Government in England (cmnd. 4040, 1969) in its search for a definition of community found that the great majority of people identify themselves with a "home area" not larger than a parish in rural areas and rarely extending to more than a group of streets in urban areas of more than sixty thousand population'. E. Hutchinson, (1974) reprinted in A. N. Fairbairn, *The Leicestershire Community Colleges and Centres*, p. 50.

32 ibid., 148–49.

33 'In Liverpool the unskilled and semi-skilled working-classes have borne the brunt of the redevelopment process and this has added to their misfortunes by disrupting community life. Thus in the Liverpool EPA there are no working-class "communities" in the old sense of the word, but merely individuals seeking to come to terms with a new environment.' T. Lovett, 'Community Adult Education', pp. 5-6.

34 'Adult educators will themselves learn a great deal from association with such programmes.' Jackson, (1970), pp. 161-2.

B. Stewart, 'A community adult education service', *Adult*
35 *Education*, vol. 49, no. 2, (1976).

36 Jackson, 'Adult education and community development', *Studies in Adult Education*, (1970), pp. 161-2.

37 Lovett, 'Community adult education', *Studies in Adult Education* (1971), p. 2.

38 'Adult educators should be trying to find an appropriate role for their agencies, not attempting to take over for themselves what

is a complex exercise.' Jackson, (1970), p. 162.

39 W. C. Hallenbach, *et al., Community and Adult Education,* (Adult Education Association of USA), quoted in Jackson (1970), fn. 18.

40 Jackson, (1970), p. 156.

41 Stewart, 'A community adult education service' (1976), p. 73.

42 Lovett, 'Community adult education' (1971), p. 25.

43 Stewart, 'A community adult education service' (1976), p. 73.

44 C. Kirkwood, 'Adult education and the concept of community' (1978), p. 147.

45 Stewart, (1976), p. 71.

46 Sheldon, *et al.* (1970) quoted in R. Ruddock, 'The sociology of adult education: a plea for humanism'. *Studies in Adult Education* vol. 3, no. 1, (1971), p. 21.

47 Jackson, (1970), p. 172.

48 ibid., p. 169.

49 Lovett, (1971), p. 10.

50 P. Freire, *Pedagogy of the Oppressed* (Penguin, 1972) p. 88.

51 '. . . in Liverpool CDP, for example, adult education workers became drawn into a political campaign against the Housing Finance Bill in 1972.' *Gilding the Ghetto: the State and the Poverty Experiments* (CDP, 1978).

52 P. Collins, 'Presentation of Workshop by Focus 230' in Anders *et al., Community Education Seminar Report* (2), pp. 32–33.

53 Anders *et al.,* 'Summary of Discussion Groups' in ibid., pp. 22–23.

54 Stewart, (1976), p. 74.

55 Jackson, (1970), p. 177.

56 B. R. Harvey, 'When adult tutors were appointed at Ashby their joint appointment — 40 per cent school, 60 per cent adult/community — set the pattern which has persisted on paper ever since'. 'The community college in Leicestershire — an interim report', *Studies in Adult Education,* vol. 3, no. 3, pp. 140–53.

57 Lovett, (1971), p. 2.

58 '. . .the provision made in the county, and particularly that made by the community colleges, attracts larger proportions of the accessible population than is suggested by enquiries elsewhere or by national statistics.' Hutchinson in A. N. Fairbairn, *The Leicestershire Community Colleges and Centres,* p. 51.

59 'Seminars aimed to clarify the nature of different neighbourhood problems and . . . move towards a clearer picture of the

community development methods appropriate to British urban areas'. Jackson, (1970), p. 166.

60 'Some of those who have greatest responsibility for advising on community education seem to be least able to resist the elegant seductiveness of the armchair theoretician.' Anders, *et al.*, *Community Education Seminar Report* (2), pp. 59–60.

4   Adult education and the disadvantaged

1   Michael Rutter and Nicola Madge (eds.), *Cycles of Disadvantage* (Heinemann, 1976).

2   John Bowlby, *Maternal Care and Mental Health* (WHO, 1951).

3   L. Casler, *Maternal Deprivation: A Critical Review of the Literature*, Monograph of the Society for Research into Child Development, no. 26 (1961).

4   W. G. Runciman, *Relative Deprivation and Social Justice*.

5   B. Ekland and D. P. Kent, 'Socialisation and social structure' in *Perspectives on Human Deprivation: Biological, Psychological and Social* (UD Dept. of Health Education and Welfare, 1968).

6   H. Ginsberg, *The Myth of the Deprived Child* (Prentice-Hall, 1972); and Norman Freidman, 'Cultural deprivation; a commentary in the sociology of knowledge', *Journal of Educational Thought* (1967).

7   M. D. Ainsworth, 'The effects of maternal deprivation: a review of findings and controversy in the context of research strategy' in *Deprivation of Mental Care: A Reassessment of its Effects* (WHO, 1962).

8   Rutter and Madge, *Cycles of Disadvantage*.

9   Jim Callaghan, Home Secretary, 'Introduction to the Urban Aid Programme', *Hansard* (2 December 1968).

10   Home Office Press Release (16 July 1969).

11   Coventry CDP Final Report, Part 1 (1975).

12   i.e., *Oxford and Working Class Education*, 1908; *The Final Report of the Adult Education Committee of the Ministry of Reconstruction*, 1919; *The Ashby Report*, 1954; and *The Russell Report*, 1973.

13   E. and E. Hutchinson, *Learning Later* (Routledge & Kegan Paul, 1978).

14   H. A. Jones in his Foreword to Peter Clyne, *The Disadvantaged Adult* (Longman, 1972).

15   H. A. Jones, ibid.

16 H. A. Jones, ibid.
17 Peter Clyne, ibid.
18 See, for example, the recommendations made as a consequence of the New Communities Project in Leigh Park and outlined in Fordham, Poulton and Randle, *Learning Networks in Adult Education*, (Routledge & Kegan Paul, 1979).
19 The ACACE Report *A Strategy for the Basic Education of Adults*, 1979, also supervised by Henry Arthur Jones with Clyne as a committee member, was more obliged than Russell had been to take account of the economic crisis and escalating unemployment of the mid 1970s. But the emphasis in this report is still essentially on personal inadequacy in circumstances in which structural unemployment and redundancy, however, distressing, are taken as 'given' and with solutions seen to lie in 'coping skills' and 'basic education available wherever needed to *counter* the loss of personal dignity, the waste of human resources and the *vulnerability to political extremism* that hopeless unemployment can bring' (my italics).
20 K. H. Lawson, 'Community education: a critical assessment', *Adult Education*, vol. 50, no. 1.
21 Graham Mee and Harold Wiltshire, *Structure and Performance in Adult Education*, (Longman, 1978).
22 Keith Jackson, 'Adult education and social action', Jones and Mayo (eds.), *Community Work One* (Routledge & Kegal Paul).
23 See Freidman, 'Cultural deprivation'.
24 Christopher Jencks, 'Johnson vs poverty', *New Republic*, no. 150 (1964).
25 Jencks in the *Moynihan Report* (1965).
26 Norman Freidman, 'Cultural deprivation: a commentary on the sociology of knowledge', *Journal of Educational Thought*, vol. 1, no. 2.
27 Basil Bernstein, 'Education cannot compensate for society', *New Society*, (26 February 1970).
28 'Mainstream culture' is a term which writers like Keddie have utilized to refer to the dominance of middle-class cultural values.
29 Kenneth Clark, *Dark Ghetto-Dilemmas of Social Power* (1965).
30 Bernstein, 'Education cannot compensate for society'.
31 William Ryan, 'Savage Discovery' in the *Moynihan Report* (1965).
32 Jenny Headlam Wells, 'Adult education and disadvantage: the

special needs of physically handicapped students', *Adult Education*, vol. 49, no. 6.

33 Baratz and Baratz, *Early Childhood Intervention: The Social Science Base of Institutional Racism* (1970).

34 Nell Keddie, *Social Differentiation* (2), Unit 10, E.282. (Open University).

35 Cole and Bruner, *Preliminaries to a Theory of Cultural Difference* (1972).

36 Giles and Woolfe, Units 25 and 26, E.202 (Open University).

37 Introduction and guide to Reading Development PE.231 (Open University).

38 Raymond Williams in *Keywords* (Fontana, 1976).

39 ibid.

40 ibid.

41 ibid.

42 Herbert Bowles and Samuel Gintis, *Schooling in Capitalist America* (Routledge & Kegan Paul, 1976).

43 Fordham, Poulton and Randle, *Learning Networks in Adult Education.*

44 *A Strategy for the Basic Education of Adults*, para 70.

45 Bowles and Gintis, *Schooling in Capitalist America.*

46 See R. W. K. Paterson, *Values, Education and the Adult* (Routledge & Kegan Paul, 1979).

47 Fordham, Poulton and Randle, *Learning Networks in Adult Education.*

48 Smith and Harris, 'Ideologies of need and the organisation of social work departments', *British Journal of Social Work*, vol. 12, no. 1.

49 Ivan Illich, *Deschooling Society* (Penguin, 1973).

50 Jenny Headlam Wells, 'Adult education and disadvantage'.

51 Colin Fletcher, Chapter 3 in this book.

52 Thomas La Belle, 'Goals and strategies of non-formal education in Latin America', *Comparative Education Review*, vol. 20, no. 3.

53 Colin Kirkwood, 'Adult education and the concept of community', *Adult Education*, vol. 51, no. 3.

54 Keith Jackson, *Adult Education in a Community Development Project*, (1973).

55 Simon Frith and Paul Corrigan, 'The politics of education', Geoff Whitty and M. F. D. Young, in *Society, State and Schooling*, (Falmer Press, 1977).

56 ibid.

57   ibid., and Guy Neaves' article 'The free schoolers' in Douglas
      Holly, (ed.) *Education for Domination*, (Arrow Books, 1974).
58   See, for example, Richard Pring, 'Knowledge out of control',
      Education for Teaching, (November 1971); Jim Campbell and
      Martin Merson, 'Community education: instruction for
      inequality, *Education for Teaching* (Spring 1974); and John and
      Pat White, 'Slogan for crypto-elitists?', in *TES* (5 January 1973).
59   Martin Yarnit, Chapter 9 in this book.
60   Keith Jackson and Bob Ashcroft, *Adult Education, Deprivation
      and Community Development – A Critique*, (1972).
61   ibid.
62   Frith and Corrigan, 'The politics of education'.
63   In October 1978, Basil Bye, lecturer in Industrial Relations at
      Southampton University, resigned his post. During the pre-
      ceding 12 years, together with local shop stewards and regional
      trade union officials he had helped to establish the *Southern
      Region Trade Union Information and Research Unit*. At first this
      organization worked in close co-operation with the university,
      as it did with the WEA, the TUC and individual trade unions.
      Increasingly it was felt that the University's definition of
      'liberal adult education' was being used to imply an unaccept-
      able bias in the work of its Industrial Studies Unit. The
      SRTUIRU felt under sufficient restriction to declare its
      independence from the university connection. It now operates
      independently but in close harmony with the TUC and
      individual unions. Its work is flourishing. The university's
      provision of trade union education, on the other hand, is, at the
      time of writing (July 1979), now confined to three part-time
      certificate courses in Industrial Relations which draw students
      from both sides of industry.
64   School of Barbiana, *Letter to a Teacher*, (Penguin, 1970).
65   See Chapter 8 by Tom Lovett in this book.
      Keith Jackson is now Senior Tutor at the Northern College,
      Barnsley.
66   See Chapters 7 and 9 in this book.
67   Keith Jackson, 'Notes on the background to an appointment
      of an action researcher in adult education for a working class
      neighbourhood', University of Liverpool internal paper.
68   David Evans, Chapter 7 in this book.
69   Colin Kirkwood, 'Adult education and the concept of
      community'.

70 Paul Thompson, *The Voice of the Past: Oral History* (Opus, 1978).

71 Jackson and Ashcroft, *Adult Education, Deprivation and Community Development.*

72 *A Strategy for the Basic Education of Adults* (ACACE, 1979).

5   Independence and incorporation

1 By the Labour College movement I mean the Plebs League, the Central Labour College and its provincial classes, and after 1921 the National Council of Labour Colleges.

2 Figures for the WEA from S. G. Raybould, *The WEA; the Next Phase* (London, 1949), p. 102; and for the Labour College movement from J. F. Horrabin, 'Independent working-class education' in *Journal of Adult Education*, vol. 1, no. 1. (September 1926), and T. Kelly, *A History of Adult Education in Great Britain* (Liverpool, 1970 edn) p. 283.

3 J. P. M. Millar, 'Socialist Education' in *Plebs* (Summer 1969 — the final issue).

4 See A. J. Corfield, *Epoch in Workers' Education* (London, 1969), p. 41.

5 For an indication of the WEA's record see two WEA pamphlets: *The Adult Student as Citizen* (1938) and *Workers' Education in Great Britain: a Record of Educational Service to Democracy Since 1918* (1943); and for something of the Labour College movement's contribution see W. W. Craik, *Central Labour College* (London, 1964), esp. Appendix 2.

6 James Griffiths, *Pages From Memory* (London, 1969), p. 48.

7 The standard work on the history of adult education, that of Kelly, mentioned above, contains only a handful of insubstantial references to the Labour College movement, whereas it has a great deal of substance on the WEA. Brian Simon's books, *Education and the Labour Movement, 1870–1914* (London, 1965) and *The Politics of Educational Reform, 1920-1940* (London, 1974), are hostile to the WEA, whilst containing much, often of an uncritical nature, on the Labour College movement.

8 *Oxford and Working-Class Education* (Oxford, 1908), pp. 47–48. For accounts of the Ruskin Strike see Craik, *Central Labour College*; Paul Yorke, *Education and the Working Class, Ruskin College 1899–1909* (Oxford, 1977); Bernard Jennings, 'Revolting students' in *Studies in Adult Education*, vol. 9, no. 1 (April 1977)

and for the Oxford Report, see Jennings, 'The Oxford Report
Reconsidered' in ibid., vol. 7, no. 1, (April 1975).

9 Quoted in Richard Lewis, 'The South Wales miners and the
Ruskin College strike of 1909' in *Llafur*, vol. 2, no. 1 (Spring
1976), p. 61.

10 Lenin, *State and Revolution* (Peking, 1965 edn), p. 8. For the
Labour College on the WEA and the state, see, for example,
Plebs (May 1913).

11 For a fine attempt to look at the complexities involved in the
historical development and operation of capitalist democracy,
see G. Therborn, 'The rule of capital and the rise of
democracy', *New Left Review*, 103 (May–June 1977); and for a
polemic against a general rhetoric, dismissive of democratic
practices, passing itself off as Marxism: see E. P. Thompson,
'The secret state', *Race and Class*, vol. XX, no. 3 (Winter 1979).

12 William Mellor, *Direct Action* (London, 1920), pp. 129–30.

13 On the WEA in Yorkshire see J. F. C. Harrison's account,
centred round the work and attitudes of its District Secretary,
G. H. Thompson, in *Learning and Living, 1790-1960* (London,
1961), pp. 289-99.

14 Cole in *Students' Bulletin* (November 1924).

15 W. E. Styler, *Yorkshire and Yorkshire North* (Leeds, 1964), p. 17.

16 G. P. Jones, *A Report on the Development of Adult Education in
Sheffield* (Sheffield, 1932), p. 31. For a similar position at the
same time in Leeds, see J. F. C. Harrison, *Learning and Living,
1790-1960*, p. 289.

17 NCLC, *Education for Emancipation*, Report for 1935.

18 *Tutors' Bulletin* (July 1938).

19 Barbara Wootton, *Plan or No Plan* (London, 1934), p. 7.

20 B. Wootton, 'A plea for constructive teaching', *Adult Education*
(December 1937).

21 John Brown, *I Was a Tramp* (London, n.d., 1936), p. 221.

22 Bradford ILP Commission, *Report on Education*, (n.d., 1931),
para 437.

23 See A. J. Allaway and J. Rawson, *The Rossendale Branch of the
WEA* (Manchester, n.d.? 1954) p. 7., and D. M. Emmet, 'Joseph
Dietzgen: the philosopher of proletarian logic', *Journal of Adult
Education*, vol. III, no. 1 (October 1928).

24 John Dover Wilson, *Milestones on the Dover Road* (London,
1969) p. 80.

25 *I, James Whittaker* (London, 1934), p. 311, and J. L. Stocks,

'Theory and Practice', *Adult Education*, vol. IX, no. 2 (December 1936).

26 Headlam and Hobhouse's report, reproduced in A. Mansbridge, *University Tutorial Classes* (London 1913), pp. 147 and 151.

27 R. H. Welch, quoted in T. Kelly, *Outside the Walls* (Manchester, 1950), pp. 65-6.

28 See on this T. W. Price, *The Story of the WEA from 1903 to 1924* (London, 1924) esp. Ch. VII, 'The WEA and the Working Class Movement'.

29 Board of Education, Educational Pamphlet no. 59. *Report on Adult Education in Yorkshire*, (HMSO, 1928), pp. 26-27.

30 John Thomas, 'The economic doctrines of Karl Marx and their influence on the industrial areas of South Wales, particularly among the miners', unpublished essay for the National Eisteddfod, Ammanford 1922 (Copy in South Wales Miners' Library, Swansea).

31 Report in North-Eastern District Supplement to *The Highway* (November 1934).

32 A. Mansbridge, *University Tutorial Classes*, p. 119.

33 *Tutors' Bulletin* (November 1922).

34 See, for example, T. C. Barker, 'The Beginnings of the Economic History Society', *Economic History Review*, 2nd series, vol. XXX, no. 1 (February 1977).

35 G. D. H. Cole, 'The Place of Marx in Economic Teaching', *The Highway* (November 1919).

36 See Craik, *Central Labour College*, pp. 154-55 for the effects of the closure. For an imaginative attempt to introduce elementary Marxism to new students, see Fred Casey, 'Beginning with the Beginner', *Plebs* (April 1920), reprinted with introduction by Tim Putnam in *Capital and Class* (Spring 1979).

37 Frank Hodges, 'Adult Education in South Wales', *The Welsh Outlook*, vol. V (1918), p. 322.

38 Letter in *The Highway* (January 1926), and Jack Hilton, *Caliban Shrieks* (London, 1935), pp. 126-27.

39 J. F. Horrabin, 'Independent working-class education'.

40 *The Burning Question of Education*, (Oxford, no date 1909), p. 7.

41 Noah Ablett, *Easy Outlines of Economics*, first published by Plebs League 1919. See also Ablett's long, though sometimes too flippant, review of one of the standard WEA textbooks, Henry Clay's, 'Economics for the general reader', in *Plebs* (August and September 1916).

42   Margaret T. Hogden, *Workers' Education in England and the United States* (London 1925), p. 143, and pp. 146-47 on Cole's role in the attempts at unity.
43   There has already been some progress in this direction. See, for a discussion, P. Caldwell, P. Gerhardt and R. Kohn, 'Policies for the future: from above . . . or from below?', *WEA News* (Spring 1979).

7   Writers' workshop and working-class culture

1   *Writing* is published by the Federation of Worker Writers and Community Publishers (1978).
2   The *Morning Star* (19 October 1978) devoted a full page to the worker writers' movement. Reviews of *Writing* have since appeared in *Time Out* (29 September – 5 October), the *TGWJ Record* (October 1978) and other trade union journals. See also Ken Worpole, 'Alternative Publishing' in *New Society*, 3 May 1979.
3   First published in *Voices of Scotland Road and Nearby* (2) and later in the coincidentally named national *Voices* (no. 16, Winter 1977/78).
4   Ken Worpole of the Centerprise Publishing Trust in the 'Afterword' to *Writing*. Greg Wilkinson of Commonword Workshop, Manchester and I assisted in the drafting of the 'Afterword': sometimes it is impossible to remember which part came from whom.
5   ibid.
6   See also Martin Yarnit, Chapter 9 in this volume.
7   They included a fireman, a young man who had failed his 'O'-levels but later went on to university, a timber storeman, a dockgate man, two cleaning women and a former factory hand.
8   I served on the committee which campaigned for the community centre and helped it and Heriot Tenants' Association on communications questions.
9   That is the convention that adult education classes which drop below a certain number — usually 10 or 12 — should be discontinued.
10   I do not believe that bourgeois education encourages individualism; it encourages licence within conformity which is a different thing altogether.
11   Paulo Freire, *Pedagogy of the Oppressed*, p. 47. Freire is, of course, leaning heavily on Simone de Beauvoir's formulation.

12 A study of the nineteenth century, particularly the Chartist period, suggests a lively interest in writing and culture among working-class people, and their allies: 'Go ye and write likewise . . . all join hands to create a library of your own, your own prose and poetry; you ought to be resolved to create these.' Thomas Cooper as quoted in Patricia Hollis, *The Pauper Press*.

13 The quotation is from Pears' Cyclopaedia (87th Edition). There the apathy of the masses is characteristically blamed.

14 The Netherley group saw *Voices of Scotland Road* (2), *19 from 8* and *Writing* and decided to try their hand. Initially, the group had been (and still is) the core of the Anti-Nazi League in its area; once again social action preceded cultural activity.

15 Most of the middle-class members are writers sympathetic to the working-class cause. Because of their education they usually do the editing and correcting of mistakes. They also tend to become the managers of groups, a split of function which reflects the nature of our society and troubles the movement.

16 In a paper to the Universities Council for Adult Education Conference in 1978.

17 Rather than force the examples of the 'great tradition' on working-class students, there is a case for developing their creativity first and then looking at classical or traditional models.

18 I ran a literature class in Vauxhall for a year. Though useful it declined, largely, I suspect, because I was handing down received bourgeois wisdom from the position of 'expert'.

19 There have been heated arguments on such matters as rape, abortion, political violence, hanging and homosexuality. Also race and immigration, though our friendly relations with the Liverpool 8 group seem to have enhanced sympathy for black working-class people in Britain and created a sense of common problems.

20 Unity Theatre, a 'socialist' group with a history of good productions going back to the 1930s, has produced plays by three workshop writers. Our own productions included performances in the bistro of the Everyman Theatre under the sponsorship of Liberty Hall, at Centerprise in London and in a Scotland Road school. The drama section of Ethel Wormald College of Teacher Training staged one play also.

21 The full poem has been printed as a wall poster.

22 One of the three Everton 'piggeries' frequently shown on television programmes about Liverpool.

23 'Good Old Albie' in (Manchester) *Voices* (16). In a McGovern
    play, 'Lost City Echoes', a crippled woman starves herself
    because her husband is risking a heart attack pulling her wheel-
    chair up the steps of a high-rise block where the lifts are wrecked.
24 'Whatever happened to the Good Samaritan?' in *Voices* |(15).
25 Ralph Peacock, 'Jack Wilson' in the *Scottie Press* (February
    1978).
26 'Annie Married' in *Voices of Scotland Road* (2); reproduced in
    Writing.
27 *Voices of Scotland Road* (1); reproduced in *Writing*. Ann Blunt is
    a pseudonym the writer reluctantly accepted. She has since
    written equally forceful pieces under her own name.
28 Val Newall was a Second Chance to Learn student. The target
    might well be a middle-class man. I have not quoted the whole
    poem.
29 Cheryl Dudt, 'A Prayer' in *19 from 8*.
30 See also my paper to the UCAE (which is due to be printed in the
    International Journal of University Adult Education).

8 Adult education and community action

 1 J. Harrison, 'Community work and adult education', *Studies*
    in *Adult Education*, vol. 6, no. 1 (April 1974).
    K. H. Lawson, 'Community education — a critical assessment',
    in *Adult Education*, vol. 50, no. 1 (May 1977).
 2 T. Lovett, *Adult Education, Community Development and the
    Working Class* (Ward Lock, 1975).
 3 K. Jackson, 'The marginality of community development —
    implications for adult education', *International Review of Com-
    munity Development,* (Summer 1973).
 4 ibid.
 5 Lovett, *Adult Education, Community Development and the
    Working-Class.*
 6 Jackson, 'The marginality of community development', p. 27.
 7 M. Coady, *Masters of Our Destiny* (New York: Harpers and
    Bros., 1939).
 8 A.F. Laidlaw, *The Man from Margaree – Writings and speeches
    of M. M. Coady*, (Toronto: McClelland and Stewart Ltd, 1971).
 9 ibid., p. 57.
10 ibid., p. 15.
11 A. F. Laidlaw, *The Campus and the Community – The Global*

Impact of the Antigonish Movement, (Montreal: Harvard House Ltd, 1961), p. 116.

12 ibid., p. 97.
13 ibid., p. 90.
14 J. Lotz, 'The Antigonish Movement', in *Understanding Canada; Regional and Community Development in a New Nation* (Toronto: N.C. Press Ltd, 1977), Ch. 10, p. 113.
15 ibid., p. 112.
16 *The Campus and the Community*, p. 78.
17 F. Adams, 'Highlander Folk School: getting information, going back and teaching it', *Harvard Educational Review*, vol. 42, no. 4 (November 1972).
18 ibid., p. 516.
19 F. Adams, and M. Horton, *Unearthing Seeds of Fire – The Idea of Highlander* (N. Carolina: J. F. Blair, 1975), p. 206.
20 ibid., p. 208.
21 ibid., p. 33.
22 *Highlander Folk School*, p. 509.
23 J. Perlman, 'Grassrooting the system', *Social Policy* (New York: September/October, 1976).
24 For an analysis of these changes and how they have affected a Protestant working-class community in Belfast, see: R. Weiner, *The Rape and Plunder of the Shankill, Community Action: The Belfast Experience.* (Belfast: Notaems Press, 1975).
25 C. Cockburn, *The Local State – Management of Cities and People* (London: Pluto Press, 1978).
26 E. Evason, 'Poverty: The Facts in N. Ireland', *Poverty Pamphlet*, no. 27 (Child Poverty Action Group, 1976).
27 T. Lovett and R. Percival, 'Politics, conflict and community action in N. Ireland', in P. Curno (ed.), *Political Issues and Community Work* (Routledge & Kegan Paul Ltd, 1978).
28 1973 Brochure — New University of Ulster (Institute of Continuing Education, Londonderry).
29 T. Lovett, 'Adult education and community action — the N. Ireland experience', *Community Education '77*, (ed.) C. Fletcher (University of Nottingham, Department of Adult Education, 1977).
30 T. Lovett, 'Community education and local radio' in *Collective Action – a Selection of Community Work Case Studies.* Ed. M. Pungate, P. Henderson and L. Smith (Community Projects Foundation and Association of Community Workers, 1979).

31 L. Mackay and T. Lovett, 'Community based study groups — a N. Ireland case study', *Adult Education*, vol. 51, no. 1 (May 1978).

32 R. M. Pirsig, *Zen and the Art of Motor Cycle Maintenance* (Corgi Books, 1978).

33 Weiner, *The Rape and Plunder of the Shankill.*

34 Lovett and Percival, 'Politics, conflict and community action in N. Ireland'.

35 Paulo Freire, *Pedagogy of the Oppressed* (Penguin, 1972).

36 R. Miliband, 'The future of socialism in England', *The Socialist Register* (1977).

37 ibid., p. 42.

9 Second Chance to Learn, Liverpool

1   Keith Jackson and Bob Ashcroft, *Adult Education, Deprivation and Community Development – a critique* (Nuffield Teacher Inquiry, University of York).

2   Eric Midwinter, 'Educational Priority Areas: the philosophic question', *Liverpool EPA Project Occasional Papers, no. 1* (1969), p. 5.

3   From an undated duplicated Home Office paper circulated in 1971. *Gilding the Ghetto* analyses the aims and achievements of the CDPs from the point of view of its left-wing workers (published by the National CDP).

4   Coventry CDP quickly set itself the aim of helping 'people exercise increased control over their own lives' in a way that eventually brought it into collision with local politicians. (*CDP in Coventry: The Second Phase*, 1972).

5   See, for example, the five studies compiled by North Tyneside CDP, esp., *North Shields: Living with Industrial Change* (Benwell CDP, 1968).

6   Bob Ashcroft and Keith Jackson, 'Adult education and social action'. David Jones and Marjorie Mayo in *Community Work One*, (eds.) (1974), describes our involvement in the early stages of the rent strike.

7   The results in the Metropolitan County elections, April 1973. Labour 1760 (56 per cent) Tenants 1184 (38 per cent), Tory 202 (6 per cent). Liverpool CDP's final report *Government Against Poverty*, (which provides an interesting contrast to the account I have given, see pp. 89–93 and 97–101).

8 The Committee's composition is: 2 from the LEA; 2 from the WEA; 2 from the Institute of Extension Studies; 2 from the staff of Second Chance; 3 student representatives; 1 from the Northern College and 1 from Liverpool Inner Areas Adult Education Consortium.

9 The Consortium's members include: Second Chance, Home Link (a project for parent and child education which grew out of the EPA), Charles Wootton Centre (black community's adult education centre), Scotland Road Writers' Workshop and the Vauxhall Education Project and the WEA.

10 The survey, carried out by Bob Ashcroft, would have produced quite different results a year or two later after the Time Off scheme began to operate. Classes in social, leisure and vocational subjects, run by ourselves and the CDP, revealed a largely untapped demand for accessible education.

10 150 Hours

1 A Fiat worker from the south interviewed in 'Italy 1969–70', in *Red Noted – Big Flame.*

2 The *Economist* (12 July 1969).

3 Italian unions are organized into three national confederations: Christian Democratic, Socialist and Communist — each of which has an engineering section. The FLM is an unusually successful attempt at uniting these three separate engineering unions.

4 The School of Barbiana, *Letter to a Teacher* (Penguin, 1970), p. 27.

5 *Reviews of National Policies for Education: Italy*, (Paris: OECD, 1969), p. 84.

6 *Annuario Statistico Italiano* (1963), Tables 113-14.

7 Theoretically, education is compulsory until the age of 14. After five years of elementary school, children move up to the middle school for three years. These two phases of compulsory schooling (*scuola dell' obbligo*) from 6–14 leads to the middle school certificate for about one-third of all those who started the race. A major cause of casualties are the end-of-year exams which determine whether children are promoted or have to re-do their year.

8 Youth unemployment in Italy is currently amongst the worst in Europe.

Ratio of youth (under 25) to adult unemployment rates

	1970 per cent	1976 per cent
UK	1.2	3.4
West Germany	0.8	1.7
Italy	6.8	9.0

(Source: *The Economist* (25 February 1978), p. 91)

There are nearly two million unemployed, three-quarters of whom are under 30; more than 400,000 of them are graduates. (The student population quintrupled to 750,000 between 1960 and 1972). Young unemployed, school drop-outs and unemployed graduates provide a large proportion of students and teachers for the 150 Hours.

9   *Letter to a Teacher*, p. 90.
10 *I Lavoratori – studenti: testimonianze raccolte a Torino* (Feltrinelli, 1969).
11 *I Consigli – 26.*
12 Article 10 gives 'worker students protection to carry on their studies and exemption from duties which could prevent them from attending classes.'
13 *L'educazione degli adulti in Italia*, p. 317.
14 *Tra scuola e lavoro, Nadio Delai*, p. 26.
15 Although the employers agreed to the 150 Hours provisions in October 1973, union talks with Franco Malfatti dragged on until February 1974 so that courses started late and the take-up of available places was low.
16 'In a society which was changing at a very slow pace, teachers taught in the same types of schools in which they themselves had been taught, and they could therefore use the same teaching methods as were employed by their own masters.'
    Reviews of National Policies for Education: Italy (OECD, 1969), p. 143.
17 The data in this section is taken from Delai's analysis of the two CENSIS surveys. Information about the teachers is only available in the 1974 survey.
18 Although university courses are usually shorter; 80-100 hours, two mornings a week over maybe 4 months.
19 From a document by the Naples Secretariat of the three union federations, quoted in Steve Boddington, 'Italy: new

approaches to workers education' in *Workers' Control Bulletin*, no. 37.

20 From the introduction to the FLM, Reggio-Emilia, *Suggestions about the Teaching of Maths.*

21 Some examples: *Emigration, a Study through Personal Accounts*, carried out in Milan in 1974; *Factory, School and Society by 120 (sic) Hours students in Prato; Working conditions and health at Alfa Romeo, Milan*, a factory of some 20,000 workers which has provided 300 students for the 150 Hours.

22 Paola Piva, national co-ordinator of the FLM for the 150 Hours interviewed in *Panorama*, 5 April 1977.

23 Lotta Continua — La nuova sinistra, *Scuola e lotta di classe nel 1973–74*, (Savelli, 1974).

24 From the Sesto San Giovanni 150 Hours Bulletin.

11 Adult education for a change

1 K. H. Lawson, *Philosophical Concepts and Values in Adult Education*, (Department of Adult Education, Nottingham University in association with NIAE, 1975); R. W. K. Paterson, *Values, Education and the Adult* (Routledge & Kegan Paul, 1979).

2 Colin Fletcher, Chapter 3 in this book.

3 ibid.

4 Thomas Kuhn, *The Structure of Scientific Revolution.*

5 See Chapters 7, 8 and 9 in this book.

6 Wiltshire and Mee, *Structure and Performance in Adult Education* (Longman, 1978).

7 Nell Keddie, Chapter 2 in this book.

8 ibid.

9 See Chapters 1 and 5 in this book.

10 'Towards continuing education: discussion paper one' (ACACE, 1979).

11 *A Strategy for the Basic Education of Adults* (ACACE, 1979).

12 Nell Keddie, personal communication.

Index